Intergenerational Mobility

Intergenerational Mobility

How Gender, Race, and Family Structure Affect Adult Outcomes

Jean Kimmel
Editor

2021

W.E. Upjohn Institute for Employment Research
Kalamazoo, Michigan

Library of Congress Cataloging-in-Publication Data

Names: Kimmel, Jean, editor.
Title: Intergenerational mobility : how gender, race, and family structure affect adult
  outcomes / Jean Kimmel, editor.
Description: Kalamazoo, Michigan : W.E. Upjohn Institute for Employment Research,
  2021. | Includes bibliographical references and index. |
Summary: "This volume presents a complex portrait of the interrelationships among
  parents' marital status and education, child gender, and the nature and success of
  children's transitions into adulthood. The first three chapters focus on differences in
  parents' investments in their children, while the final three chapters focus directly
  on intergenerational income mobility"— Provided by publisher.
Identifiers: LCCN 2021035853 (print) | LCCN 2021035854 (ebook) |
  ISBN 9780880996785 (paperback) | ISBN 9780880996808 (ebook)
Subjects: LCSH: Social mobility. | Child development. | Families—Economic aspects.
Classification: LCC HT612 .I58 2022 (print) | LCC HT612 (ebook) |
  DDC 305.5/13—dc23
LC record available at https://lccn.loc.gov/2021035853
LC ebook record available at https://lccn.loc.gov/2021035854

Cover design by Carol A.S. Derks.
Index prepared by Diane Worden.
Printed in the United States of America.
Printed on recycled paper.

I dedicate this edited volume to David and Lizzie,
my two grown children, both making their single mother
proud by graduating from college and growing into
such unique and intellectually curious adults.

Contents

Acknowledgments

Thanks to the authors of this volume for their flexibility and commitment to this series through the disruption caused by the Covid-19 pandemic. The 56th Werner Sichel Lecture Series for the 2019–2020 academic year was organized by the Department of Economics at Western Michigan University, with financial support from the Department of Economics, the Western Michigan University College of Arts and Sciences, and the W.E. Upjohn Institute for Employment Research.

1

Introduction and Overview

Intergenerational Mobility in the Modern Era

Jean Kimmel
Western Michigan University

There is a growing literature examining the decline in labor market status experienced by lesser-educated men in the past half century. Despite workplace advances in automation and rising real wages for most workers during much of this period, lesser-educated men have experienced declining employment rates and real wages, along with declining marriage rates. At the same time, intergenerational mobility has waned, and there is growing concern that achieving a comfortable middle-class lifestyle has become unattainable for those Americans not born into privilege. Of particular concern, and a key focus of this edited volume, is that linkages between labor market and marriage declines are serving to exacerbate inequality due to a potentially lifelong burden on the children, particularly males, who do not grow up in stable, two-parent households. These burdens experienced during childhood seem to hinder both future economic independence and marriage probability, thereby contributing to an ever-worsening gap between the "haves" and "have-nots" in our society. Autor and Wasserman (2013) argue that the social and economic problems associated with the labor market decline for low-skilled men are exacerbated because low-income children are becoming increasingly likely to grow up without fathers in the household, a family structure that confers, on average, disadvantage to these children that is greater for male children.

The inspiration for this Sichel Series was drawn from the narrative that there is a gendered disadvantage associated with being raised by a single parent, specifically that boys suffer more from disadvantaged family structures than do girls. Of most concern is the potential intergenerational impacts—namely, that these struggling men are less likely to become financially independent adults and less likely to marry the mothers of their children, leading to more children being raised by unmarried mothers.

This volume includes written versions of all six public lectures from the 2019–2020 Sichel Series. The first three chapters focus on differences in parents' investments in their children, while the final three chapters focus directly on intergenerational income mobility.

Chapter 2, written by Rachel Connelly and Jean Kimmel, is titled "A Comparison of U.S. Parents' Time with Children by Child Gender and Family Structure." The authors begin by discussing Autor and Wasserman (2013), who paint a concerning picture of a gendered intergenerational connection in economic status that exacerbates the disadvantage experienced by children who grow up in single-mother families. One element of this narrative is the presumption of a gendered single parent disadvantage that the authors suggest could be explained in part by single mothers' spending more time with their daughters than their sons. Connelly and Kimmel focus their empirical research on measuring parenting time input to determine if it varies by child gender and parents' marital status. Their chapter attempts to answer two related questions: 1) Do boy children raised by single mothers receive less parenting time than female children raised in similar family circumstances, and 2) Is there a child gender difference in parenting time for children residing with their married parents? The authors use regression-based methods in order to control relevant and possibly confounding factors, such as parents' education and children's ages.

Connelly and Kimmel's chapter includes an expansive review of the literature focusing on the challenges faced by children who grow up in single-mother families. Most relevant, Lundberg (2005) presents a conceptual framework to explain why parenting behavior may vary by child gender. She explains that the two basic sources of these differences by child gender are systemic bias by gender in the utility that parents receive (or believe they may receive) from parenting boys versus girls and cost differences associated with raising boys versus girls. Another possible explanation is that girls may simply be easier to manage than boys, particularly at younger ages. Lundberg, McLanahan, and Rose (2007) document that married fathers of both sons and daughters devote more time to their sons than to their daughters, and that the daughter advantage in single mothers' parenting time is a greater relative advantage (compared to time with their sons) than the daughter advantage seen for married mothers.

As Connelly and Kimmel explain, there is a theoretical basis within the economics literature for the presumption that parental time inputs influence children's development. As described in the chapter, economists have provided the framework to explain that differential parental time inputs may explain variation in adult outcomes. However, the question of whether there are actually differences by child gender in the time that parents spend with their children (and whether this gender gap varies by parents' marital status) is an empirical question.

Connelly and Kimmel use data from the American Time Use Survey (ATUS) for the years 2003 through 2017 and examine parenting time constructed with two separate ATUS measures: primary child care time and time engaged in any activity in which children are present. As Connelly and Kimmel explain, these ATUS data are best suited for the task of the chapter. The empirical strategy in the chapter is threefold: comparison of means, regression that permits controlling both parent and child characteristics, and then using the regression results to construct predicted time use measures for a "representative" person. Connelly and Kimmel describe three main findings. First, parents of preschool children devote approximately equal time to their sons and daughters. Second, there are large differences in the time that parents spend with their teenaged children, based on child gender and parents' marital status. Mothers, both married and single, spend more time with their teenage girls, while fathers, both married and single, spend more time with their (cohabiting) teenage boys. Third, focusing on race, there are only small differences in primary child caregiving time between Blacks and non-Blacks in similar family situations, and there are no substantive differences in the existence, size, or direction of the child gender gap. The results presented by Connelly and Kimmel suggest that if male children suffer a greater single-mother disadvantage than female children, the cause is not differences in parenting time. Perhaps boys are more vulnerable to family stress, or maybe boys actually need more parenting time than girls at young ages.

Chapter 3 is titled "Behavioral Insights, Parental Decision Making, and Investments in Children's Development," by Ariel Kalil and Susan Mayer. The authors begin by documenting weak economic mobility in the United States. As they note, about half of children raised in the bottom quintile of the income distribution will remain in this quintile when they reach adulthood, and 70 percent remain in the bottom half of the income distribution. The authors explain that parenting styles play a substantial role in influencing child outcomes. They suggest that "applying behavioral science to the study of parenting can potentially yield new insight into why parents make (or fail to make) decisions to spend time, money, attention, or affection promoting their children's development and why these decisions are likely to differ by parental advantage. The assumption we make is that if advantaged and disadvantaged parents made equally optimal parenting decisions, differences in future academic and financial outcomes of their children would also narrow, and intergenerational mobility would increase" (p. 84).

Kalil and Mayer explain that the most common theories used to explain intergenerational mobility fail to provide adequate explanation for the widely acknowledged correlation between child and adult outcomes. Those explanations rely on measures of parent advantage based on economic or social factors. However, the link between economic advantage and child outcomes is weak, and there is little evidence that supplementing disadvantaged parents' income influences child outcomes to any substantive degree.

One reason the traditional approaches fail to adequately explain the persistence of disadvantage, according to Kalil and Mayer, is that so much of children's critical human capital development occurs in the first few years of life, before even starting formal schooling, and before differences in parental economic resources could play a meaningful role in passing on parental advantage to children. The authors suggest that there may be systematic differences in parents' interactions with their children that may be playing a meaningful role in their development. Understanding the sources of these differences could inform policy that might increase intergenerational mobility.

The authors note that empirical evidence shows no meaningful gap between advantaged and disadvantaged parents in their understanding of what is important for their children, and most parents seem to have access to the resources and time needed to implement these goals. However, disadvantaged parents are less likely to follow through and actually do the things with their children that they believe are important. Drawing from the relatively new field of behavioral economics, the authors assert that these differences are driven by cognitive biases that differ, on average, by the degree of parental disadvantage. The three biases described in this chapter are present bias, attribution bias, and automacity. According to Kalil and Mayer, narrowing this gap will also narrow the gap in outcomes between advantaged and disadvantaged parents. By gaining a better understanding of how these biases might influence parents' decision making, behavioral tools could be developed to help narrow the gap between aspirational and actual parenting.

Present bias, also known as hyperbolic discounting, describes the tendency to overweight the present over the future and can result in less willingness to delay gratification. Parents whose decisions suffer from excessive present bias will be less likely to engage in activities with their children that have future payoffs but little immediate benefit. Attribution bias involves mistakes parents make when trying to understand their children's behavior, making it more difficult for parents to modify misbehavior or encourage better choices.

The third type of cognitive bias Kalil and Mayer describe is what they call automacity—the spontaneity with which many parenting decisions are made. This bias arises from the fact that many daily parenting decisions that are important for children's longer-term development are made quickly, automatically, instead of deliberately. Automacity bias can be difficult to correct because it results from learned behavior that has become habit. The authors suggest that automacity in parenting may be more likely to produce ineffective automatic responses with disadvantaged parents.

Kalil and Mayer devote the remainder of their chapter to descriptions of local, small-scale interventions designed by the Behavioral Insights and Parenting Lab at the University of Chicago to improve parenting by mitigating cognitive biases in parenting. These studies were implemented with experimental design (including treatment and control groups) to permit rigorous study of their impacts. The Parents and Children Together Study targets families with children participating in Head Start with a behaviorally informed intervention to increase the time that parents read with their children. As part of the process to design a meaningful program, extensive surveying of parents was undertaken in advance, revealing that the parents understood the importance of reading to their children and confirming that they had access to appropriate reading material. The researchers designing the intervention hypothesized that parents were struggling to follow through on their own beliefs due to "present bias," and therefore reminders about reading and specific goal setting were incorporated to assist parents in meeting their own goals with their children. Evaluation of program impacts revealed that the intervention produced meaningful increases in reading with children for those parents who had been, prior to the intervention, falling short of their own desired reading goals. Importantly, the cost of this intervention was relatively low, suggesting that it is feasible to implement these sorts of behaviorally based interventions.

A second example of a behavioral intervention described by the authors is a program called Show Up to Grow Up (SUGU), which was an intervention designed to improve attendance in Chicago-area preschool programs. Chronic absence and lateness can contribute to children's failing to develop the behavioral skills necessary for kindergarten success, and one problem identified by the researchers can be described as "inaccurate beliefs." Parents tend to underestimate both the number of days their own children have been absent and their children's absences relative to that of other children. Another aspect of inaccurate beliefs that this program was designed to address is the mistaken impression of some parents that preschool is not important for their children's development. The SUGU program adopted an approach in which parents would receive text messages describing what their children were learning in school, serving both to inform the parents about what has been going on in the classroom and to emphasize that substantive activity occurs daily and should not be missed without good cause. Texts also were sent to remind parents about attendance and absences. Evaluation of the SUGU program showed that the program reduced chronic absences by 9.3 percentage points, with a smaller impact on increased attendance days. The biggest impacts were seen for children whose parents who had expressed, at the start of the study, less concern about absences.

Chapter 3 provides convincing evidence that disadvantaged children could be beneficiaries of the adoption of interventions informed by behavioral science. By identifying parents' cognitive biases that may exacerbate preexisting inequalities experienced by disadvantaged children, and designing thoughtful, low-cost interventions designed to nudge behavior in positive directions, child development in the first few years of life could be improved, and disadvantaged children could enter kindergarten on a more equal footing with children from more advantaged backgrounds. These interventions could lead to improvements in intergenerational mobility.

Chapter 4, "Gender Differences in (Some) Formative Inputs to Child Development," is written by Michael Baker. He begins with the fundamental observation that early childhood environmental factors play an important role in child development and help determine adult outcomes. The more favorable these environmental factors, the stronger the opportunity for successful human capital development and the better these adult outcomes. He notes that some previous evidence suggests that parenting time may vary by child gender.

Given what has already been cited about differences by gender in parents' time and interactions with children, Baker examines gender differences at the earliest stage of life. As Baker explains, the bulk of the existing empirical research examining the impact of early life environmental factors has focused on socioeconomic status, given its close association with the average quality of these early life factors. Baker extends this research to examine gender, motivated by the argument that gender differences that seem to emerge later in life may be linked to very early gender differences. Baker examines four such early life factors: medical care at birth for low birth weight (LBW) newborns, breastfeeding, maternal depression, and differential parenting style. He relies on a variety of different data sources for both the United States and Canada. Wherever possible, to be comfortable assuming that child gender is randomly assigned, he focuses on first-born children.

Baker begins his empirical analyses with an examination of gender differences in the need for and receipt of medical care upon birth for LBW newborns. Particularly for very low birth weight (VLBW) male children, providing additional care (as measured via hospital costs and hospital length of stay) improves survival rates as well as improved child development. Male LBW and VLBW newborns experience somewhat lower survival rates than comparable female newborns, with contributory factors being higher rates of sudden infant death syndrome deaths and respiratory system-related deaths. Baker's examination of medical interventions for at-risk newborns shows that interventions, on the margin, matter more for male VLBW newborns, suggesting that reallocating medical resources (or providing extra resources) towards VLBW males may be beneficial. He suggests that the medical intervention guidelines currently based on a single threshold for VLBW newborns might be modified to produce separate thresholds for male and female newborns.

Next, Baker examines the child gender difference in the incidence and duration of breastfeeding, an environmental factor associated with (somewhat minor) positive benefits. His data and empirical analyses reveal that while male and female newborns are breastfed at the same rate, female babies are breastfed slightly longer than males, with a very small difference of a handful of days at most.

Baker's empirical analyses continue with an examination of gender differences in parenting style that includes two elements: new mothers' mental state and the nature of parent-child interactions. Interestingly, his results show that mothers of newborn boys suffer higher rates of maternal depression than mothers of newborn girls. Although his research cannot identify the cause(s) of this newborn gender difference in maternal depression rates, Baker notes that it is possible that mothers' bodies experience a greater inflammatory response to male fetuses. Regardless of the cause, maternal depression may impact the mother-newborn interaction and with maternal depression rates that vary by the newborn's gender, male newborn babies may experience reduced quality mothering very early in life. The final early life intervention that Baker examines is the nature of the parent-child interaction. Canadian survey data reveal that, on average, boys are considered more difficult and that the boy child-parent interaction is more confrontational. It is not possible to know the source of these gendered parent-child interaction patterns, but one could speculate that it arises from multiple factors that could include gender differences in child behavior or maternal mental status.

Baker concludes that his results "paint a picture of male disadvantage" in the outcomes that he studies, a disadvantage that may place boys on a different life trajectory than girls. These carefully documented gender differences speak to the possibility of gender differences in opportunity and economic mobility that arise very early in life but could carry lifetime implications.

The final three chapters of this volume focus specifically on intergenerational income mobility. Chapter 5, "Household Structure and Socioeconomic Mobility: The Role of Mothers," is written by Sarah Kroeger.

Kroeger examines the intergenerational link between mothers and their daughters. While there has been a good bit of previous research examining intergenerational mobility through connections between fathers and sons, there has been little corresponding research focusing on mothers and their daughters. Her analysis focuses on the relationship between mothers' marital status and education and their adult daughters' outcomes.

The chapter begins with a summary of the relationship between maternal marital status and child outcomes, focusing on both the theory underlying this relationship and empirical evidence. Marital status is closely linked to household income, making it difficult to disentangle the individual, direct effects of marital status versus family income (and possibly other related factors) on children. Kroeger explains that it is important to understand the mechanisms by which marital status and income interact to influence child outcomes because single motherhood is becoming more common, particularly for lesser-educated women. If there is an interaction between marital status and economic status on children's outcomes, this could further widen gaps over time in income, education, and health.

As Paula Fomby notes in Chapter 7, there has been substantial evolution in family structure over time in the United States. In 1960, nearly three-fourths of children grew up with two married parents in their first marriage, while only 9 percent lived with a single parent. Just over half a century later, less than half of children were residing with two married parents, while over a quarter were living with a single parent. The percentage of all births to an unmarried woman increased from 5.3 percent to nearly 40 percent over the same time period. As Kroeger explains, the rise in single motherhood is attributable to a change in marriage patterns, not a change in underlying fertility behavior.

Kroeger carefully ties her research on the link between single mothers' circumstances and their children's adult outcomes to the existing literature on intergenerational economic mobility. Although the specific mechanisms are unclear (as Fomby explains in her chapter), the link between maternal marital status and child outcomes is quite strong, with these children faring less well on any number of outcome measures. As one example, children of single mothers are three times more likely to live in poverty as adults compared to children who grew up with two married parents. However, if the single parent family structure were the key causal factor, then we would expect to see increases in child poverty consistent with the increase in single parent families; yet, this is not seen in the time trend data. Additionally, were single mother-hood the key, we would see comparable child outcomes for all single mothers, without differences by the mother's education. Kroeger also explains that single mothers, on average, have completed fewer years of education than their married counterparts; as is well established in the education economics literature, low education is strongly linked to lower lifetime earnings. This suggests a third independent source of the single-mother disadvantage—having a parent with less education could affect child outcomes via lower household income.

The new empirical research presented in Chapter 5 asks the question, Is there any interaction between maternal marital status and the intergenerational correlations in household income and education? She uses data from the Child/Young Adult Survey of the National Longitudinal Survey of Youth 1979 (NLSY79). This Child/Young Adult Survey is a sampling of the children born to female respondents in the NLSY79, respondents who were aged 14–22 at the start of the survey in 1979. Kroeger begins her empirical work by establishing baseline correlations between parent and child education and income. She regresses child outcomes on maternal outcomes (with adjustments for birth cohort to reflect average changes over time) and finds the intergenerational education elasticity (between child and mother) is estimated to be 0.26, while the intergenerational income elasticity is 0.45. She states that these results are consistent with previous research. Note that a higher elasticity indicates a closer link across generations, implying less intergenerational mobility.

Next, Kroeger stratifies regressions by the mother's marital status at the time of the child's birth, producing an education elasticity of 0.243 for married mothers and 0.299 for cases of unmarried mothers, suggesting less education mobility with single-mother families. However, the pattern is opposite when looking at the intergenerational income elasticity, with a greater elasticity (less income mobility) for married mothers (0.361 for unmarried mothers and 0.411 for married mothers). Kroeger notes that her results suggest there are subtle differences in the influences of maternal income versus maternal education. Kroeger says, "A reasonable interpretation of these estimates is that maternal education becomes a more important determinant of child outcomes when mothers are unmarried. This is intuitive, since we would expect maternal intergenerational effects to be especially pronounced for mothers who are the only caregiver for their child. But with respect to household income, the relationship is more nuanced" (p. 157).

These findings point to complex interrelationships among maternal marital status, maternal education, and household income in intergenerational impacts. For example, Kroeger's results suggest that having a mother who was married at the time of the child's birth is associated with a stronger intergenerational education link. Kroeger notes that maternal marriage increases the effect of a mother's college education by 0.39 years of school. Focusing on household income, she finds that maternal marital status does not affect the strength of the correlation between maternal household income and the child's income as an adult.

Kroeger concludes that a mother's education has a bigger impact on her children's educational attainment than her marital status at the time of the child's birth. Additionally, children are influenced more by their mothers' level of educational attainment when the mother is unmarried. Overall, her results point to mother's educational attainment as a potential policy lever because, as she explains, the positive impacts of improving maternal education carries the potential for improving outcomes for generations. She suggests that policy measures that support postsecondary degree completion for single mothers would be effective, given their relative low cost and potential for high return.

Chapter 6, by Bhashkar Mazumder, is titled "Race and Intergenerational Mobility in the United States." Mazumder provides a thoughtful review of the research literature, much produced himself, on race differences in rates of intergenerational mobility. He begins by noting that the gap in median household income between white and Black households is 42 percent—and that this gap has held constant since 1972. The contribution of Mazumder's chapter lies both in his coverage of the topic and in his careful presentation of the associated methodological developments. His review offers evidence on the magnitude and persistence over time of this intergenerational mobility gap, as well as some insight into the various contributory factors. By identifying the factors that contribute to intergenerational linkages in economic outcomes, he seeks to identify policy suggestions that might help ameliorate this race gap.

As noted by Mazumder, the earliest studies of intergenerational economic mobility were conducted by sociologists who examined the link across generations in social status, in which status was proxied by the parent's occupation. These studies of social mobility revealed that parents' social status is linked more closely to that of their adult children for whites than for Blacks. Economists expanded on this research by focusing on a broader array of adult outcomes, particularly income. The earlier economics research relied on measuring linkages across generations with two methods: intergenerational earnings elasticities and transition probabilities. The first studies that used these methods relied on what perhaps could be considered the gold standard of data sources: longitudinal survey data in which socioeconomic data are available both for parents and their adult children.

Looking back at the history of economics research examining the connections across generations in economic status, Mazumder notes that the earliest historical research was conducted by Collins and Wannamaker (forthcoming), who use merged census data and find substantial evidence of large racial economic mobility gaps. Turning to the modern era, Datcher (1981) relied on longitudinal data to show that intergenerational linkages are much stronger for whites than Blacks. Following the work of Datcher, economics research focused on the persistence of poverty across generations. Corcoran and Adams (1997) found much more poverty persistence across generations in Black families, with childhood economic factors found to be important.

The modern approaches of studying intergenerational income mobility rely largely on two measures: the intergenerational elasticity and transition probabilities (likelihood of moving from one point in income distribution to another), developed by Solon (1992) and Zimmerman (1992) in their broader studies of intergenerational mobility that did not examine race. The first economics research to use these techniques with a focus on race was Hertz (2005). Hertz's results showed that the expected income of Black children (conditioned on parent income) is 40 percent lower than that of whites. Examining adult children born into the bottom income decile showed that 42 percent of Blacks remained in the same income decline while only 17 percent of white children did.

Mazumder (2014) offered the dual contribution of better data along with a revised methodological approach that he refers to as "mobility in ranks." He finds that Black children are far less likely than white children to achieve a higher rank in the income distribution, as adults, than that of their parents. He also finds racial differences in the probability of downward mobility, noting a nearly 20 percentage point gap favoring whites in the probability that a child born into the top half of the income distribution will fall into the bottom half of the distribution as an adult. Mazumder calculates quintile transition matrices that show that "51 percent of Blacks who start in the bottom quintile will remain there as adults compared to just 26 percent of whites. The matrices imply that if this mobility process continued over time, the 'steady state' distribution of income would converge to one in which there is a permanent Black underclass, where 39 percent of Blacks would perpetually remain in the bottom quintile and only 8 percent in the top quintile. This is, of course, a stunning and sobering finding and suggests that there is a fundamental lack of opportunity for African Americans in the United States" (pp. 176–177).

Pathbreaking work by Chetty et al. (2018) relies on the use of population-wide data drawn from administrative databases with a modified empirical approach. They note that the expected rank of Black children (holding constant parent characteristics) falls substantially below that of white children. A key finding of Chetty et al. is gleaned from their stratification by both race and gender. When focusing on individual income for women, there is no race difference in expected rank, but there are large race differences in expected rank when focusing on individual income for men. The absence of a race gap for women serves to inform the discussion of the source of the race gap noted for men.

Mazumder presents new empirical evidence in this chapter that the overall income elasticity increased from 0.21 in the cohort born around 1950 to 0.50 for the cohort born about 10 years later. (A larger elasticity means that an adult child's income is more closely associated with the income of his parents.) Mazumder's new research focuses on race and finds that, despite the substantial decline in overall mobility, there has been no discernible closing of the race mobility gap.

The most striking conclusion of Mazumder's careful review of both previous and new evidence is the depressing persistence of the racial gap in intergenerational mobility, making clear that the so-called American Dream of economic mobility is an illusion for nonwhite America. Its persistence through the most recent data shows that declines in unionization, worsening monopsony power in local labor markets, and skill-biased technological change—factors that may be responsible for declines in overall economic mobility—are not to blame for the persistence in the racial mobility gap.

Chapter 6 concludes with a brief discussion of possible policy solutions that might prevent what appears to be movement toward a permanent large Black underclass. Mazumder points to the evidence that quality human capital plays some role in limiting intergenerational mobility for Blacks and offers suggestions for how to reduce the gap in the quality of human capital investment that may be depressing intergenerational mobility. He also suggests that other early life interventions may also be helpful, including addressing environmental concerns such as lead in paint, and water or air pollution. He notes that without a substantial shift in policy, there will be no income convergence and no closing of the income gap or the gap in intergenerational mobility.

The final chapter, "Accounting for Race Differences in How Family Structure Shapes the Transition into Adulthood," is written by Paula Fomby. It expands on Mazumder's review of the literature on the racial gap in intergenerational mobility by delving into the question of how family structure shapes the transition into adulthood, with a focus on differences by race. She notes that the extensive literature that examines intergenerational mobility concludes that growing up in a stable two-parent family confers substantial long-term benefits to children that persist well into adulthood. When researchers talk about evolving family structures in the United States, the standard framework looks to the immediate post–World War II period (the time period from 1946 to about 1964), when most adults got married early in adulthood, women had several babies, two-parent families resided in single-household dwellings, and health improvements produced declining child and adult mortality. This portrait of family life is treated as the long-term historical norm, and deviations from that norm beginning in the 1960s are treated as such. However, according to Fomby, household and family organization in this post–World War II era was largely a historical aberration. Examining the causes and consequences of the evolution of family and household organization that began 20 years after World War II must be considered in this context.

In the mid-1960s, well over 90 percent of adults were married, and nearly the same percent of children lived in two-parent households.

Moving into the 1970s and beyond, divorce rates grew, and although fertility rebounded from its low from the baby bust in the early 1970s, it never returned to the three or more children per mother seen at the peak of the baby boom. The rate of single parenthood grew, as did the percentage of couples living together outside of marriage. Currently, about 40 percent of children do not reside in two-parent households. When this "traditional" family structure was at its peak, there were notable differences between white and Black children. According to Fomby, there was an approximate 25 percentage point racial gap that favored white children in the percentage of children living with two parents in 1960. Family structures have evolved since that time—44 percent of Black children resided with two parents in 2019 compared to about 77 percent of white children.

Not only are there differences in the evolution of family structure by race, but also in the transition to adulthood. The racial gap in high school graduation has closed in recent years, but there has been a persistent gap of about 10 percentage points in college graduation rates. There are also substantial differences in fertility patterns, with about 70 percent of births to Black women occurring outside of marriage, compared to about 28 percent of births for white women.

Along with these changes in family structure, equally substantive social and cultural changes include the introduction of birth control, which made it possible for women to control their own fertility, and the relaxation of divorce laws. Economic changes include dramatic increases in female labor force participation, real-wage stagnation, and rising rates of return to education, all of which contribute to increasing inequality. At the same time, supportive systems like health insurance, child care, unionization, and criminal justice have not evolved correspondingly, and thus they continue to favor the "traditional" family structure of two married parents living in two-generation households. This failure to evolve harms children who are not raised in these "traditional" structures, resulting in a disproportionate burden on Black children.

Given the dramatic qualitative differences in the experiences of family structure during childhood and in the transition into adulthood among white and Black youth, are racial differences in adult transitions the result, at least in part, of different family structures? Empirical evidence suggests that the link between family structure and adult outcomes is less strong for Blacks than for whites. Fomby argues that family structure does not actually matter more for one racial group than another; instead, "The social construction of the family as it is theorized, measured, and articulated in social science research and public expression reflects the biases of the actors who predominate in that discourse" (p. 199). There has been the presumption that the "traditional" two-parent family is optimal, overlooking strengths of other family forms.

This deficit model is based, at least in part, on the patriarchal norms of the 1970s, when this literature was in its infancy. Father absence has been blamed for compromised transitions to adulthood experienced more often for Black children. Research in the 1980s worked to debunk this notion, disentangling the interrelated factors associated with difficult adult transitions, focusing on economic strain and family stress as causal factors. Unfortunately, despite some progress in this reorienting, the bulk of research continues to frame the single-mother upbringing in terms of a "deficit model."

An important development in the study of family structure has been to rethink how family is defined. Black children are more likely to be raised in three-generation households (about 1 out of 9 Black families versus about 1 out of 20 for white families). Interestingly, studies of the relationship between residing with a grandparent and child cognitive development suggest that such coresidence is favorable for Black children but not for white children. Another development (made possible by the increased availability of better data sources) is increased study of involvement of nonresident fathers in their children's lives. Finally, contributions from sociologists have offered a better understanding of the importance of extended social networks for Black families (beyond multigenerational households and involvement of nonresident fathers) in managing the hardships of minority life.

Fomby reminds the reader both that the evidence linking family structure to more difficult transitions to adulthood is not particularly convincing, and that this framing of single-mother families as providing a disadvantaged upbringing to the children raised in these families reflects more the norms for those creating the research than some objective ideal. More research is needed into the various types of extended family/extended networks that provide the protective umbrella for Black children to understand the implications for their adult transitions and to design any needed policy solutions to address any accompanying deficits.

These chapters present a complex portrait of the interrelationships among child gender, parents' marital status, and the intergenerational transmission of inequality. No chapter addresses the precise hypothesis proposed by Autor and Wasserman (2013), namely, that the gendered single-mother disadvantage that disfavors boys is contributing to growing intergenerational inequality. Instead, each of these six chapters offers evidence on various pieces of this puzzle.

Connelly and Kimmel examine mothers' and fathers' parenting time with an eye toward identifying systematic differences by marital status and child gender that might provide evidence of gendered parenting time driving the so-called gendered single-mother disadvantage—that is, the notion that sons are damaged more than daughters from being raised by a single mother. Connelly and Kimmel show that parenting time for preschool children does not vary by child gender, leading them to reject the notion of a gendered single-parent disadvantage arising from gendered parenting time. Kalil and Mayer use insights from psychology to explain differences in parenting strategies. They use the results of small-scale experiments to show that inexpensive policy interventions can modify parenting behavior in ways that would be expected to improve child development. Baker focuses on differences in maternal health investments by gender that manifest very early in life. He starts with a focus on gender differences in health outcomes for low (and very low) birth weight newborns, noting that very low birth weight male infants may be receiving a suboptimal amount of health care at the time of their birth. Baker's data show no meaningful difference in breastfeeding patterns by child gender, but he does show that mothers interact, on average, somewhat more negatively with young sons than young daughters.

Kroeger finds that mothers' education and household income play important independent roles in influencing their daughters' economic status in adulthood, with maternal education particularly important for children raised by unmarried mothers. Mazumder describes the existing literature along with original research to document the lack of progress in narrowing the race mobility gap and offers the warning that, without innovative policy interventions, this gap is likely to become permanent. His policy suggestions include improvements in the quality of human capital investments and improvements in health investments, particularly reducing environmental health disparities, especially early in life. Fomby examines potential race differences in the role of family structure, including parents' marital status and multigenerational households. She observes that policy development has been hindered by bias in how family structures are described by researchers and policy makers, concluding that better, less biased research is necessary for developing specific policies that might contribute to narrowing race gaps in intergenerational mobility.

What common lessons can be drawn from these six very distinct chapters? First, there appears to be sufficient evidence to conclude that gender matters, but in complex ways. Male fragile newborns may merit more medical resources than current agendered policy permits. Girls may be more influenced by their mothers' educational attainment than that of their fathers. Second, while education is not a panacea, there is some evidence that education (formal and within the family) may be able to reduce the intergenerational transmission of disadvantage in part by mitigating the negative impact of growing up in a single-mother family. Finally, and perhaps most important, it is clear that more research is needed to connect all the pieces of the puzzle. We need stronger evidence of the precise nature of the gendered single-mother disadvantage along with a better understanding of its specific causes, particularly since we have ruled out the mothering time-deficit hypothesis. For example, the experimental approach of Kalil and Mayer could be applied to studies of school interventions to examine whether boys would benefit from increased schooling support. Perhaps the structure of school places a disproportionate burden on boys, particularly at young ages, and if so, targeted support might be particularly useful for boys. The combination of improved parenting strategies along with targeted school support, along with expanded access to higher education, could serve to help ameliorate the gendered single-mother disadvantage, resulting in improved intergenerational mobility.

References

Autor, David, and Melanie Wasserman. 2013. *Wayward Sons: The Emerging Gender Gap in Labor Markets and Education.* Washington, DC: Third Way.

Chetty, Raj, Nathaniel Hendren, Maggie R. Jones, and Sonya R. Porter. 2018. "Race and Economic Opportunity in the United States: An Intergenerational Perspective." Working Paper No. 24441. Cambridge, MA: National Bureau of Economic Research.

Collins, William J., and Marianne H. Wannamaker. Forthcoming. "African American Intergenerational Economic Mobility Since 1880." *American Economic Journal: Applied Economics.*

Corcoran, Mary, and Terry Adams. 1997. "Race, Sex, and the Intergenerational Transmission of Poverty." In *Consequences of Growing Up Poor*, Greg J. Duncan and Jeanne Brooks-Gunn, eds. New York: Russell Sage Foundation, pp. 461–517.

Datcher, Linda. 1981. "Race/Sex Differences in the Effects of Background on Achievement." In *Five Thousand American Families: Patterns of Economic Progress*, vol. 9, Martha S. Hill, Daniel Hill, and James N. Morgan, eds. Ann Arbor: Institute for Social Research, University of Michigan, pp. 359–390.

Hertz, Tom. 2005. "Rags, Riches and Race: The Intergenerational Economic Mobility of Black and White Families in the United States." In *Unequal Chances: Family Background and Economic Success*, Samuel Bowles, Herbert Gintis, and Melissa Osborne Groves, eds. Princeton, NJ: Princeton University Press, pp. 165–191.

Lundberg, Shelly. 2005. "Sons, Daughters, and Parental Behaviour." *Oxford Review of Economic Policy* 21(3): 340–356.

Lundberg, Shelly, Sara McLanahan, and Elaina Rose. 2007. "Child Gender and Father Involvement in Fragile Families." *Demography* 44(1): 79–92.

Mazumder, Bhashkar. 2014. "Black-White Differences in Intergenerational Economic Mobility in the United States." *Economic Perspectives* 38(1).

Solon, Gary. 1992. "Intergenerational Income Mobility in the United States." *American Economic Review* 82(3): 393–408.

Zimmerman, David J. 1992. "Regression Toward Mediocrity in Economic Stature." *American Economic Review* 82(3): 409–429.

2

A Comparison of U.S. Parents' Time with Children by Child Gender and Family Structure

Rachel Connelly
Bowdoin College

Jean Kimmel
Western Michigan University

During the past 50 years, in the face of workplace advances in automation, improvements in health care, and rising real wages for most workers (at least for the first 30 of those 50 years), lesser-educated men have been left behind. These men have suffered declining real wages and employment rates along with declining marriage rates. At the same time, intergenerational economic mobility has declined, putting the American Dream out of reach for millions of Americans not born into privilege. While there are many labor market explanations for the declines in wages and employment, there is a growing concern on the part of researchers that the linkages between labor market and marriage declines are serving to exacerbate growing economic inequality, particularly racial economic inequality, due to a potentially lifelong burden on the children, particularly male children, who do not grow up in stable, two-parent households. These burdens seem to be further reducing the likelihood that these children will achieve economic independence and marry as adults, thereby contributing to an ever-worsening gap between the "haves" and the "have-nots" in our society, with a particular concern for Black male children who historically have been less successful in escaping the economic circumstances into which they are born. (See Mazumder 2005). In the remainder of this introductory overview, we describe these interrelated concerns in more detail.

As noted in detail by Binder and Bound (2019), real hourly earnings for prime-aged males with a high school diploma fell by 18.2 percent from 1973 to 2015, and their labor force participation rates fell by more than 10 percentage points. (See also Sum et al. 2011.) The authors argue that because these two factors did not decline uniformly over this time period, it does not appear that labor demand shifts, resulting in declining wages, are the primary cause of the declining attachment to the paid workforce. Instead, they suggest that there is evidence of some role of growing disability insurance coverage along with increasing incarceration rates. However, Binder and Bound assert that even these traditional labor market–based explanations are insufficient to explain the full labor force decline. They argue that "changing family structure shifts male labor supply incentives independently of labor market conditions, and that, in addition, changing family structure may moderate the effect of a male labor demand shock on labor force participation. Because male earnings potential is an important determinant of new marriage formation, a persistent labor demand shock that reduces male earnings potential could impact male labor force participation through its effects on the marriage market" (p. 164). Edin et al. (2019) also examine the link between employability and marriage in their sociological study. They describe their findings as follows:

> Work, family and religion have traditionally played an important role in furnishing working-class Americans with economic resources, moral guidance, and opportunities for civic engagement. Ongoing attachments to work, family, and religion connected working-class men to social bonds and defined identities that kept them in the formal labor market and forestalled health problems. Conversely, precarious attachments to these key social institutions, we argue, may now dilute their power to shepherd and shift men's trajectories and may place them at risk of a host of negative outcomes. (p. 211)

A disturbing consequence of Binder and Bound's and Edin et al.'s (2019) narrative is outlined in Autor and Wasserman's (2013) paper, in which the authors argue that the social and economic problems associated with the well-documented labor market decline for low-skilled men over the past four decades is magnified across generations, in part, because low-income children are now more likely to be growing up without fathers in the household.[1] Autor et al. (2019) and Autor and Wasserman (2013) present evidence that these cross-market reinforcements (labor market and marriage market) produce outcomes that are exacerbated further by intergenerational transmission effects. Coile and Duggan (2019) document the dramatic increase in the age at first marriage for both men and women, along with the increase in never-married rates at midlife. For example, the percentage of men aged 45–54 who have never married increased from 6 percent in 1980 to 16 percent in 2017. According to the authors, "Marriage rates were nearly identical across all education groups in 1980, but by 2018 had dropped by roughly 20 percentage points among all groups with less than a college education, while dropping only slightly for college graduates" (p. 203).

As marriage rates fall, more children are being raised by single parents, typically single mothers. Coile and Duggan (2019) argue that sons are particularly disadvantaged by growing up in a single-mother family, leading to an increasing gender gap favoring women both in educational attainment and in labor market outcomes. As the authors note, the mechanisms by which this intergenerational effect may be transmitted are not well understood. One hypothesis focuses on differential parental time inputs, suggesting that not only do sons in single-parent families have less contact with their fathers than sons in married households, but also that single mothers themselves spend more time with their daughters than their sons, resulting in boys growing up in single-mother families receiving less overall parenting time than girls growing up in like circumstances.

This discussion of the so-called single-parent disadvantage relies on two logical assumptions (often without supporting data): first, that children who grow up in single-parent families enjoy less total parenting time (considering the sum of the time of the resident parent plus the time of the nonresident parent); second, and more specifically, that boys receive less parenting time than girls in single-mother families, but not in married-parent families. Our chapter seeks to provide the missing supporting data concerning the potentially complex interrelationships between family structure and gender differences in parenting time with the goal of better framing the discussion of the well-documented labor market concerns of lesser-educated men. We answer two questions with this chapter. First, do the data support the suggestion that boys who grow up in single-mother families experience less parenting time than do similarly raised girls? Relatedly, do boys and girls who live with married parents experience comparable parenting time investments? Second, what factors explain these differences or similarities? We expand the set of possible family relationships to include the oft ignored but potentially important parenting time by nonresident parents. We employ a regression-based approach to facilitate comparison of parents' time with children adjusted for differences in relevant and possibly confounding factors such as parents' education and children's ages.

THE (GENDERED) SINGLE-PARENT FAMILY DISADVANTAGE AND ITS POTENTIAL FOR INTERGENERATIONAL TRANSMISSION

The underlying premise of Autor and Wasserman's (2013) intergenerational transmission concept is the assumption that there is a gendered disadvantage to growing up in a single-mother family, and there is considerable research to support this narrative. Research evidence documenting the myriad difficulties experienced by children who grow up with a single mother has existed for over half a century. Perhaps the first widely known publication that describes concerns for such children is the infamous Moynihan report (Moynihan 1965), titled *The Negro Family: The Case for National Action*, published with the expressed intent of convincing policymakers that racial inequalities in the United States could not be solved solely with civil rights legislation. According to the author, worsening racial inequalities in the United States were the result of a growing racial gap in marriage rates. While this report has been controversial since it was first published, it played a substantive role in framing the conversation around family structure, with the clear implication that family structure plays a meaningful role in influencing child outcomes that persist into adulthood.[2] This conversation lays the foundation for the intergenerational transmission concern discussed in this chapter.

Nearly 30 years after the release of the Moynihan report, with the racial gap in single parenthood stabilized and many more years of data available to analyze, McLanahan and Sandefur's (1994) monograph provided a thorough empirical analysis of the nuances of single parenthood, including how the single-parent family originated (never married versus divorce), the implications for the children, and potential policy solutions. McLanahan and Sandefur provide evidence that shows that children growing up in single-mother families, whether from never married or divorce, are less likely to graduate from high school, the daughters are more likely to experience an early first birth, and the sons are less likely to be involved with paid work in young adulthood. This empirical research also forms the groundwork for discussions of intergenerational transmission of the disadvantage arising from single motherhood.

Waldfogel, Craigle, and Brooks-Gunn (2010) delineate five pathways by which family structure and child well-being are linked: 1) parental resources, 2) parental mental health, 3) parental quality, 4) parental relationship quality, and 5) father involvement. Parental resources and quality are interrelated: both reflect the quantity of resources devoted to children (including time resources) as well as the quality of those resources (e.g., the sensitivity and responsiveness to children during parents' time with children). The authors provide empirical evidence of the disadvantage experienced by children growing up in single-parent families, demonstrating that the primary concern is behavior problems along with some health problems (greater incidence of asthma, for example). According to the authors, "Behavioral development is compromised in stable single-parent families" (p. 104). Waldfogel et al. determine that child development is not hindered so much directly from the single-parent family structure but instead from the family disruption (i.e., divorce) that led the children into that structure (p. 103).

The single-mother disadvantage is described succinctly and clearly by Sawhill (2014):

> Children raised by single mothers are more likely to fare worse on a number of dimensions, including their school achievement, their social and emotional development, their health and their success in the labor market. They are at greater risk of parental abuse and neglect (especially from live-in boyfriends who are not their biological fathers), more likely to become teen parents and less likely to graduate from high school or college. Not all children raised in single parent families suffer these adverse outcomes; it is simply that the risks are greater for them.

More recent evidence cited by McLanahan and Sawhill (2015) also focuses on children's disadvantage resulting from family instability. The authors say that "family instability undermines parents' investments to their children, affecting the children's cognitive and social–emotional development in ways that constrain their life chances" (p. 3). While this research does not make the intergenerational transmission argument, it certainly lays the foundation for it.[3]

Bertrand and Pan (2013) examine gender differences in noncognitive skill formation for children growing up in different family structures using data drawn from the Early Childhood Longitudinal Study: Kindergarten Cohort. Their goal is to explain the gender gap in disruptive behavior, specifically, to determine the importance of home versus school in explaining this gender gap. Their data show little gender gap in disruptive behavior among young children in kindergarten, but there are differences in the family environment that explain the gender gap in disruptive behavior that emerges by fifth grade. They find that "family structure is an important correlate of boys' behavioral deficit. Boys raised outside of a traditional family (with two biological parents present) fare especially poorly" (p. 34). Bertrand and Pan attempt to identify the pathways by which this gender gap in disruptive behavior develops, and they conclude that some portion of the gap can be explained by single mothers' treating their boys differently than their daughters. As they explain, "Single mothers seem relatively more emotionally distant from their sons and are also more likely to have reported spanking their sons" (p. 34). "Most important though are gender differences in the noncognitive returns to parental inputs. On average, across children, broken families are associated with lower levels and lower quality of parental inputs and the noncognitive development of boys seems extremely responsive to such inputs" (p. 34). Bertrand and Pan link their findings to parenting time, suggesting that boys may need more parenting time than girls because such time may be particularly important for boys' noncognitive development.

More recent evidence is provided by Mencarini, Pasqua, and Romiti (2019) who examine the time that children spend studying in married versus single-mother families in Italy. They find that children living in single-mother families spend less time studying than children living with married parents, and this gap is greater for boys than for girls. They note that "the increase in the gender gap due to living with a single mother is stronger for older boys, boys with lower-educated or less-well-off mothers, or boys with working mothers" (p. 152).

College enrollment and graduation is a "child outcome" that varies substantially by gender, and some portion of the growing female advantage in college enrollment may be attributable to gender differences in the single-parent disadvantage. According to Buchmann and DiPrete (2006), the "female advantage in college completion remains largest in families with a low educated or absent father" (p. 515). However, there are other important correlates with this growing gender gap, including a greater relative return to college (versus high school) for women than for men (DiPrete and Buchmann 2006). Fortin, Oreopoulos, and Phipps (2015) show that the growing college gender gap is attributable primarily to changing preferences; girls are growing more motivated to attend college and even pursue postgraduate education, and this preferences gap is manifesting in a gender difference in middle school grade distributions. But the authors also explain that, "among eighth graders, our second dominant factor accounting for the lower grades of boys is a measure of the frequency of having been sent to the office or to detention over the previous year. This suggests that motivation and misbehavior may go hand in hand" (p. 577).[4]

There is empirical evidence, however, to contradict the notion that the single-mother disadvantage particularly disadvantages boys. Lundberg (2017) finds that the gender gap in the disadvantage children experience from growing up with a single parent does not systematically differ by the gender of the child. Brenoe and Lundberg (2018) show that for Denmark, while it appears that boys are more sensitive than girls to family environment, girls' outcomes as young adults are more responsive to parents' characteristics, particularly their mothers'. Finally, Buchmann and DiPrete (2006) find that girls are outperforming boys in two-parent families as well as single-parent families, suggesting that factors beyond family structure are contributing to the gender gap in school performance and other outcomes.

One implication of the phenomenon of intergenerational transmission of the single-mother disadvantage is that it has the potential to partially explain racial inequalities observed in U.S. society. Rates of single motherhood are higher for Blacks than for whites, suggesting that racial inequality will worsen as these higher single motherhood rates produce more disadvantaged children who then become adults who are less likely to marry, thereby exacerbating this disadvantage in future generations. However, there is little empirical evidence of differences in the single-mother disadvantage by race. Gennetian and Rodrigues (2020) examine differences in parenting time in the U.S. by race and ethnicity for specific ranges of income, in order to identify time investments differences not arising from income differences. They focus on possible trade-offs between paid work and parenting time for mothers and fathers who are white, Black, and Hispanic. Notably, while their estimates reveal little difference in parenting time (with income held constant) by race, they note that Hispanic fathers' parenting time is reduced more per hour of paid work time than non-Hispanic fathers'. Cross (2018, 2019) focuses explicitly on potential differences in the single-motherhood disadvantage by race. According to Cross, who studies the impact of growing up in single-mother families on children's educational attainment, Black children are impacted less negatively by growing up in single-mother families than white children, a result she largely attributes to the fact that the gap in socioeconomic resources by family structure for Black families is smaller than for white families. A second factor is the greater incidence of protective extended family networks for Black households. Specifically, Cross explains that the greater incidence of single-mother families is mitigated somewhat by the counterbalancing larger percentage of extended family households. While 57 percent of Blacks and 35 percent of Hispanics reside in extended family households, only 20 percent of white families live in such families (Cross 2018).

FAMILY STRUCTURE AND PARENTING TIME

Our empirical approach in this chapter is largely descriptive; however, there is a theoretical basis for our presumption that parental time inputs matter for children's development. Becker and Tomes (1986) describe intergenerational mobility in the context of a single time period of a child's skills production function. Cunha and Heckman (2007) expand on earlier work in their development of an economic model of skill formation (also referred to as an economic model of child development) that incorporates multiple investment periods during childhood, with complementarity of inputs across these time periods. The model reflects the authors' attempt to organize the existing empirical evidence into a cohesive model that supports, in particular, the evidence that earlier investments are more efficient than later ones—"abilities are created, not solely inherited, and are multiple in variety"—and that reflect their conclusion from the existing evidence that "the nature versus 'nurture' distinction is obsolete" (p. 31). Fuller development and testing of this theory using dynamic factor models is found in Cunha and Heckman (2008). The authors conclude that parental investments are more effective in the production of noncognitive skills more than cognitive skills, although this varies by the age of the child. Additionally, they find that noncognitive skill development enhances the production of cognitive skill development, but not vice versa.

The underlying theory describing the relationship between parenting inputs and child outcomes developed by Cunha and Heckman permits the impact of parenting to vary by parent's education level. Becker et al. (2018) rely on the notion that higher-educated parents (typically wealthier parents) devote more resources to their children, which tends to decrease intergenerational mobility. This theoretical framework is consistent with the frequent finding in the parenting time-use literature that higher-educated parents, on average, devote more time to caring for their children, regardless of how one measures child care and independent of the parent's employment status. Guryan, Hurst, and Kearney (2008) describe this positive educational gradient in child care (and income as well), explaining that it is evidence that parenting time "behaves" more like paid work time than leisure or household production time.[5]

Research focusing on the impacts of family structure concludes that father absence is detrimental for children's well being.[6] The mechanisms by which married biological parents confer their advantage are not well understood. Beyond the obvious income differences by family structure, there is the parental time constraint that is worsened when only one adult is present in the household. One theory suggests that the gendered disadvantage for children growing up in single-mother families is the result, at least in part, of maternal time focused on daughters more than on sons. There also may be substantial selection issues in which the characteristics of individuals who marry contribute to better outcomes for children, rather than the marriage itself. For example, personal traits that are useful in keeping a marriage together (ability to empathize, problem solve, compromise) may also contribute to better parenting skills. Finally, married biological parents may provide more long-term stability, while cohabiting parental relationships are more likely to fail, resulting in change and uncertainty that can be disruptive to children's lives and emotional well-being.

The parenting time literature most relevant for our project lies in two interrelated areas: the implications of family structure on parenting time and differences in parenting time by child gender. Conceptually, there are several reasons that one might expect to observe different unpaid time-use patterns by marital status. First, average differences in family income or parents' educational attainment, or persistent gender differences, may be associated with differences in time allocation choices. Second, differences in time resources and the inability to exploit economies of scale or specialization may result in observed differences in time-use patterns by marital status.[7]

Kalenkoski, Ribar, and Stratton (2007) expand on the above listed mechanisms by which family status could affect parenting time with notions drawn from sociology's theories of socialization and gender theory. "These theories," they write, "consider how individuals come to internalize certain values or roles and how societies and institutions—including the institution of the family—reinforce those roles and possibly construct gender itself" (p. 356). In their paper, the authors use data from the ATUS for the United States along with the United Kingdom Time Use Survey to examine the effects of family structure on parenting time in primary and passive child care and market work. According to the authors, "A major finding in our study is that single parents in both countries spend more time in child care than married or cohabiting parents" (p. 354).

Ermisch (2008) links parenting time by family structure to child outcome gaps by family structure, arguing that for the United Kingdom, more favorable developmental outcomes for children growing up in two-parent families can be explained, at least in part, by a gap in parenting time in developmental activities. Also using data from the United Kingdom, Kalenkoski, Ribar, and Stratton (2005) analyze time-use patterns across parent gender and marital status. The authors find that both single men and single women spend more time in child care and less time in paid work than their married counterparts (p. 196).

Connelly and Kimmel (2014) find small differences in parental time with children across marital status, with no significant difference in primary child caregiving time. According to the authors, "Single mothers devote a larger percentage of their time to physical care, controlling for the age of the youngest child, compared to coupled mothers" (p. 89). For men, single fathers spend less time on child caregiving than married men, but for single fathers, the percentage of child caregiving that is developmental care is greater than for married men. A drawback of all of the studies cited thus far is that they do not consider differences by child gender.

Lundberg (2005) provides a conceptual framework to explain why parental behavior with regard to their children might vary based on that child's gender, concluding that there are two basic explanations: "Systematic bias in the utility generated by male and female children (or their attainment) or by the differences in the net costs of raising boys and girls" (p. 344). According to Lundberg, "The preference- and constraint-based models of child-gender effects have the same predictions with respect to parental time allocation and child involvement. Increased time with a same-sex child can result from the enjoyment of time spent with the child who is most like you, perhaps engaged in familiar and gender-typical activities, or from the belief that you are a more effective, productive parent with this child. Differences in the market work or other activities of parents of boys and girls may occur as indirect outcomes of differences in optimal child care time or as a reaction to different expectations about relationship stability" (p. 348). Empirical evidence cited by Lundberg supports these predictions; specifically, fathers spend more time with their sons than daughters, and fathers are more likely than mothers to treat their sons differently than their daughters.

Baker and Milligan's (2016) international comparative study of parental time investments in their children provides detailed analyses of gender differences of these investments. They analyze panel data for first-born children up through age five for Canada, the United States, and the United Kingdom, and they document greater parental time investment in girls in developmental activities (reading and teaching activities). The bulk of their empirical work is regressions in which parenting time per child is explained with a male child dummy and a list of controls that does not include the mother's marital status because, according to the authors, marital status may be endogenous and dependent upon child gender (p. 406).[8] For children under the age of three, despite the advantage that girls receive in parental time investments in developmental activities, total parenting time does not differ by child gender. Once children reach the age of three, the balance of total parenting time tips in favor of boys due to a dominant time advantage for boys observed in play time and secondary time, especially for fathers (p. 402).

Baker and Milligan (2016) consider several different sources of girls' advantage in reading and teaching time before age three, and although they do not draw any decisive conclusions, they note that other researchers have identified a girl developmental advantage representing approximately one month's worth of development for infants younger than one year of age. It is possible that parents are more motivated to engage in reading and teaching activities with girls than boys simply because girls are more ready for such activities at younger ages.

Mammen (2011) uses American Time Use Survey data to examine married fathers' time with their children with a focus on child gender. Fathers sacrifice their own leisure to increase their time with their children when one of the children is male, and more of this paternal time is devoted to their sons than daughters. Girls with male siblings receive more parental time than girls with just female siblings, although this increased time is observed just in watching television.[9]

There is limited research that examines the relationship between children and their nonresident parents. One example is the Pronzato and Aassve (2019) study of the impact of parent separation on child outcomes in the United Kingdom. They rely on data on children under the age of 11 to examine the consequences of parent separation on child outcomes. Most relevant for our research is their finding that children who experience family disruption fare better when they maintain a quality relationship with the nonresident parent (as measured by the frequency with which the child sleeps at the nonresident parent's home).

A related issue is studied by Lundberg, McLanahan, and Rose (2007), who draw their data from the Fragile Families and Child Well-being Study, an ongoing panel survey of U.S. children born in large U.S. cities between 1998 and 2002. They examine the quality of the relationship of nonresident fathers with their children as it relates to the child's gender, the father's marital status at the time the child was born, and the father's financial commitment to the child. As the authors note, "The association between child gender and father involvement is of particular interest. If children benefit from close connections with their fathers, and if boys are more likely than girls to maintain such connections following a nonmarital birth, the recent increase in nonmarital childbearing may have important implications for future gender equality" (p. 79). After the child is one year of age, their results suggest that for unmarried parents, the child's gender is not correlated with the involvement of nonresident fathers in their children's lives or the likelihood that the father and mother will cohabit.

Hook and Wolfe (2012) study residential fathers' time with their first-born children in the United States, Germany, Norway, and the United Kingdom. Using 2003 ATUS data, they find that for the United States, fathers spend more time in physical care of their children when the mother is employed full time, and fathers' parenting time is greater on the weekend.

Bringing the two literatures together (gender of the child and family structure), Lundberg, Wulff Pabilonia, and Ward-Batts (2007) provide some empirical evidence of differences in parenting time inputs both by parent/child gender and family structure. Using data from the PSID, they find that married fathers with both sons and daughters devote more time to their sons than their daughters. Also, they find that the daughter advantage in single mothers' parenting time is a greater relative advantage than the daughter advantage observed for married mothers. "Overall, we find that same-sex parent-child time in stereotypically gendered activities is pervasive and becomes increasingly evident in the teen years" (g. 6).

The research closest to ours is Bibler (2020), who analyzes parenting time with children across both family structure and child gender using Panel Study of Income Dynamics (PSID) data.[10] These data on children's time use are collected in the 1997, 2002/2003, and 2007 surveys. Bibler estimates fixed effects time-use equations with the child as the unit of analysis, focusing on total time spent in activities with his/her mother or father as the time-use measure. As a result of the fixed effects strategy, his resulting estimated coefficients are driven solely by those children who experienced changes in family structure from two parent to single parent between 1997 and 2007. There are a number of problems with this approach, not the least of which is that the bulk of single-mother families (and the ones potentially most at risk of transmitting disadvantage) are families in which the mother has never married, and whose children have not experienced a change in family structure.[11] In addition, each observation represents only two days: one weekday and one weekend day. Single-day diaries are appropriate for finding differences across large numbers of observations in average time-use patterns, but not for identifying differences within a single individual, given the high percent of time use that is idiosyncratic (Frazis and Stewart 2012).

Our research strategy, which is described below, uses the ATUS data on parental time use treating their marital and parental status as exogeneous on the diary day. While gender of one's child may indeed have a small effect on the probability of the marriage of that child's parents, marital status is not endogenous to a specific day's time choices. We rely on the large sample sizes of the ATUS over the full range of years available to take a closer look at parental time use by current marital status and the gender of one's children.[12]

CONCEPTUALIZING, MEASURING, AND DESCRIBING PARENTING TIME

Conceptualizing and Measuring Parenting Time

We use the full combined sample of the ATUS data from the years 2003–2017, combining many years of ATUS data to yield subgroup samples of sufficient size.[13] The ATUS yearly samples comprise a subsample of the outgoing rotation group of the Current Population Survey. The ATUS is a retrospective time diary in which individuals are contacted via telephone and asked to report their primary activities for the 24-hour period immediately preceding the phone interview. In reporting on the primary activity, individuals are also asked to report which household members are in the room with the survey respondent during the activity.

In order to measure child caregiving time, we rely on two distinct measures of time with children: primary child care time and time engaged in any activity in which children are present (i.e., "who was in the room" information). The ATUS also includes a measure of secondary child care time, time when children are under one's care when engaged in non–child caregiving activities, but we have chosen not to use this measure, as previous research and our current exploration have found it unreliable.[14] Early in the results section we also report more limited time-use categories: time in the presence of children when the adult is engaged in nonwork (i.e., nonemployment and nonhousework) time (labeled in-room, nonwork) and primary caregiving time when the activity is reading or playing with one's child (developmental child caregiving).

Exploiting the two primary child caregiving time measures and the two in-room measures permits us to capture as best we can two of the three categories of parents' time expenditures devoted to their children as described by Mammen (2011). Mammen focuses on fathers' time with their children and claims that there are three categories of fathering time: interaction, availability, and responsibility. Interaction involves fathers' time use that encompasses direct engagement with their children, whereas time during which the father is engaged in some other primary activity but is also available to the children can be categorized as availability. Responsibility includes fathers' time devoted to tasks undertaken on their children's behalf, along with fathers' time with their children when the mother is not present. Our primary child caregiving and developmental child caregiving time can be thought of as interaction time, with developmental time more interaction intensive than all primary child caregiving time. In-room time and in-room, nonwork time includes both interaction and availability time; we expect the greater portion of the time in in-room, nonwork is interaction time.

Description of Data

We use a merged sample comprising all parents of minor children from the 2003–2017 ATUS, with initial sample selection contingent on age restrictions (18–65), the presence of at least one own child under the age of 18 in the household, or the existence of at least one own non-resident child under the age of 18.

While the ATUS data are appropriate for this project for many reasons, the survey and the resulting database have their deficiencies. The most significant drawback of the ATUS survey is that the bulk of survey respondents are adults, and when child care time is reported, the identity (and thus the gender) of the child is not clearly identified except to differentiate among own resident children, own nonresident children, and non-own children. We address this data deficiency by examining subsamples of the ATUS of parents with just one child in order to be certain about that child's sex: single mothers with just one own resident child, married mothers with just one own resident child, and likewise for fathers, though the sample size for single fathers with own resident children is quite limiting.[15] In addition, we have a sample of fathers with one own nonresident child.[16] In the case of just one child, we know this one child's gender for all the parent's child caregiving activities. In addition, in later analyses not reported here, but described briefly in the text, we consider single mothers with exactly two own resident children, married mothers with exactly two resident children, single fathers with exactly two own resident children, and married fathers with exactly two resident children. For two children, we include dummies for the gender mix of the children: both daughters, a son and a daughter, and both sons. While we still cannot tell which time is spent with which child, we can observe general patterns across these three cases. Including those with two children in the analysis allows us to consider whether patterns observed for one child carry over to parents juggling the needs of two children.[17]

There is a relatively small loss of sample size resulting from our selection of parents with just one child or just two children. For men, 91.9 percent of the sample of single fathers and 78.7 percent of the married fathers have exactly two or exactly one child. For women, 83.8 percent of the sample of single mothers and 78.5 percent of the married mothers have exactly two or exactly one child. However, the primary focus on parents with only one child does substantially restrict our sample sizes. Only 36 percent of the full sample of married mothers and 52 percent of the single mothers, both with own resident children, have one child. For married fathers, the corresponding percentages are 36 percent and 63 percent, respectively, for married and single fathers. For mothers and fathers with own nonresident children, the percentages with one child are 69 percent and 67 percent. The resulting sample sizes are still fairly large. Considering fathers with exactly one own resident child under the age of 18, there are 8,819 married fathers and 1,390 single fathers; in the case of exactly two resident own children in the household under the age of 18, there are 10,277 married fathers and 651 single fathers. Considering mothers with exactly one own resident child under the age of 18 in the household, there are 10,211 married mothers and 5,633 single mothers; in the case of exactly two own resident children in the household under the age of 18, there are 11,760 married mothers and 3,470 single mothers. In each of these samples, approximately 50 percent of the children are male.[18]

The sample sizes of those with a single own nonresident child are much smaller, especially for mothers. Considering mothers with exactly one own resident child under the age of 18 in the household, there are 177 married mothers and 164 single mothers; for fathers the comparable numbers are 471 for married fathers and 653 for single fathers. Considering mothers with exactly two own resident children under the age of 18 in the household, there are 63 married mothers and 57 single mothers; for fathers the comparable numbers are 137 for married fathers and 270 for single fathers.[19]

Empirical Strategy

Our empirical strategy comprises a comparison of means, regression, and then using the regression results to construct predicted time-use measures for a "representative" person. These three steps in our empirical approach are described below.

1) We compare mean child caregiving time across family structure, child gender, parent gender, and coresident status (i.e., does the parent reside with the child) using t-tests to determine which of the observed differences are statistically significant differences.

2) We estimate time-use equations using our various measures for parenting time separately by parent gender and marital status.[20] This regression approach permits us to control characteristics of both the respondent and his/her children. Among the regressors that we include are: dummy variable for weekend diary, dummy variable for summer month diary, parent works for pay part-time or not employed (with full-time employment as the omitted category); completed education as a set of dummies; ATUS survey year dummy variables; and the gender composition of their children. See Appendix Tables 2A.1A–2A.1D for the full set of regressors.[21]

3) Using the estimated coefficients from the regressions, we construct predicted mean minutes for the "representative" parent defined with the key characteristic of lesser education, as this is the focus of our chapter. More completely, the "representative" parent is described as not foreign born, employed full time, who dropped out of high school, resides in an urban area, in the western portion of the United States, with a nonsummer 2017 diary day (averaged between five identical weekdays and two identical weekend days). The race and ethnicity of our representative parent and the probability of living with adults other than one's spouse are in proportion to the population's race and ethnicity and "other adult" profile of the relevant subsamples. The predicted mean minutes for mothers and fathers are added together to provide estimates of total parent time for boys and girls in married and single households.[22]

Descriptive Findings

In Table 2.1A, we present selected means for married and single mothers with a single child under age 6 and then a single teenage child (aged 13–17), and in Table 2.1B, we present selected means for married and single fathers with a single child under the age of 6 and then a single teenage child. We include the results of t-tests, which indicate significant differences between single and married parents by gender and age of their only child.

Both tables show that there are significant differences across marital status for many of the observable characteristics of the parent and the household within which he or she resides. Compared to the married samples, a larger percent of all the single-parent samples are Black and Hispanic. For example, 15.5 percent of the single mothers whose child is under 6 are Black, while 5.2 percent of the married mothers whose only child is under 6 are Black. Single and married mothers of an only child under 6 are equally likely to not be employed (32 percent), but single fathers with an only child under 6 are significantly more likely than married fathers to not be employed (18.6 percent versus 7.6 percent). Single parents have a much higher proportion with low educational attainment (high school graduate or below) except for the comparison of single and married mothers with a single teenage child in

Table 2.1A Selected Means for Married and Single Mothers with Exactly One Child under Age 6 or Teenaged (13–17)

	Single mother, child under 6 (%)	Married mother, child under 6 (%)	Significant difference single vs. married	Single mother, child 13–17 (%)	Married mother, child 13–17 (%)	Significant difference single vs. married
Black	28.5	5.2	***	24.3	6.8	***
Hispanic	17.3	14.2	***	13.8	11.9	**
Foreign born	11.7	18.9	***	14.0	16.0	**
Not employed	31.2	32.4		22.0	23.0	
HS grad or below	45.6	22.8	***	36.5	34.2	*
Some college	35.7	26.9	***	35.0	30.7	***
College grad	18.6	51.1	***	28.4	35.0	***
Other adult	37.5	7.5	***	32.1	42.0	***
Summer	24.6	26.0		25.5	25.8	
Son	50.4	51.0		51.0	51.4	
In-room minutes	423	475	***	209	227	***
In-room, nonwork minutes	309	352	***	144	153	
Primary child caregiving minutes	109	149	***	27	24	*
Developmental child caregiving minutes	41	64	***	2	1	*
N	1,687	4,212		1,861	3,265	

NOTE: *** p < 0.01, ** p < 0.05, * p < 0.1.
SOURCE: ATUS 2003–2017.

residence. This pattern with regard to educational attainment by marital status has been noted by other researchers.

There are also notable differences in the percentage of households with another adult in the household (not the spouse in the case of married parents) for households with a preschooler. Only 7.5 percent of married mothers and 10.0 percent of married fathers with a child under

Table 2.1B Selected Means for Married and Single Fathers with Exactly One Child under Age 6 or Teenaged (13–17)

	Single father, child under 6 (%)	Married father, child under 6 (%)	Significant difference single vs. married	Single father, child 13–17 (%)	Married father, child 13–17 (%)	Significant difference single vs. married
Black	15.5	5.2	***	13.0	6.9	***
Hispanic	21.4	14.2	***	9.4	11.1	
Foreign born	11.8	19.9	***	9.2	15.0	***
Not employed	18.6	7.6	***	18.4	11.8	***
HS grad or below	46.6	27.8	***	44.7	35.3	***
Some college	39.1	26.1	***	24.6	38.4	***
College grad	14.3	46.1	***	30.7	26.3	**
Other adult	44.7	10.0	***	30.7	43.1	***
Summer	24.5	24.8		24.8	23.6	
w/son	50.6	50.8		59.0	51.6	***
In-room minutes	306	344	***	194	183	
In-room, nonwork minutes	244	275	***	140	135	
Primary child caregiving minutes	77	82		16	12	**
Developmental child caregiving minutes	40	43		2	2	
N	322	3,654		544	2,875	

NOTE: *** $p < 0.01$, ** $p < 0.05$, * $p < 0.1$.
SOURCE: ATUS 2003–2017.

age 6 live with another adult in the household, while that percentage is 37.5 percent for single mothers and 44.7 percent for single fathers. The situation is reversed for those with a child aged 13–17, with 42.0 percent of the married mothers and 32.1 percent of the single mothers with another adult present. One presumes that many of these other adults are actually older children of these parents of one minor teenager. Single and married fathers exhibit the same relative pattern and approximately the same levels, 30.7 percent for single fathers and 43.1 percent for married fathers. Two characteristics in which single and married samples do not differ is in the percentage whose single child is a boy (both are approximately 50 percent) and the percentage of time diaries collected in the summer (both are approximately 25 percent).

Finally, looking at mean minutes spent with children, there are significant and sizable differences by marital status, by gender, and by the measure of child caregiving used. The mean number of total minutes the parent reports being in the same room as his/her only child is the highest for married mothers with preschoolers, at 475 minutes, and the lowest for married fathers of teenagers, at 183 minutes. In-room time is higher for married fathers versus single fathers and married mothers versus single mothers for young children. The same is true for married versus single mothers of teenage children, while married and single fathers spend similar minutes with their teenage children (194 minutes for single fathers and 183 for married fathers).

Not all time with a child in the room involves interaction. To narrow this time-use measure a bit, we consider the minutes spent with a child in the room in which the parent is engaged in primary child caregiving or in a leisure activity (in-room, nonwork). With this more focused measure, the basic pattern described above still holds, with married mothers of preschoolers spending 352 minutes compared to 308 for single mothers of preschoolers and married fathers of preschoolers spending 275 minutes compared to 244 for single fathers of preschoolers. The differences across marital status by gender are quite small for time spent with teenagers.

Alternatively, we can look at time specifically characterized by the parent as child caregiving time. This measure of child caregiving time differs substantially by the age of the child. Married mothers of preschoolers spend 149 minutes on the diary day, on average, on those activities compared to 109 for single mothers; for fathers, average minutes are 149 for both married and single fathers. Married and single fathers spend approximately the same number of minutes on primary child caregiving for their preschoolers, about 80 minutes a day. Finally, with a nod to Baker and Milligan (2016), we record the minutes spent in reading or playing, a sub-category of primary child caregiving. As others have found, the differences here between fathers and mothers are much smaller (fathers get to do the fun stuff), but the differences between single and married mothers of preschoolers is substantial (41 versus 64 minutes).

Tables 2.1C and 2.1D present similar selected means for the samples of parents with a single nonresident child. The sample size for mothers with a nonresident child under age 6 is very small, thus we do not report those data. Single nonresident parents are more likely to be Black and have another adult living with them than married parents. Single fathers of a nonresident teenager are more likely to be nonemployed than similar married fathers. There are no significant differences in child caregiving times across marital status for this group. We should note that a substantial number of these parents have other own coresident children, with significant differences by marital status, particularly for fathers.

Table 2.1C   Selected Means for Married and Single Mothers with Exactly One Nonresident Teenaged Child (13–17)

	Single mother with nonresident child 13–17	Married mother with nonresident child 13–17	Significant difference single vs. married
Black	26.1	8.4	***
Hispanic	15.9	8.0	*
Foreign born	3.4	7.5	
Not employed	31.8	35.5	
HS grad or below	42.0	43.9	
Some college	38.6	35.5	
College grad	19.3	20.6	
Other adult	26.1	13.1	**
Summer	28.4	23.4	
w/own resident child	43.2	65.4	***
w/nonresident son	68.2	48.6	***
In-room minutes	23	29	
In-room, nonwork minutes	31	14	
Primary child caregiving minutes	12	3	
N	88	107	

NOTE: Sample sizes for mothers with a single nonresident child under 6 too small to report. *** $p < 0.01$, ** $p < 0.05$, * $p < 0.1$.
SOURCE: ATUS 2003–2017.

Table 2.1D Selected Means for Married and Single Fathers with Exactly One Nonresident Child under Age 6 or Teenaged (13–17)

	Single father with nonresident child under 6	Married father with nonresident child under 6	Significant difference single vs. married	Single father with nonresident child 13–17	Married father with nonresident child 13–17	Significant difference single vs. married
Black	29.0	14.7	*	25.4	14.1	***
Hispanic	24.5	17.6		16.3	12.6	
Foreign born	14.8	14.7		12.0	11.5	
Not employed	21.3	11.8		21.0	14.5	**
HS grad or below	55.5	47.1		42.4	45.4	
Some college	29.7	26.5		31.9	28.2	
College grad	14.8	26.5		25.7	26.3	
Other adult	41.9	11.8	*	20.7	13.0	**
Summer	22.6	20.6		26.1	28.6	
w/own resident child	9.7	52.9	***	11.6	68.3	***
w/non-resident son	44.5	47.1		50.4	47.7	
In-room minutes	92	64		38	27	
In-room, nonwork minutes	49	26		28	16	
Primary child caregiving minutes	36	2		4	3	
N	155	34		276	262	

NOTE: *** p < 0.01, ** p < 0.05, * p < 0.1.
SOURCE: ATUS 2003–2017.

Tables 2.2A and 2.2B present the mean child caregiving times for parents with sons versus daughters. Table 2.2A presents the results for parents with only one own resident child. Looking first at time spent with sons and daughters under the age of 6, both single and married mothers spend comparable time with their young sons and daughters. There are no significant differences for any of the four alternative measures of child caregiving time. On the other hand, fathers of preschoolers consistently spend more time with sons than daughters, with the differences significant in the case of married fathers. Married fathers spend an extra 10 minutes a day in primary child caregiving time with their sons than their daughters, with all the extra minutes devoted to developmental child caregiving.

For teenage children, there is a clear pattern of parents spending more time with their same-sex teenage child; that is, fathers spend more time with their sons, and mothers spend more time with their daughters. These differences are significant for the in-room and in-room, nonwork caregiving time measure and for primary child caregiving for married mothers and fathers. However, in this latter time category, the magnitude of the difference is quite small.

Table 2.2B presents the same comparison for mothers and fathers with one nonresident child. The results show that there are no statistically significant differences between the time mothers and fathers spend with their nonresident teenage sons and daughters and no statistically significant differences between the time nonresident fathers spend with preschoolers. Sample sizes are too small to report for mothers with children under the age of 6. Thus, nonresident parents who acknowledge their nonresident child do not follow the same gendered pattern of time with the children that resident parents do.

EMPIRICAL RESULTS

Baseline Regression Results

The patterns of time use in Table 2.2A reveal some differences by child gender in child caregiving for mothers and fathers. We noted earlier substantial differences in the observable characteristics across single and married samples, with single samples more likely to be Black, low educated, and having other adults present in the household. Since these characteristics are themselves correlated with child caregiving time, we need to consider the effect of child gender controlling for these other characteristics. In this section, we report results of estimating ordinary least squares (OLS) regressions using two of our four time-use categories: in-room time and primary child care time.[23]

Table 2.2A Mean Child Caregiving Minutes by Sex of Child for Sample with Only One Own Resident Child

	Single mothers w/ 1 child < 6		Married mothers w/ 1 child < 6		Single mothers w/ 1 child 13–17		Married mothers w/ 1 child 13–17	
	With son	With daughter	With son	With daughter	With son	With daughter	With son	With daughter
In-room	429	418	475	476	183	237*	208	246*
In-room, nonwork time	318	300	353	350	126	163*	143	163*
Primary child caregiving	111	107	150	147	25	28	22	26*
Developmental child caregiving	42	41	65	62	2	2	1	1
N	850	837	2,148	2,064	956	905	1,664	1,601

	Single fathers w/ 1 child < 6		Married fathers w/ 1 child < 6		Single fathers w/ 1 child 13–17		Married fathers w/ 1 child 13–17	
	With son	With daughter	With son	With daughter	With son	With daughter	With son	With daughter
In-room	329	284	347	341	215	164*	192	172*
In-room, nonwork time	265	223	280	271	154	119*	141	129*
Primary child caregiving	81	72	87	77*	16	17	14	11*
Developmental child caregiving	42	38	48	38*	3	2	2	1*
N	163	159	1,855	1,799	321	223	1,484	1,391

NOTE: * indicates significantly different by gender of child at 5% level based on two tailed t-tests (p < 0.05).
SOURCE: ATUS 2003–2017.

Table 2.2B Mean Child Caregiving Minutes by Sex of Child for Sample with Only One Own Nonresident Child

	Single mothers with a nonresident child 13–17		Married mothers nonresident child 13–17	
	With son	With daughter	With son	With daughter
In-room	41	37	16	29
In-room, nonwork time	32	28	15	14
Primary child caregiving	15	6	0	6
N	60	28	52	55

	Single fathers non-resident child 13–17		Married fathers non-resident child 13–17	
	With son	With daughter	With son	With daughter
In-room	22	43	37	18
In-room, nonwork time	22	34	21	12
Primary child caregiving	4	3	3	4
N	139	137	125	137

	Single fathers non-resident child 0–6		Married fathers non-resident child 13–17	
	With son	With daughter	With son	With daughter
In-room	77	61	66	104
In-room nonwork time	40	26	26	56
Primary child caregiving	34	3	1	38
N	69	16	18	86

NOTE: No significant differences between those with sons versus daughters at the 5% level based on two tailed t-tests. Sample sizes for mothers with a nonresident child 0–5 are too small to report.

SOURCE: ATUS 2003–2017.

Regression results for the dependent variable of total minutes of child care, for subsamples with exactly one child in the household, are presented in Appendix Tables 2A.1A and 2A.1B for in-room time for children under age 6 and 13 to 17, respectively, and Appendix Tables 2A.1C and 2A.1D for primary child caregiving time. Note that we have combined married fathers and single fathers of nonresident children because of sample size concerns. Coefficients can be interpreted as the number of extra minutes the parent with that characteristic reported being engaged in the time use activity as compared to the excluded group. For example, in Appendix Table 2A.1A we see that for single mothers with an only child under the age of 6, not employed mothers spend 118 more minutes in the same room with that single child compared to those mothers who are employed full time.

Effects of Child Gender on Child Caregiving Time of Parents of One Child

Table 2.3 reports only the marginal effect of the son dummy variable for the in-room and primary child caregiving measures of child caregiving time. The pattern of significant difference or lack thereof in terms of the gender of the child is quite similar to those reported in Tables 2.2A and 2.2B, with the difference being that variation in other observable characteristics is now controlled for via OLS. Considering in-room time, we find that mothers and fathers, both single and married, spend the same amount of time with their preschool sons as preschool daughters. However, substantial gender differences emerge for in-room time spent with teenage children. Mothers, both single and married, spend more time in the presence of their daughters, while fathers, both single and married, spend more time with their sons. The differences are larger for single parents than married, with single mothers spending 53 fewer minutes a day with their teenage son than if their child were female, compared to 36 fewer minutes a day for married mothers of teenage sons versus teenage daughters. For fathers, the comparison is 46 more minutes for single fathers with teenage sons and 26 minutes for married fathers with teenage sons. There are no significant differences of time spent by fathers with nonresident sons versus nonresident daughters. Also, once other factors are controlled, the child gender effects are muted for primary child caregiving time, with very small child gender differences by the child's age for mothers versus fathers.

Table 2.3 Marginal Effect of Having a Son on Minutes of Child Caregiving Time

	Aged 0–5	Aged 13–17
In-room minutes		
Single mothers w/ resident child	4.05	−53.02***
Married mothers w/ resident child	−5.01	−35.75***
Single fathers w/ resident child	26.95	46.21**
Married fathers w/ resident child	8.51	26.00***
Fathers w/ nonresident child	−18.08	1.61
Primary child caregiving minutes		
Single mothers w/ resident child	2.96	−3.67
Married mothers w/ resident child	2.70	−4.67**
Single fathers w/ resident child	−1.41	−0.73
Married fathers w/ resident child	10.06***	3.61**
Fathers w/ nonresident child	0.30	0.23

NOTE: *** $p < 0.01$, ** $p < 0.05$, * $p < 0.1$. The number in the cell is the coefficient on Son Indicator from separate regression by marital status of the parent, the parent's sex, and the age category of their only child. Other variables included in the OLS regression were: indicators for Black, Hispanic, foreign born, nonemployed, employed part time, low education level, high education level, region of the country, MSA, summer, weekend, and a full set of dummies for year of survey. Full results save for the year in survey dummies are available in Appendix Tables 2A.1A–2A.1D.
SOURCE: ATUS 2003–2017.

Determinants of Average In-Room Child Caregiving Minutes beyond Child Gender

Tables with the full regression results are presented in Appendix 2A.[24] Tables 2A.1A and 2A.1B display regression results for parents with exactly one resident child, focusing on in-room child care minutes, and Tables 2A.1C and 2A.1D focus on primary child caregiving minutes. In the discussion of regression results that follows, ceteris paribus is implied. Focusing first on in-room time, for all five family types, there is no statistically significant difference in time spent with children in the room for parents who are foreign born. Compared to the excluded category of non-Black, Black single fathers do not report any statistically significant difference in parenting time as compared to the excluded category of white. Black married fathers report spending 48 fewer in-room minutes with their preschool child and 29 minutes fewer with their teenage child. Both married and single Black mothers report spending less time in the same room with their child than non-Black mothers. Black married mothers report spending 47 fewer minutes with their single preschool child overall than non-Black mothers and 51 fewer minutes with their single teenager. Black single mothers report, on average, 34 fewer minutes of time spent in the same room as their preschool child, as compared to non-Black single mothers, and 18 fewer minutes with their teenager, although that effect is imprecisely measured.

An indicator variable for Hispanic ethnicity is also included in the regression. The coefficient is significant only for single mothers. Single Hispanic mothers spend more in-room time with their child than non-Hispanic single mothers for both preschoolers (30 minutes) and teenagers (44 minutes).

In our analysis of sample means above, we observed large differences across samples in the proportion of households with other adults beyond the partner. A larger proportion of single parents with young children have other adults living with them (these should not be partners, since partnered but unmarried couples are included in our married sample). For the parents with teenagers, married parents have a larger proportion of other adults living with them, and we expect that many of these are older children (now adult aged). It is interesting to observe what effect if any the presence of another adult in the household has on child caregiving time. Theoretically, the effect with grandparents could be to supplement or replace parental caregiving. The results in Appendix Tables 2A.1A and 2A.1B show that for married mothers and fathers with young children, the presence of other adults reduces in-room time by about 25 minutes. There is no significant effect for single mothers and fathers of preschoolers. For parents of older children, only single fathers show a negative effect of other adults on their in-room time. For single mothers of teenagers, their in-room time is increased by 22 minutes in the presence of other adults (these also could be older children).

There are two employment dummy variable measures included in the regressions, a dummy for not employed and a dummy for employed part time; the excluded category is full time employment. Notably, nonresident fathers reveal only a weak link between time with their child and employment status (results not shown). For all four family type subsamples with resident parents, those who are not employed report statistically significantly more minutes of time spent in the same room with their only preschool child compared to full-time employed parents. Similarly, not employed resident parents of teenagers spend between 20 minutes to an hour more time a day with their teenagers, although the result is not significant for single fathers. For those who are employed part time, married mothers and fathers spend an extra three-quarters of an hour with their preschoolers. For those with teenagers, part-time employed mothers, both single and married, spend more time with their teenagers than those employed full time.

There is extensive evidence in the literature to show that education is related consistently to differences in time spent with children; *ceteris paribus*, higher-educated parents report spending more time with their children.[25] We do not find an entirely consistent education gradient for in-room time, using the three levels of education we have chosen. Low-education-level married mothers spend 20 fewer minutes in-room with their preschoolers than mid-level-education married mothers, and high-level-education married fathers spend 17 more minutes with their preschoolers than mid-level education married fathers; however, the other coefficients for education are the opposite in sign or insignificant. Below we report stronger positive education gradients for primary child care time, but again, mostly for married parents.

We include in our regressions dummy variables for whether the diary was collected during the summer and whether the diary was collected on a weekend day. For each of the four samples, there is no impact on time with young children reported during the summer, but sizable effects on time spent with teenagers. On the other hand, as expected, in-room time with children is substantially greater for all parents on weekends. Mothers' time is increased more than fathers' time, and time with younger children is increased more than teenager time. Even for fathers of teenagers, the increases on the weekend are more than two hours a day. For nonresident fathers, the increase of time with children on the weekend is also evident, but the magnitudes are much smaller, one hour for young children and 45 minutes for teenagers (results not shown).

Determinants of Average Primary Child Caregiving Minutes beyond Gender of the Child

Next, we discuss the full regression results for parents with a single resident child for primary child caregiving time. As a reminder, primary child caregiving is time that the parent reports as being spent directly involved in an activity with the child, including reading to the child, bathing an infant, and helping with homework. As described previously, average daily minutes that parents devote to primary child caregiving are considerably lower than minutes reported in-room with the child. The full regression results for parents with a single resident child are shown in Appendix Tables 2A.1C and 2A.1D. We describe the most notable results here. Race and ethnicity have some significant predictive power in parents' primary child care minutes devoted to their single resident child. Being Black predicts fewer minutes of such care for residential mothers and fathers of young children, with 41 minutes fewer for married mothers, 32 fewer minutes for single mothers, 14 fewer minutes for married fathers, and 37 fewer minutes for single fathers. The father coefficients are noisier. For teenagers, the only significant coefficient on race is for married Black mothers who spend 8 fewer minutes on primary child caregiving than non-Black mothers. For those who are Hispanic or foreign born, the relationship is negative for married mothers and fathers of young children. As would be expected, reporting nonemployment is associated with more minutes devoted to primary child caregiving in each subsample of residential parents (the effect for single fathers of young children is not significant, but that sample size is quite small). As was the case for the in-room measure of child caregiving, nonresidential fathers' time with their child is not significantly related to employment status (results not shown).

As noted previously, there is a long literature that speaks to the relationship between parents' educational attainment and their time devoted to child caregiving. For the most part, our results on primary child care for parents with exactly one resident child are consistent with the literature; namely, that lesser-educated parents report spending less time in such care and more-educated parents spend more time. For married parents of preschoolers these results are more precisely estimated, showing that the lowest education group devotes 20 fewer minutes for mothers and 12 fewer minutes for fathers than the mid-level education group.

The high education group (college degree or beyond) spends 30 minutes more for mothers and 13 minutes more for fathers than the mid-education group. Nonresidential fathers of preschoolers also display a positive education gradient (results not shown). For parents of teenagers, married mothers and fathers in the high education group spend significantly more minutes on primary child caregiving than the mid-level group though the differences are small (about five minutes a day). Both married mothers and fathers are observed devoting fewer minutes to primary child caregiving when there is another adult in the household (in addition to the spouse), suggesting that these parents consider this other adult as a substitute for their own care. This relationship is opposite for single mothers who report spending 13 more minutes in primary child caregiving when there is another adult in the household.

Turning to the effects of weekends and summer on primary child care time, the key finding is that the direction of this relationship is small and largely negative, in contrast with the mostly positive findings for the in-room minutes child care measure. Married mothers report relatively small declines in primary child care time on both weekends and the summer (ranging from 0 to 5 minutes for the summer and 10 to 15 minutes for the weekend), and single mothers' results are very similar. The one contrary case is a fairly substantial positive impact for fathers' weekend time for preschool children for both married and single fathers, of about 20 minutes extra.

Predicted Mean Minutes for a "Representative" Low-Education Parent

Using the estimated coefficients from the regressions presented in Appendix Tables 2A.1A–2A.1D and the equivalent regression for non-resident fathers, we construct predicted mean minutes for two types of child care time—in-room and primary child caregiving time—for the "representative" parent whom we define as a parent who dropped out of high school. We chose our representative parent to be a low-educated parent in light of the research of Autor and Wasserman (2013) and others reported above, which focuses attention on the negative outcomes of low-income young men. In addition to being lesser-educated, this representative parent is not foreign born or Hispanic, is employed full time, resides in an urban area in the western portion of the United States, with a nonsummer 2017 diary day (averaged between five identical week-days and two identical weekend days). The race and presence of other adults in the household of our representative low-education parent is in proportion to the race and presence of other adults of their relevant subsample of the population. Using these predicted time-use measures constructed for the individual parent, we combine predicted mean min-utes for the mothers and fathers to produce a measure of the mean total parenting time received by the child. We present these predicted mean minutes in Table 2.4.

The estimated values in columns 1–5 of Table 2.4 for the individual parents are similar to the raw sample means presented in Table 2.2A and 2.2B, indicating that the included variables do a relatively good job of predicting care time. The fact that they are somewhat lower than the means from the raw data is mainly the result of the choice to focus on the low-education population and on those employed full time. In addi-tion, the ATUS oversamples weekend days, which we have seen have higher levels of child caregiving time, while the predicted values are the average for a week of days with five weekdays and two weekend days. The predicted time differentials for sons versus daughters presented in Table 2.4 when measured by in-room minutes are substantial for resi-dent fathers of teenagers in favor of boys and for resident mothers of teenagers in favor of girls. Nonresident fathers spend 18 more minutes in-room with their preschool daughters, while single fathers spend more time in-room with their preschool sons; however, both these estimates are made with a small number of observations. The predicted time dif-ferentials for primary child caregiving time are all small in magnitude, with the only notable difference (10 minutes) for married fathers with a preschool child, in favor of boys.

The last three columns of Table 2.4 (columns 6, 7, and 8) present a comparison of total parent time spent with one's child from the child's perspective. We construct this predicted measure of mean total parent time by adding the mean predicted times for mothers and fathers. We use these data to construct a lower and upper bound of parents' mean total time with child, first by assuming that none of this time with the child is overlapping (the upper bound) and then by assuming that all of the time is overlapping (the lower bound). Our data do not permit the construction of an observed total nonoverlapping parent time with child, nor does the economic theory underlying the child development

Table 2.4 Predicted Minutes a Day in Child Caregiving for a Child of Low-Education Parents

	(1) Single resident mother	(2) Married resident mother	(3) Single resident father	(4) Married resident father	(5) Nonresident father	(6) Single resident mother and nonresident father	(7) Married resident mother and father, upper bound	(8) Married resident mother and father, lower bound
In room 0–5								
Son	393	360	298	271	104	497	631	360
Daughter	389	365	271	263	122	511	627	365
Primary child caregiving 0–5								
Son	98	95	85	88	97	195	183	95
Daughter	95	92	86	78	97	192	170	92
In room 13–17								
Son	77	134	176	161	65	142	295	161
Daughter	130	170	130	135	64	194	305	170
Primary child caregiving 13–17								
Son	10	22	4	15	−4	6	38	22
Daughter	14	27	5	12	−5	9	39	27

NOTE: Parent characteristics are assumed to be low education, employed full time, non-Hispanic, non-foreign born, western region, lives in an MSA, diary collected in the nonsummer of 2017. Black and other adult in proportion to the sample. The value reported is the average time spent per day over a week with five weekdays and two weekend days. Upper bound for married parents assumes the child is with one or the other parent, but not both. Lower bound assumes all parent time is with both parents together up to the smaller of the two parent estimates.
SOURCE: ATUS 2003–2017.

production function tell us whether parents' overlapping time is less meaningful than nonoverlapping time.

Interestingly, for children aged 0–5, girls of low-education households receive 14 extra minutes of in-room time while sons receive 3 minutes extra of primary child caregiving time. However, mostly what this exercise shows us is the time devoted to young children is very similar across gender of the child. Young boys receive more caregiving time than girls in married households, with the total amount of time quite comparable to the single mother/nonresident father combination. Thus, it seems clear that a gender gap in parents' time with children is not the "smoking gun" in the search for the source of the boy/girl achievement gap in kindergarten and fifth grade described by Autor et al. (2019).

Teenage boys living with their single mothers and having a nonresident father spend almost an hour less per day in the presence of one of their parents than daughters, while teenage sons with married parents spend 10 minutes a day less in the presence of one of their parents. In addition, the total amount of time in the presence of parents is substantially less for both sons and daughters of single mothers and nonresident fathers compared to even the lower bound for married parents. Overall, teenagers experience very low amounts of primary child caregiving time, so while there are gender gaps as noted here, they are not particularly meaningful.

HETEROGENEITY IN SON EFFECTS BY EDUCATION AND RACE

Given the importance of race in the literature that motivates our research (as described in the introductory section to this chapter), we delve deeper into differences in parents' child caregiving patterns for sons versus daughters, as observed for Black versus white parents. In the regression results discussed above, race enters the model as a simple indicator variable, serving to shift the number of minutes without allowing for the effect of the gender of the child to differ by race. Previous researchers have hypothesized that the single-parent differential may be more substantial for Black sons, while others have argued that Blacks may be less disadvantaged by growing up in a single family because of the role of extended family and because Black single families are less disadvantaged relative to married Black families (Cross 2018). Because low education plays an important role in Autor and Wasserman's (2013) narrative, we also explore whether son coefficients differ across educational attainment groups. It is possible that a gender gap in parenting time exists for some, but not all, educational groups.

To better explore racial and education differentials, we modify our regression specification in three ways, presenting these results in Tables 2.5, 2.6, and 2.7. Our first new specification adds a race/son interaction term, and our second new specification adds education/son interaction terms (for both low education and high education). Changing the specifications in these two separate ways allows the differential time afforded to boys versus girls to differ first by race, then by educational achievement level. The third new specification is a fully interacted model with interactions for the presence of a son, race, and education.

Table 2.5 shows the resulting son coefficients for the original baseline specification and then separately for non-Blacks and Blacks. For young children, we continue to find mostly insignificant son coefficients, meaning that parents, regardless of race, spend approximately equal time with their sons and daughters. The two exceptions are Black married mothers, for whom in-room time with young sons is an hour less per day for sons, and for married Black fathers, who spend 12 more minutes with their preschool boys than their girls (although this latter estimate is noisier). The other exception is extra time that married fathers spend in primary child caregiving appears to be only the case for non-Black fathers.

For teenage children, the pattern of more in-room time with same-sex children holds for race groups, with the differences somewhat larger for Blacks. Black single mothers spend 68 minutes fewer per day in the presence of their son compared to their daughter, whereas the comparable difference for non-Black single mothers is 48 minutes. For primary child caregiving, non-Black married mothers spend five minutes a day less with daughters, and married non-Black fathers spend four minutes a day more with sons. None of the son coefficients are significant for primary child caregiving time differentials for Black parents of teenagers.

Table 2.5 Son Coefficients for Black and Non-Black Parents

	Aged 0–5			Aged 13–17		
	Base specification	Race interacted specification		Base specification	Race interacted specification	
		Non-Black	Black		Non-Black	Black
In room						
Single mothers	4.05	−5.041	27.13	−53.02***	−48.07***	−68.32***
Married mothers	−5.01	−1.84	−62.61**	−35.75***	−35.47***	−39.67
Single fathers	26.95	21.98	54.25	46.21**	40.86*	82.75
Married fathers	8.51	8.307	12.13	26.00***	25.74***	29.52
Nonresident fathers	−18.08	−12.92	−31.00	1.61	0.55	5.95
Primary child caregiving						
Single mothers	2.96	−1.73	27.13	−3.67	−3.461	−4.32
Married mothers	2.70	2.37	8.72	−4.67**	−5.055**	0.70
Single fathers	−1.41	−1.10	−3.14	−0.73	−1.842	6.89
Married fathers	10.06***	11.45***	−15.37	3.61**	3.88**	−0.13
Nonresident fathers	0.30	0.79	−0.93	0.23	0.54	−1.03

NOTE: *** p < 0.01, ** p < 0.05, * p < 0.1. The coefficients reported here were obtained from an OLS estimation of the model where race and son were interacted. The reported coefficients for Black parents is the sum of the coefficient for the son dummy and the Black × son interaction coefficient. The significance was determined by a post estimation test of the linear combination of these two variables. The other variables included in the regression are the same as those used throughout the analysis and reported in Appendix Tables 2A.1A–2A.1D.

SOURCE: ATUS 2003–2017.

Table 2.6 Son Coefficients for Low-, Middle-, and High-Education Parents

	Aged 0–5			Aged 13–17		
	Low-education	Mid-education	High-education	Low-education	Mid-education	High-education
In room						
Single mothers	7.68	14.55	−24.68	−52.84***	−53.65***	−52.49***
Married mothers	13.37	−6.25	−12.58	−57.91***	−37.78***	−11.97
Single fathers	−17.01	56.33	92.74	81.27**	55.56	−27.00
Married fathers	10.70	−8.67	16.93	28.91**	25.45*	23.71**
Nonresident fathers	−45.48	2.96	26.39	14.88	−28.43	13.00
Primary child caregiving						
Single mothers	9.60	5.64	−18.28	−2.57	−7.33	−0.61
Married mothers	−7.64	4.34	6.47	−4.69	−3.90	−5.31
Single fathers	−21.06	20.79	2.08	−1.08	3.07	−4.95
Married fathers	8.91	0.32	16.27***	5.60**	−0.25	4.37*
Nonresident fathers	−15.23	2.82	41.32	3.79	−6.34*	1.57

NOTE: *** p < 0.01, ** p < 0.05, * p < 0.1. The coefficients reported here were obtained from an OLS estimation of the model where education and son were interacted. The reported coefficients for low-education parents is the sum of the coefficient for the son dummy and the low-education × son interaction coefficient with a parallel construction for high-education parents. The significance was determined by a post estimation test of the linear combination of the two variables. The other variables included in the regression are the same as those used throughout the analysis and reported in Appendix Tables 2A.1A–2A.1D.

SOURCE: ATUS 2003–2017.

Table 2.6 presents the results of son coefficients that are allowed to vary by education level. No clear patterns of difference across education levels in boy/girl differences emerge for young children. The one interesting finding for this age group is that the previously noted extra primary child caregiving time sons receive from married fathers appears to be driven by fathers who have graduated from college. For teenagers, we find that single mothers at all education levels spend about the same reduced minutes with sons than daughters. For married mothers, the son time deficit is much larger for low-educated mothers, while the married father surplus time with sons is consistent across education levels at just under 30 minutes.

Our third and final new specification is a fully interacted regression model with gender of the child, race, and education level. Instead of reporting the son coefficients, we have calculated the predicted average minutes of child caregiving time as we did in Table 2.4. Only the results for the low-educational-level parents are reported in Table 2.7. The results in 2.7 mirror those from Table 2.4. For primary child caregiving, sons and daughters receive similar minutes of parenting time regardless of family structure. The biggest primary caregiving gender gaps are observed for Black married households where the gap favoring girls is between 14 and 30 minutes (upper bound estimate versus lower bound estimate). In-room estimates for preschool children show a big son deficit for Black households for both single mother/nonresident father and married mother and father. The estimated time across parents' marital status is similar unless all married parent time is performed together and not additive (the lower bound estimate).

For teenage children, the primary child caregiving time is similar by child gender, but married parents of teenagers spend substantially more time in primary child caregiving than single parents (10 minutes compared to 20–30 minutes for Blacks, 8 minutes versus 25–40 minutes for non-Blacks). The in-room minutes are similar by child gender but low for Black teenagers who live with their single mothers (130 minutes) compared to 168 to 215 minutes for non-Black teenagers who live with their single mothers (168 for sons, 215 for daughters). Similarly, for married parents of teenagers, Black parents spend up to an hour less with their teenagers in the room than non-Black parents, with the upper bounds higher for children of married parents than children of single parents. The size of the child gender gap in in-room minutes depends

Table 2.7 Predicted Minutes a Day in Child Caregiving for a Child of Low-Education Parents by Race

	(1) Single resident mother	(2) Married resident mother	(3) Single resident father	(4) Married resident father	(5) Non-resident father	(6) Single mother and nonresident father	(7) Married mother and father upper bound	(8) Married mother and father lower bound
In room 0–5								
Black low-ed. son	385	288	237	225	25	409	513	288
Black low-ed. daughter	373	347	251	224	211	584	571	347
Non-Black low-ed. son	399	373	275	274	73	472	647	373
Non-Black low-ed. daughter	394	354	294	263	73	468	617	354
Primary child caregiving 0–5								
Black low-ed. son	86	69	51	61	101	187	130	69
Black low-ed. daughter	68	46	69	99	118	186	144	99
Non-Black low-ed. son	107	91	79	88	73	180	179	91
Non-Black low-ed. daughter	102	101	100	76	88	190	177	101
In room 13–17								
Black low-ed. son	42	72	180	156	92	134	228	156
Black low-ed. daughter	90	119	98	101	34	124	220	119
Non-Black low-ed. son	99	128	189	162	70	168	289	162
Non-Black low-ed. daughter	150	186	109	135	65	215	321	186
Primary child caregiving 13–17								
Black low-ed. son	14	19	4	13	–3	11	31	19
Black low-ed. daughter	16	19	–7	8	–7	9	27	19
Non-Black low-ed. son	10	22	4	17	–2	8	39	22
Non-Black low-ed. daughter	13	28	7	11	–6	7	39	28

Table 2.7 (continued)

NOTE: Parent characteristics are assumed to be low education, employed full time, non-Hispanic, non–foreign born, western region, lives in an MSA, diary collected in nonsummer 2017. Other adult in proportion to the sample. The value reported is the average time spent per day over a week with five weekdays and two weekend days. The regression model used fully interacts race, education, and the gender of one's child. All other control variables are the same as reported in Appendix Tables 2A.1A–2A.1D. Upper bound for married parents assumes the child is with one or the other parent, but not both. Lower bound assumes all parent time is with both parents together up to the smaller of the two parent estimates.

SOURCE: ATUS 2003–2017.

on whether we consider the upper or lower bound estimate. The biggest gap is 37 minutes in favor of sons for children of married Black couples looking at the lower bound, but if we use the upper bound, there is only an 8-minute difference in favor of sons. For non-Black married couples, there is a 20-minute gap favoring girls.

CONCLUSION

While the evidence of the increasing struggles of lesser-educated men is growing, as seen in declining employment and marriage rates, it has proven difficult for researchers to identify causal factors. Our goal with this chapter has been to bite off just one small piece of that very large apple by answering two specific questions: 1) Do the data support the suggestion that boys who grow up in single-mother families experience less parenting time than do similarly raised girls? And relatedly, do boys and girls who live with married parents experience comparable parenting time investments? 2) What factors explain these differences or similarities?

Importantly, there was no a priori requirement or expectation that substantive child gender differences in parenting time within and across family structures would be identified. The purpose of this project, instead, is to examine whether parents' time with children (and how it may vary by gender and family structure) could be an explanation of the presumed gendered single-mother family disadvantage. Our results reject that hypothesis.

Preliminary descriptive statistics suggest some differences, but not widespread gender-specific advantages, in parenting time for girls, regardless of family structure. However, even in the presence of time input similarities, it still would be interesting to examine the role of different factors in producing those time inputs.

Providing evidence of parenting time inputs and possible differences by child and parent gender and family structure contributes to the public policy debate in myriad ways. Most importantly, it helps determine whether the problems faced by boys growing up in single-mother families (as described by Autor and his coauthors) are at their core "boy problems," "family structure problems," or both. If meaningful parenting time differences had been identified, then suggested policy solutions might include further support for quality nonparental care, or even parenting interventions (guided by insight gleaned by small-scale experiments like those undertaken by the Behavioral Insights Parenting Lab at the University of Chicago's Harris School of Public Policy).

The four main findings from our analysis are listed and described briefly below.

1) For preschool children, we find that parents treat their sons and daughters quite similarly. Table 2.3 shows that the son coefficient is not significantly different from zero for any group except married fathers who provide 10 more minutes of primary child caregiving time to their young sons than their young daughters. Table 2.4, which provides predicted minutes of caregiving time for low-education modal parents, shows small, if any, gaps between preschool boys and girls in either in-room time or primary child caregiving time. Single mothers spend more time than married mothers with their preschool child, but combining both parents' time with children, children in married households probably receive more in-room time than children with a single mother and a nonresident father. However, if we limit ourselves to primary child caregiving time, then preschoolers in single mother/nonresident father situations receive the same amount of parenting time than children in married households.

2) On the other hand, we find sizable differences in time spent in the presence of teenagers based on child and parent gender. Mothers, both married and single, spend more time with their teenage girls, while fathers, both married and single in residence, spend more time with their teenage boys. An analysis of the sample means also shows that 60 percent of the single fathers living with a single teenager are living with a son rather than a daughter, further increasing the same gender preference of both mothers and fathers. Considering primary child caregiving time with teenagers, we do not find large child gender differences except for married parents, who spend about 4–5 minutes more with their matching gendered child.

3) Focusing on race, we do not find large differences in primary child caregiving time between Blacks and non-Blacks in similar family situations (Table 2.7), nor do we find difference in the existence, size, or direction of the child gender gap.

4) In results not presented in the text, we also find that the parenting time pattern by child gender for those with exactly two children is essentially the same as we have shown for those with only one child. Including families with exactly one or exactly two children means we are using 80–90 percent of the full sample of parents with any own minor children. It seems unlikely that the patterns identified here would be much different if we included those with more than two children.

Our empirical findings do not mitigate the importance of the Autor et al. (2019) finding that boys are disadvantaged compared to girls in all four measures of school outcomes from kindergarten readiness to high school graduation rates, and that the gap is largest for those from economically disadvantaged households. If the problem is not that these mothers (and their nonresidential fathers) are spending relatively less time with their sons, then perhaps it is the case that boys are more vulnerable to family stress or that boys, in fact, need more parental time when young.

In the face of concerns for children growing up in single-mother families and our findings that parental time investment is quite similar between young boys and girls, what are the potential policy solutions? Where do we as a society go from here? Do we pursue policies (as yet unidentified) to strengthen families in the hopes of restoring nuclear families as the core family structure? Or, do we move forward to a new model, in consideration of what has been noted by Brooks (2020): "We've left behind the nuclear-family paradigm of 1955. For most people, it's not coming back." As Brooks describes, what we once thought of as a positive development in the 1900s, the birth of the modern nuclear family ultimately may not be the model we choose for our future. It provides little in the way of security in the event of a parent's untimely death, for example, and can be isolating and leave families vulnerable to exogenous relationship, labor market, and incarceration shocks. One is reminded of the research findings by Cross (2018), referenced earlier in this chapter, who finds that extended family networks are stronger in Black communities and serve as protection from the negative consequences of growing up in single-mother families. As Brooks describes, "Americans are hungering to live in extended and forged families, in ways that are new and ancient at the same time. This is a significant opportunity, a chance to thicken and broaden family relationships, a chance to allow more adults and children to live and grow under the loving gaze of a dozen pairs of eyes, and be caught, when they fall, by a dozen pairs of arms."[26]

Notes

1. See also Lundberg, Pollak, and Stearns (2016) for a thorough analysis of the evolution of family structure by economic status and education.
2. In addition to reviewing the report itself, see also the so-called Annotated Edition (Geary 2015).
3. McLanahan and Sawhill (2015) describe the inherent instability of cohabiting families, noting that half of couples who are cohabiting when a child is born are no longer cohabiting by the time the child reaches the age of five. Perhaps not broadly known is that among new unmarried mothers, the vast majority are cohabiting with a male partner. According to the authors, "Almost all of the increase in nonmarital childbearing during the past two decades has occurred to cohabiting rather than single mothers" (p. 3).
4. Note that this linkage of motivation, misbehavior, and school performance is an example of the linkage between cognitive and noncognitive skills discussed by Cunha and Heckman (2008).
5. Kimmel and Connelly (2007) presented similar findings on the gradient of child caregiving time by mothers' wages. Kalil, Ryan, and Corey (2012) also describe the educational gradient in child care with a focus on the child's age. Fiorini and Keane (2014) provide an interesting application of a child skill's production function that incorporates parenting time, along with the child's time uses. They use data from the Longitudinal Study of Australian Children. Their results show that parenting time can enhance cognitive skills, but noncognitive skill development is more responsive to the mother's parenting style. (See also Todd and Wolpin 2007.) Bertrand and Pan's (2013) empirical research also is grounded by a theoretical child skills production model that attempts to explain gender gaps in behavioral outcomes in middle school, in part, by the quantity and quality of parental inputs.
6. For a recent review of this large literature see McLanahan and Sawhill (2015), Sigle-Rushton and McLanahan (2004), along with several chapters in Ermisch, Jantti, and Smeeding (2012).
7. See, for example, Kalenkoski, Ribar, and Stratton (2005) and Becker (1985). Becker uses the theoretical model of household production to explain observed differences in time-use patterns by gender and marital status.

8. For evidence on the potential endogeneity of marital status with respect to child gender, see Dahl and Moretti (2008).

9. Mammen (2011) notes that television watching may not represent quality time; however, TV watching is included in this study and is described as affective time.

10. PSID and ATUS analyses of child caregiving time differ fundamentally, as PSID is a record of the child's day and the ATUS is a record of the parent's day.

11. In addition, Bibler (2020) classifies a child as living with a single parent if her biological mother is living with her new husband, while we classify this child as the own resident child of a married mother.

12. Our focus is on differences in parenting time by marital status and child gender; hence, our subsamples are stratified by marital status. We do acknowledge, however, the potential for bias resulting from sample stratification using criteria that may also be related to child gender. Specifically, marital status is a choice, and there is some research in the literature that suggests the marriage decision may be influenced by child gender. Baker and Milligan (2016) explain that this concern is one reason their research focuses just on married couples. Kalenkoski et al. (2007) also allude to this problem. They note that, "While economic and sociological theories each predict that family structure affects the time that parents allocate to child care and market work, we must recognize that family structure is behaviorally determined" (p. 356). Dahl and Moretti (2008) provide empirical evidence that married fathers of exactly one child who is female are more likely to divorce than married fathers of exactly one child who is male. However, the magnitude of the effect is quite small. One explanation for Dahl and Moretti's finding is preferences; either fathers simply enjoy the activities in which their sons are (or will be) engaged, or both parents believe that sons need their fathers in the household more than daughters. Perhaps the ideal solution to this problem would be some sort of instrumental variables approach, but we have chosen to avoid introducing such complexity to our estimation.

13. We do not differentiate between married versus unmarried coupled parents. The number of coupled, but not married, parents is not large enough to do meaningful analyses. Kalenkoski, Ribar, and Stratton (2007) examine parents' time use using data from the 2003 and 2004 ATUS, and their results show that there is no significant difference in parenting time for married parents versus cohabiting parents. Our preliminary exploration of our full ATUS sample supports that finding as well.

14. The problem with the secondary care measure in the ATUS is that it is collected after the entire time diary information has been collected. At that point, respondents are asked during any of the activities having just been recorded were children under age 13 "under one's care." Examination of the data shows that some parents interpret this question to refer to all the awake time of the child while others think of the concept of "under one's care" more narrowly.

15. Theoretically, the "in-room" minutes can be linked with a specific child in a multichild family, but that requires substantial data work, which will remain a task for future work. In addition, primary child caregiving minutes cannot be linked with a specific child in a multichild family such that concentrating on one-child households is still necessary for this important measure of child caregiving time.

16. The sample of mothers with one nonresident child is too small for meaningful analysis.

17. An alternative empirical approach taken by some researchers, whose focus is not specifically on child gender, is to include a dummy variable in parent time-use equations to indicate the presence of at least one male child in the household. For an example of this approach, see Kendig and Bianchi (2008). Note, however, that this dummy variable does not provide any information linked to the actual parenting time measured in the data. Given that our research focus is squarely on child gender, we cannot rely on this approach.

18. Parents whose diary day occurred on a holiday were omitted but represent a very small percent of parents (1.7 percent of the sample of all parents with own residential children).

19. There appears to be substantial underreporting of own nonresident children. The number of fathers with nonresident children is only about 15 percent of the number of single mothers with resident children.

20. This empirical strategy is similar to that employed in Connelly and Kimmel (2014).

21. Time-use data typically include many zero values, particularly for the more narrowly defined child caregiving measures. The Tobit model and the double hurdle model are alternative econometric specifications that are often utilized in these cases in which the dependent variable is left censored. However, as Stewart (2013) explains, marginal effects calculated from Tobit coefficients are biased, with the bias worsening as the percentage of the sample that reports zero values for the dependent variable becomes larger. "OLS estimates are unbiased and robust to a number of assumptions about the relationship between the variables in the model and the probability of doing an activity" (p. 12).

22. For this back-of-the-envelope calculation, we provide two alternative assumptions: 1) that parent time is additive so that an hour spent with both parents in the same room at the same time counts as two hours of parent time, or 2) that parent time is altogether up to the amount of the parent with the lower time inputs. These clearly represent the upper and lower bound of together parental time, with the reality falling somewhere in the middle of these two estimates.

23. We have included only full regression results for two definitions of child care time. The other two are available from the authors. The results for the other two time categories are very similar to the broader category to which they are a subset. That is, the results for developmental time are similar to that of primary child caregiving time, and the results for in-room nonwork are similar to the in-room time more generally.

24. Full regression results are provided in the appendix. We restrict our discussion in the text to estimated effects that are statistically significant at least at the 10 percent level.

25. See, for example, Guryan, Hurst, and Kearney (2008); Ramey and Ramey (2010); Gimenez-Nadal and Sevilla (2016); and Kalil, Ryan, and Corey (2012).

26. Moving toward a future of more extended families and stronger community networks would be a rejection, of sorts, of the policy suggestions from the Moynihan report, which implied that the nuclear family was the gold standard. Multigenera-

tional households may also be desirable for environmental reasons, and thinking about the current Covid-19 pandemic, we've learned the benefits of household "pods" that extend beyond the nuclear family.

References

Autor, David, David Figlio, Krzysztof Karbownik, Jeffrey Roth, and Melanie Wasserman. 2019. "Family Disadvantage and the Gender Gap in Behavioral and Educational Outcomes." *American Economic Journal: Applied Economics* 11(3): 338–381.

Autor, David, and Melanie Wasserman. 2013. *Wayward Sons: The Emerging Gender Gap in Labor Markets and Education.* Washington, DC: Third Way.

Baker, Michael, and Kevin Milligan. 2016. "Boy-Girl Differences in Parental Time Investments: Evidence from Three Countries." *Journal of Human Capital* 10(4): 399–441.

Becker, Gary S. 1985. "Human Capital, Effort, and the Sexual Division of Labor." *Journal of Labor Economics* 3(1, Part 2): S33–S58.

Becker, Gary S., Scott Duke Kominers, Kevin M. Murphy, and Jorg L. Spenkuch. 2018. "A Theory of Intergenerational Mobility." *Journal of Political Economy* 126(S1): S7–S25.

Becker, Gary S., and Nigel Tomes. 1986. "Human Capital and the Rise and Fall of Families." *Journal of Labor Economics* 4(3): 2.

Bertrand, Marianne, and Jessica Pan. 2013. "The Trouble with Boys: Social Influences and the Gender Gap in Disruptive Behavior." *American Economic Journal: Applied Economics* 5(1): 32–64.

Bibler, Andrew. 2020. "Household Composition and Gender Differences in Parental Time Investments." *Demography* 57(4): 1415–1435.

Binder, Ariel J., and John Bound. 2019. "The Declining Labor Market Prospects of Less-Educated Men." *Journal of Economic Perspectives* 33(2): 163–190.

Brenoe, Anne Ardila, and Shelly Lundberg. 2018. "Gender Gaps in the Effects of Childhood Family Environment: Do They Persist into Adulthood?" *European Economic Review* 109(1): 42–62.

Brooks, David. 2020. "The Nuclear Family Was a Mistake." *Atlantic* (March). https://www.theatlantic.com/magazine/archive/2020/03/the-nuclear-family -was-a-mistake/605536/ (accessed February 17, 2021).

Buchmann, Claudia, and Thomas A. DiPrete. 2006. "The Growing Female Advantage in College Completion: The Role of Family Background and Academic Achievement." *American Sociological Review* 71(4): 515–541.

Coile, Courtney C., and Mark G. Duggan. 2019. "When Labor's Lost: Health,

Family Life, Incarceration, and Education in a Time of Declining Economic Opportunity for Low-Skilled Men." *Journal of Economic Perspectives* 33(2): 191–210.

Connelly, Rachel, and Jean Kimmel. 2014. "Gender Differences in Unpaid Time Use by Family Structure." In *Family Economics: How Households Impact Markets and Economic Growth*, vol. 2, Esther Redmount, ed. Santa Barbara: ABC-CLIO, pp. 67–114.

Cross, Christina. 2018. "Extended Family Households among Children in the United States: Differences by Race/Ethnicity and Socio-Economic Status." *Population Studies* 72(2): 1–17.

———. 2019. "Racial/Ethnic Differences in the Association between Family Structure and Children's Education." *Journal of Marriage and the Family* 82(2): 691–712.

Cunha, Flavio, and James J. Heckman. 2007. "The Technology of Skill Formation." *American Economic Review* 97(2): 31–47.

———. 2008. "Formulating, Identifying and Estimating the Technology of Cognitive and Noncognitive Skill Formulation." *Journal of Human Resources* 43(4): 738–782.

Dahl, Gordon B., and Enrico Moretti. 2008. "The Demand for Sons." *Review of Economic Studies* 75(4): 1085–1120.

DiPrete, Thomas A., and Claudia Buchmann. 2006. "Gender-Specific Trends in the Value of Education and the Emerging Gender Gap in College Completion." *Demography* 43(1): 1–24.

Edin, Kathryn, Timothy Nelson, Andrew Cherlin, and Robert Francis. 2019. "The Tenuous Attachments of Working-Class Men." *Journal of Economic Perspectives* 33(2): 211–228.

Ermisch, John. 2008. "Origins of Social Immobility and Inequality: Parenting and Early Child Development." *National Institute Economic Review* 205(1): 62–71.

Ermisch, John, Markus Jantti, and Timothy Smeeding, eds. 2012. *From Parents to Children: The Intergenerational Transmission of Advantage*. New York: Russell Sage Foundation.

Fiorini, Mario, and Michael P. Keane. 2014. "How the Allocation of Children's Time Affects Cognitive and Noncognitive Development." *Journal of Labor Economics* 32(4): 787–836.

Fortin, Nicole, Phillip Oreopoulos, and Shelley Phipps. 2015. "Leaving Boys Behind: Gender Disparities in High Academic Achievement." *Journal of Human Resources* 50(3): 549–579.

Frazis, Harley, and Jay Stewart. 2012. "How to Think about Time-Use Data: What Inferences Can We Make about Long- and Short-Run Time Use from Time Diaries?" *Annals of Economics and Statistics* 105/106: 231–245.

Geary, Daniel. 2015. "The *Moynihan Report*: The Annotated Edition." *Atlantic*. https://www.theatlantic.com/politics/archive/2015/09/the-moynihan-report -an-annotated-edition/404632/ (accessed February 17, 2021).

Gennetian, Lisa, and Christopher Rodrigues. 2020. "Mothers' and Fathers' Time Spent with Children in the U.S.: Variations by Race/Ethnicity within Income from 2003 to 2013." *Journal of Economics, Race and Policy* 4: 34–36.

Gimenez-Nadal, J. Ignacio, and Almudena Sevilla. 2016. "Intensive Mothering and Well-Being: The Role of Education and Child Care Activity." IZA Discussion Paper No. 10023. Bonn: IZA.

Guryan, Jonathan, Erik Hurst, and Melissa Kearney. 2008. "Parental Education and Parental Time with Children." *Journal of Economic Perspectives* 22(3): 23–46.

Hook, Jennifer L., and Christina M. Wolfe. 2012. "New Fathers? Residential Fathers' Time with Children in Four Countries." *Journal of Family Issues* 33(4): 415–450.

Kalenkoski, Charlene M., David Ribar, and Leslie Stratton. 2005. "Parental Childcare in Single-Parent, Cohabiting, and Married-Couple Families: Time-Diary Evidence from the United Kingdom." *American Economic Review, Papers and Proceedings* 95(2): 194–198.

———. 2007. "The Effect of Family Structure on Parents' Childcare Time in the United States and the United Kingdom." *Review of Economics of the Household* 5: 353–384.

Kalil, Ariel, Rebecca Ryan, and Michael Corey. 2012. "Diverging Destinies: Maternal Education and the Developmental Gradient in Time with Children." *Demography* 49(4): 1361–1383.

Kendig, Sarah, and Suzanne Bianchi. 2008. "Single, Cohabitating, and Married Mothers' Time with Children." *Journal of Marriage and Family* 70(5): 1228–1240.

Kimmel, Jean, and Rachel Connelly. 2007. "Mothers' Time Choices: Caregiving, Leisure, Home Production, and Paid Work." *Journal of Human Resources* 42(3): 643–681.

Lundberg, Shelly. 2005. "Sons, Daughters, and Parental Behaviour." *Oxford Review of Economic Policy* 21(3): 340–356.

———. 2017. "Father Absence and the Educational Gender Gap." IZA Working Paper No. 10814. Bonn: IZA.

Lundberg, Shelly, Sara McLanahan, and Elaina Rose. 2007. "Child Gender and Father Involvement in Fragile Families." *Demography* 44(1): 79–92.

Lundberg, Shelly, Robert A. Pollak, and Jenna Stearns. 2016. "Family Inequality: Diverging Patterns in Marriage, Cohabitation, and Childbearing." *Journal of Economic Perspectives* 30(2): 79–102.

Lundberg, Shelly, Sabrina Wulff Pabilonia, and Jennifer Ward-Batts. 2007. "Time Allocation of Parents and Investments in Sons and Daughters." Unpublished paper.

Mammen, Kristen. 2011. "Fathers' Time Investments in Children: Do Sons Get More?" *Journal of Population Economics* 24(3): 839–871.

Mazumder, Bhashkar. 2005. "Fortunate Sons: New Estimates of Intergenerational Mobility in the United States Using Social Security Earnings Data." *Review of Economics and Statistics* 87(2): 235–255.

McLanahan, Sara, and Gary Sandefur. 1994. *Growing up with a Single Parent: What Hurts, What Helps.* Cambridge, MA: Harvard University Press.

McLanahan, Sara, and Isabel Sawhill. 2015. "Marriage and Child Well Being Revisited: Introducing the Issue." *Future of Children* 25(2): 3–9.

Mencarini, Letiza, Silva Pasqua, and Agenese Romiti. 2019. "Single-Mother Families and the Gender Gap in Children's Time Investment and Non-Cognitive Skills." *Review of Economics of the Household* 17(1): 149–176.

Moynihan, Daniel Patrick. 1965. *The Negro Family: The Case for National Action.* Washington, DC: U.S. Department of Labor, Office of Planning and Research.

Pronzato, Chiara, and Arnstein Aassve. 2019. "Parental Breakup and Children's Development: The Role of Time and of Post-Separation Conditions." *Review of Economics of the Household* 17: 67–87.

Ramey, Garey, and Valerie A. Ramey. 2010. "The Rug Rat Race." *Brookings Papers on Economic Activity* 41(1): 129–176.

Sawhill, Isabel. 2014. "Are Children Raised by Absent Fathers Worse Off?" *Brookings Op-Ed*, July 15. https://www.brookings.edu/opinions/are-children-raised-with-absent-fathers-worse-off/ (accessed February 17, 2021).

Sigle-Rushton, Wendy, and Sara McLanahan. 2004. "Father Absence and Child Well-Being; A Critical Review." In *The Future of the Family*, Daniel P. Moynihan, Timothy M. Smeeding, and Lee Rainwater, eds. New York: Russell Sage, pp. 116–155.

Stewart, Jay. 2013. "Tobit or Not Tobit." *Journal of Economic and Social Measurement* 38(3): 263–290.

Sum, Andrew, Ishwor Khatiwada, Joseph Mclaughlin, and Sheila Palma. 2011. "No Country for Young Men: Deteriorating Labor Market Prospects for Low-Skilled Men in the United States." *Annals of the American Academy of Political Science* 635(1): 24–55.

Todd, Petra E., and Kenneth I. Wolpin. 2007. "The Production of Cognitive Achievement in Children: Home, School, and Racial Test Score Gaps." *Journal of Human Capital* 1(1): 91–136.

Waldfogel, Jane, Terry-Ann Craigle, and Jeanne Brooks-Gunn. 2010. "Fragile Families and Child Wellbeing." *Future Child* 20(2): 87–112.

Appendix 2A

Tables

Table 2A.1A Full OLS Regression Results for Basic Specification for In-Room Minutes for Own Child Aged 0–5

Variables	Single mothers	Married mothers	Single fathers	Married fathers	Fathers of nonresident child
Son	4.045	−5.013	26.95	8.505	−18.08
	(11.71)	(6.587)	(29.85)	(7.290)	(29.66)
Low education	21.65	−19.3	−27.1	1.308	36.07
	(13.49)	(9.746)**	(32.66)	(10.19)	(34.04)
High education	25.98	−1.9	−27.28	16.67	15.44
	(17.08)	(8.121)	(46.67)	(9.231)*	(44.05)
Black	−34.25	−47	−28.23	−47.87	43.73
	(14.05)**	(14.97)***	(43.89)	(16.65)***	(36.26)
Hispanic	30.3	5.219	14.85	17.19	−8.988
	(17.92)*	(10.56)	(44.78)	(12.26)	(45.50)
Foreign born	−23.37	3.853	−58.44	0.195	−69.32
	(20.23)	(9.172)	(53.22)	(10.30)	(49.88)
Not employed	118.1	169	85.75	158.2	−24.6
	(14.19)***	(7.757)***	(39.53)**	(13.86)***	(40.14)
Employed part-time	15	41.97	78.46	37.83	−5.343
	(15.87)	(9.106)***	(56.11)	(16.48)**	(52.15)
Other adult present	5.625	−23.64	38.02	−27.17	9.871
	(12.57)	(12.79)*	(31.31)	(12.56)**	(31.19)
Own resident child	NA	NA	NA	NA	−29.09
					(32.71)
Northeast region	20.22	10.02	32.35	−0.231	−4.592
	(19.47)	(10.57)	(50.65)	(11.66)	(50.45)
Midwest region	9.546	6.091	15.96	7.232	−5.265
	(18.25)	(9.807)	(44.28)	(10.60)	(45.17)
Southern region	−2.326	−7.108	10.04	−9.396	−41.62
	(17.00)	(8.919)	(40.93)	(9.814)	(43.46)
MSA	−11	−2.352	11.93	12.29	−5.52
	(16.34)	(9.474)	(40.63)	(10.81)	(44.70)
Summer	2.621	11.71	−35.87	−1.302	−43.61
	(13.59)	(7.508)	(34.70)	(8.444)	(35.51)
Weekend	125.4	135.7	158.9	219.3	63.39
	(11.76)***	(6.580)***	(29.88)***	(7.303)***	(31.36)**
Constant	328.7	360.9	187.3	172.3	26.29
	(28.92)***	(16.85)***	(75.88)**	(17.87)***	(73.22)

Table 2A.1A (continued)

Variables	Single mothers	Married mothers	Single fathers	Married fathers	Fathers of nonresident child
Survey year dummies	Yes	Yes	Yes	Yes	Yes
Observations	1,687	4,212	322	3,654	189
R-squared	0.134	0.186	0.176	0.229	0.155

NOTE: *** p value < 0.01; ** p value < 0.0; * p value < 0.1. Estimated OLS. Standard errors in parentheses.

SOURCE: ATUS 2003–2017; ATUS year dummies were also included but not reported here.

Table 2A.1B Full OLS Regression Results for Basic Specification for In-Room Child Caregiving Minutes for Own Child Aged 13–17

Variables	Single mothers	Married mothers	Single fathers	Married fathers	Fathers with nonresident child
Son	−53.02	−35.75	46.21	26	1.614
	(9.784)***	(7.306)***	(20.61)**	(7.643)***	(10.96)
Low education	−7.095	−4.437	43.26	−22.33	10.36
	(11.95)	(9.262)	(24.33)*	(10.14)**	(13.12)
High education	16.66	5.022	12.57	−12.12	6.209
	(12.59)	(9.114)	(28.18)	(9.873)	(14.94)
Black	−17.51	−50.92	−25.85	−29.37	−11.79
	(12.00)	(14.76)***	(31.61)	(15.42)*	(14.57)
Hispanic	43.64	19.65	63.69	6.043	−13.91
	(16.88)***	(13.62)	(39.77)	(14.67)	(18.20)
Foreign born	−0.484	15.58	−17.98	19.18	−11.84
	(16.31)	(11.92)	(39.34)	(12.64)	(19.00)
Not employed	55.62	64	23.03	42.17	−26.4
	(12.48)***	(9.091)***	(27.56)	(12.01)***	(14.66)*
Employed part time	33.62	35.58	−2.994	−1.054	−15.11
	(15.09)**	(9.720)***	(43.46)	(19.52)	(25.81)
Other adult present	21.67	1.416	−60.39	8.36	8.363
	(10.57)**	(7.469)	(22.22)***	(7.776)	(14.78)
Own resident child	NA	NA	NA	NA	−12.36
					(11.23)
Northeast region	−20.02	−23.58	−6.388	−7.382	8.962
	(16.00)	(12.06)*	(33.24)	(12.21)	(18.83)
Midwest region	7.24	−19.9	−7.79	−21.32	−21.1
	(15.33)	(11.11)*	(29.50)	(11.58)*	(17.05)
Southern region	26.99	−13.84	−7.372	−2.066	−19.89
	(13.91)*	(10.17)	(27.89)	(10.68)	(16.23)
MSA	−2.764	−26.06	−61.89	−18.23	10.47
	(13.98)	(9.531)***	(26.68)**	(10.02)*	(14.95)
Summer	14.43	33.95	36.51	15.98	−3.105
	(11.22)	(8.328)***	(23.79)	(8.980)*	(12.22)
Weekend	90.82	117.5	106.1	134.5	46.35
	(9.809)***	(7.298)***	(20.56)***	(7.624)***	(10.95)***
Constant	135.3	163.5	166.8	131.3	23.34
	(24.40)***	(17.49)***	(49.80)***	(18.46)***	(26.87)

Table 2A.1B (continued)

Variables	Single mothers	Married mothers	Single fathers	Married fathers	Fathers with nonresident child
Year of survey dummies	Yes	Yes	Yes	Yes	Yes
Observations	1,861	3,265	544	2,875	538
R-squared	0.091	0.12	0.116	0.116	0.069

NOTE: *** p value < 0.01; ** p value < 0.0; * p value < 0.1. Estimated OLS. Standard errors in parentheses.

SOURCE: ATUS 2003–2017; ATUS year dummies were also included but not reported here.

Table 2A.1C Full OLS Regression Results for Basic Specification for Primary Child Caregiving Minutes for Own Child Aged 0–5

Variables	Single mothers	Married mothers	Single fathers	Married fathers	Fathers with nonresident child
Son	2.96	2.7	−1.413	10.06	0.298
	(5.599)	(3.977)	(13.19)	(3.454)***	(11.91)
Low education	5.935	−20.06	−23.21	−11.8	−6.905
	(6.451)	(5.884)***	(14.43)	(4.826)**	(13.66)
High education	14.8	30.01	−18.77	13.35	31.81
	(8.168)*	(4.903)***	(20.63)	(4.374)***	(17.68)*
Black	−31.62	−40.73	−36.97	−13.83	20.5
	(6.721)***	(9.036)***	(19.40)*	(7.888)*	(14.56)
Hispanic	−6.911	−33.36	−24.19	−12.49	−19.64
	(8.572)	(6.375)***	(19.79)	(5.810)**	(18.26)
Foreign born	−11.88	−12.69	−6.675	−15.83	−3.675
	(9.675)	(5.537)**	(23.52)	(4.879)***	(20.02)
Not employed	24.97	70.29	22.86	51.66	3.093
	(6.788)***	(4.683)***	(17.47)	(6.567)***	(16.11)
Employed part time	0.355	28.42	5.946	23.28	0.526
	(7.591)	(5.497)***	(24.80)	(7.809)***	(20.93)
Other adult present	13.44	−6.64	−16.37	−3.674	9.999
	(6.013)**	(7.721)	(13.84)	(5.950)	(12.52)
Own resident child	NA	NA	NA	NA	−30.24
					(13.13)**
Northeast region	28.5	16.31	9.754	12.46	−17.63
	(9.312)***	(6.381)**	(22.39)	(5.523)**	(20.25)
Midwest region	21.9	8.973	26.32	7.726	−31.08
	(8.728)**	(5.920)	(19.57)	(5.024)	(18.13)*
Southern region	11.06	2.809	30.12	1.437	−41.36
	(8.131)	(5.384)	(18.09)*	(4.650)	(17.44)**
MSA	0.933	14.63	−2.951	15.42	−15.67
	(7.814)	(5.720)**	(17.95)	(5.122)***	(17.94)
Summer	−14.31	−0.273	−16.6	−5.579	−6.701
	(6.499)**	(4.533)	(15.34)	(4.001)	(14.25)
Weekend	−10.3	−13.85	23.63	17.85	6.921
	(5.625)*	(3.972)***	(13.21)*	(3.460)***	(12.59)
Constant	106.1	102.6	54.96	36.56	51.9
	(13.83)***	(10.17)***	(33.54)	(8.465)***	(29.39)*

Table 2A.1C (continued)

Variables	Single mothers	Married mothers	Single fathers	Married fathers	Fathers with nonresident child
Year of survey dummies	Yes	Yes	Yes	Yes	Yes
Observations	1,687	4,212	322	3,654	189
R-squared	0.051	0.089	0.131	0.058	0.21

NOTE: *** p value < 0.01; ** p value < 0.0; * p value < 0.1. Estimated OLS. Standard errors in parentheses.

SOURCE: ATUS 2003–2017; ATUS year dummies were also included but not reported here.

Table 2A.1D Full OLS Regression Results for Basic Specification for Primary Child Caregiving Minutes for Child Aged 13–17

Variables	Single mother	Married mother	Single father	Married father	Fathers with nonresident child
Son	−3.67	−4.665	−0.726	3.607	0.231
	(2.642)	(2.034)**	(4.022)	(1.566)**	(1.860)
Low education	−8.957	−3.22	−1.034	0.562	−1.576
	(3.227)***	(2.579)	(4.748)	(2.078)	(2.227)
High education	3.25	5.458	3.642	4.829	1.208
	(3.399)	(2.538)**	(5.500)	(2.023)**	(2.536)
Black	1.277	−8.342	−4.222	−0.977	−2.401
	(3.240)	(4.109)**	(6.168)	(3.159)	(2.473)
Hispanic	3.342	−5.885	−4.119	−6.078	−1.34
	(4.558)	(3.791)	(7.762)	(3.006)**	(3.090)
Foreign born	−3.626	−4.247	3.56	2.253	6.966
	(4.404)	(3.317)	(7.678)	(2.590)	(3.225)**
Not employed	15.74	17.24	3.234	7.705	3.43
	(3.369)***	(2.531)***	(5.378)	(2.461)***	(2.488)
Employed part time	3.114	7.401	0.268	−0.967	−1.694
	(4.073)	(2.706)***	(8.482)	(4.000)	(4.382)
Other adult present	2.321	−2.067	−7.814	−0.0461	−2.408
	(2.853)	(2.079)	(4.335)*	(1.593)	(2.510)
Own resident child	NA	NA	NA	NA	−2.044
					(1.906)
Northeast region	−4.877	−0.821	9.588	−2.989	2.949
	(4.320)	(3.358)	(6.487)	(2.503)	(3.197)
Midwest region	−1.764	0.842	3.323	−0.946	1.611
	(4.140)	(3.093)	(5.758)	(2.373)	(2.894)
Southern region	2.114	2.476	6.684	−0.152	2.616
	(3.755)	(2.832)	(5.443)	(2.188)	(2.756)
MSA	0.711	0.306	−17.01	2.711	1.91
	(3.776)	(2.654)	(5.206)***	(2.053)	(2.539)
Summer	−2.731	−5.429	−4.449	−4.372	−1.216
	(3.030)	(2.319)**	(4.643)	(1.840)**	(2.074)
Weekend	−9.738	−9.332	−6.316	−0.954	4.452
	(2.649)***	(2.032)***	(4.012)	(1.562)	(1.858)**
Constant	24.45	24.62	35.84	4.18	2.674
	(6.589)***	(4.869)***	(9.719)***	(3.783)	(4.561)

Table 2A.1D (continued)

Variables	Single mother	Married mother	Single father	Married father	Fathers with nonresident child
Year of survey dummies	Yes	Yes	Yes	Yes	Yes
Observations	1,861	3,265	544	2,875	538
R-squared	0.034	0.037	0.073	0.017	0.067

NOTE: *** p value < 0.01; ** p value < 0.0; * p value < 0.1. Estimated OLS. Standard errors in parentheses.

SOURCE: ATUS 2003–2017; ATUS year dummies were also included but not reported here.

3

Behavioral Insights, Parental Decision Making, and Investments in Children's Development

Ariel Kalil and Susan Mayer
Harris School of Public Policy Studies,
University of Chicago

PARENTAL BEHAVIOR AND THE INTERGENERATIONAL PERSISTENCE OF ECONOMIC ADVANTAGE

Economic advantage is correlated across generations. In the United States, 43 percent of adults who were raised in the poorest fifth of the income distribution now have an income in the poorest fifth of the income distribution, and 70 percent have incomes in the poorest half of the distribution. Among adults raised in the richest income quintile, 40 percent have incomes in the richest quintile, and 53 percent have incomes in the richest half of the income distribution (Pew Charitable Trusts 2012). Although a variety of factors play a role in the correlation in outcomes of adults and their parents, evidence suggests that parental decision making plays a crucial role. Parents make decisions that affect their children in a variety of domains, including, for example, where to live, how much time to spend with their children in various activities, what time to put their children to bed, whether their children brush their teeth each night, and whether to immunize their children against communicable diseases. Parental decision making interpreted in this way probably accounts for around half of the variance in adult outcomes and is therefore an important contributor to the level of intergenerational mobility in a country (Bjorklund, Lindahl, and Lindquist 2010).

Across disciplines, dozens of studies have demonstrated differences in the way advantaged and disadvantaged parents raise their children and how these differences matter to children's adult success. Among other things, advantaged parents spend more time in educational activities with their children (Guryan, Hurst, and Kearney 2008; Kalil, Ryan, and Corey 2012), produce more cognitively stimulating home learning environments (Harris, Terrel, and Allen 1999), and are more likely to read to their children (Noel, Stark, and Redford 2015) and to do math-related activities with their children (Lazarides et al. 2015). Furthermore, because highly educated mothers have increased the amount of time they spend in educational activities with their children more than mothers with less education, the gap between the amount of time that advantaged and disadvantaged parents spend with their children overall and in educationally relevant activities has widened over the past 20 years (Altintas 2012; Hurst 2010; Ramey and Ramey 2010).

James Heckman and his colleagues find that more engaged parents have greater success in producing both cognitive and noncognitive skills in their children, and that both types of skills are crucial to social and economic success (e.g., Cunha, Heckman, and Lochner 2006; Heckman and Masterov 2004). Other research finds that the amount of time parents spend with their children has a direct and causal effect on children's cognitive test scores (Fiorini and Keane 2014; Villena-Rodán and Ríos-Aguilar 2011). Price and Kalil (2018) find that a one standard deviation increase in mother-child reading time increases children's reading achievement by 0.80 standard deviations on average.

In this chapter, we propose that applying behavioral science to the study of parenting can potentially yield new insights into why parents make (or fail to make) decisions to spend time, money, attention, or affection promoting their children's development and why these decisions are likely to differ by parental advantage. The assumption we make is that if advantaged and disadvantaged parents made equally optimal parenting decisions, differences in future academic and financial outcomes of their children would also narrow, and intergenerational mobility would increase. In domains as varied as financial services, medicine, education, and the law, both experts and laypersons systematically make decisions that are, by their own evaluation, suboptimal due to cognitive biases (e.g., Castleman and Page 2014; Chabris et al. 2008; Gilovich, Griffin, and Kahneman 2002; Meier and Sprenger 2010; Rodgers et al. 2005; Sharek, Schoen, and Loewenstein 2012). Parental decision making is no different. However, advantaged and disadvantaged parents make different decisions about how to raise their children, and these differences account for variances in children's success. Understanding differences in cognitive biases by parental advantage can point to low-cost ways to narrow the parenting differences and hence the differences in child outcomes.

In what follows, we first describe the differences between our approach and traditional approaches to the study of parenting. We then describe characteristics of parental decision making that make it subject to cognitive biases, and why the experience of cognitive biases may differ by parental advantage. We then discuss how using behavioral insights can point to new directions for research and the development of new programs and policies to support parents.

MECHANISMS LINKING PARENT AND CHILD OUTCOMES

Theories across several disciplines try to explain why child outcomes are highly correlated with parent outcomes. The dominant theories fail to adequately explain this correlation. One of the most prevalent theories is that poor parents cannot afford the goods and services that can improve their children's life chances, including high-quality education and health care. Other prevalent theories are that because of their social and economic circumstances, advantaged and disadvantaged parents have access to different information about parenting, or different parent groups estimate differently the returns to the time they spend in parenting activities.

Economic and social structural factors undoubtedly play a role in the intergenerational transmission of advantage. But how large that role is remains unclear. While parental income consistently has a substantial correlation with important child outcomes, the causal impact of parental income in rich countries is much less certain. Most studies find small or no average causal effect of parental income on child outcomes, including cognitive and noncognitive skills, and even smaller effects on adult outcomes, including income and education (for reviews on this literature, see Mayer [2010] and Cooper and Stewart [2013]). However, studies that examine nonlinearities in the effect of income usually find greater effects for families with less income (e.g., Shea 2000; Dahl and Lochner 2012; but see also Blau [1999], who finds no additional effects for children from low-income families).

Although raising the income of the poorest parents might increase their children's adult income, there is uncertainty about the potential size of this increase. For example, Akee et al. (2010) studied the effect of an income windfall from casino earnings on members of a Native American tribe. They find no effect of an increase in parental income on high school graduation or educational attainment for children who were never poor; however, for children in poor families, additional parental income increased schooling by nearly one year and increased the chance of graduating high school by 30 percent. However, the average income increase for poor families in that study was very large—as much as 100 percent—and out of the range likely to be implemented by public policies in the United States.

In our own survey of parents of children in Head Start programs in Chicago, over 95 percent of parents report that they have all the materials that they need to help their children learn math. Almost no parents report that they ever failed to read to their child because they had no books to read (Mayer et al. 2018).

In the United States, differences in access to and quality of schooling may also play a role in intergenerational mobility; again, the size of the effect is unclear. The education of parents is highly correlated with the education of their adult children, which suggests that differences in school quality in the parents' generation is replicated in the children's generation, or that having highly educated parents conveys other advantages. However, the substantial differences between advantaged and disadvantaged children in cognitive skills emerge well before the start of formal schooling (Washbrook and Waldfogel 2011), and conventional measures of school quality (such as teacher/pupil ratios and teacher salaries) have small effects on creating or eliminating gaps after the first few years of schooling (Carneiro and Heckman 2003; Cunha and Heckman 2007). The importance of family influences relative to schooling is perhaps not surprising, considering children in the United States will spend only about 13–15 percent of their waking hours in school between birth and age 18 (Mayer et al. 2018). Finally, school outcomes reflect many child characteristics, such as orientation toward the future, sense of personal efficacy, work ethic, and other characteristics sometimes referred to as "noncognitive skills" (see, for example, Cunha and Heckman 2007; Carneiro and Heckman 2003; Heckman and Kautz 2012). These skills are largely shaped by family influences and not by schools. This body of research suggests that differences in schools do not account for a large portion of differences in educational outcomes.

Other research shows that increasing the schooling level of parents does not necessarily increase schooling levels for children. Black, Devereux, and Salvanes (2005) use a policy change in Norway that exogenously changed educational levels for a cohort of students to estimate the effect of a change in schooling level on the schooling level of their children. They found little causal relationship between the education of parents and their children, with the possible exception of a modest effect of maternal education on sons' education.

Differences in parenting also do not seem to arise because disadvantaged parents do not know what to do to foster their child's skills. For example, surveys show that virtually all parents say that reading to their preschool-aged child is important or very important. Yet substantial numbers of disadvantaged parents do not read to their children on a regular basis (Aud et al. 2012).

Some parents with basic reading skills may *expect* a lower return from reading to their children. Our research (Mayer et al. 2018) and research by Cunha, Elo, and Culhane (2013) find that low-income parents expect a substantial return from the time they spend in educational activities with their children. Agee and Crocker (1996) use an instrument for the parents' discount rate on time investments in their children and find that less-educated and lower-income parents discount their investments at about twice the rate as more advantaged parents. However, in a survey of British parents of school-aged children in England, Attanasio, Boneva, and Rauh (2018) find no difference in expected returns to time or money investments in children by parental income or education. In a companion survey, Boneva and Rauh (2018) find that low-income parents expect a lower rate of return from investments during early childhood compared to higher-income parents, but they find no difference in the expected rate of return for parental investments at older ages. In any case, a lower expected rate of return could lead to either less or more investment in children, depending on whether parents try to make up for a lower expected return by spending more time engaging their children or forego investing because of the lower expected return.

Another explanation for the gap in the amount of time that advantaged and disadvantaged parents invest in their children is that disadvantaged parents have less time to engage their children. However, evidence from time diary data shows that even when researchers account for the number and ages of children in the home, whether the parent is married, and how much time the parent works, differences by education in the amount of time that parents spend with their children persist (Guryan, Hurst, and Kearney 2008). National Center for Education Statistics data show that the proportion of parents who report that they or someone else in the household read to their three-year-old children at least three times a week does not vary by the employment status of the mother, except that the proportion of parents reading to their children was lower when the mother was unemployed (Nord et al. 1999).

Developmental psychology is the academic discipline that perhaps has been most influential in setting the agenda for how researchers think about parenting. A primary tenet of developmental psychology is that "good parenting" cannot be understood in purely quantitative terms and that the quality of parent-child engagement is equally if not more important than the quantity. There is little consensus about how to measure quality except by using classifications of "parenting style" as first described by Baumrind (1991). Her classifications included authoritarian or disciplinarian, permissive or indulgent, uninvolved or authoritative, with authoritative considered to be the most effective style. Developmental psychology has long focused on classifying parent behaviors into these parenting styles (or their variants), and correlating the different typologies with child outcomes. Darling and Steinberg (1993) noted that parenting style is a characteristic of the parent that is distinct from specific parenting practices; the former represents a constellation of parent attributes and attitudes that interact with specific parental socialization practices to shape children's development. Notable in this conceptualization, however, is the thesis that the influence of specific parent behaviors on children's development can be understood only in the context of the emotional milieu, or "parenting style" in which they occur.

Nevertheless, the primary objective of developmental psychology is not to explain why parenting styles differ or explain the decision-making process that leads to differences in specific, measurable behaviors such as reading to young children, enrolling children in early education programs, or taking children to school on time every day. Research on parenting styles acknowledges that in this definition of parental behavior the influence of any one specific parenting practice cannot be disaggregated due to its being part of a typology of other behaviors (Darling and Steinberg 1993). But the aggregation of parental behavior across a wide range of dimensions into a global parenting characteristic or "style" hinders our understanding of how the behavior arises and what can change the behavior, short of changing parents' style of interaction with their children—a task that has proven to require intensive and often expensive interventions.

Increasing intergenerational mobility requires narrowing the differences in how advantaged and disadvantaged parents raise their children. However, evidence on why parenting practices differ by parent advantage leads to a puzzle: advantaged and disadvantaged parents seem to know what is important for their children, and both groups have the time and resources to do what is important for their children, but advantaged parents are more likely to actually do the things that are important. We argue that this difference arises in large part because of differences by parental advantage in the experience of cognitive biases, and that using behavioral tools to reduce these differences can greatly narrow the gap in child outcomes.

A BEHAVIORAL LENS ON PARENTAL DECISION MAKING

Behavioral tools are intended to help people make optimal decisions by overcoming cognitive biases. Because what parents need to do to protect and nurture their children may differ in some respects by parental advantage (for example, some research shows that harsher parenting may be required in dangerous neighborhoods; Ceballo and McLoyd [2002]), when we refer to "optimal" decision making we do not necessarily mean that disadvantaged parents should make the same decisions as advantaged parents. Instead, by optimal decision making we mean the decision that the parent believes is optimal or, put another way, the decision the parent would make in the absence of a cognitive bias. Disadvantaged parents seem to want to do the same things as advantaged parents but are less likely to actually do those things. That is, there is a wider gap between what disadvantaged parents aspire to do and what they actually do. Behavioral tools can help narrow the gap between aspirational and actual parenting.[1] If this gap narrows, so will the outcomes of children from advantaged and disadvantaged families, increasing intergenerational mobility.

The gap between knowing what one ought to do and actually doing it is not unique to parenting. In many situations, people's intentions are not matched by their actions. For example, people often intend to complete tasks on time but routinely miss their self-imposed deadlines, a phenomenon known as the "planning fallacy" (Buehler, Griffin, and Ross 1994; Kahneman and Tversky 1979). Similarly, most people understand the importance of maintaining a healthy diet and taking medications as prescribed. However, research finds that large numbers of people fail to do either of those things because of a variety of decision errors and biases (for review, see John, Loewenstein, and Volpp 2012).

Behavioral science has documented biases that characterize much of human decision making. By understanding how these impede parental decision making and how this differs by parental advantage, researchers can design low-cost interventions to manage the biases, thereby narrowing the gap in the decisions that advantaged and disadvantaged parents make. Like many other decisions, parenting decisions are complex, constraining parents' capacity to make optimal decisions simply because human judgment cannot readily master the complexity associated with parenting. For this reason, parents are prone to rely on heuristics (cognitive "shortcuts") to simplify their decisions and make them "computationally cheap" (e.g., Gigerenzer and Selten 2001). Advantaged and disadvantaged parents can experience this complexity differently, resulting in different patterns of decision making. Here we describe three potentially important characteristics of parenting that make it especially susceptible to cognitive biases and to differential adaptions to biases by parental advantage.

1) Parenting requires making temporal trade-offs. The payoff to many parenting decisions does not materialize until many years into the future. Decisions about spending money and time on educational activities with children, their children's schooling, health-promoting behaviors, and other activities meant to improve child outcomes can be likened to investments with uncertain returns. Research suggests that people systematically overweight present outcomes compared to future outcomes, often leading to suboptimal choices (Castillo et al. 2011; Chabris et al. 2008; Meier and Sprenger 2010; Sutter et al. 2013). Present bias can result in parents prioritizing spending time on activities that provide immediate gratification rather than on investing in time with their children that has a payoff sometime in the future and then regretting those decisions once their children have grown.

Time preference varies across countries and within countries. While present bias exists in the populations of every country where it has been measured (Wan, Rieger, and Hens 2016), the discount rate varies across and within countries (see Frederick, Loewenstein, and O'Donoghue 2002, for a survey of this literature). There is no consensus on what causes differences in time preference. However, Becker and Mulligan (1997) propose that the more financial resources one has to imagine the future, the lower the discount rate on the future, and empirical evidence supports the hypothesis that lower-income adults have a greater discount rate on the future (Hausman 1979; Harrison, Lau, and Williams 2002; Golsteyn, Grönqvist, and Lindahl 2014; Dohmen et al. 2010; Eckel, Grundy, and Zimmet 2005; Lawrance 1991; Pabilonia and Song 2013). Many early studies in sociology provide observational evidence that time preference is culturally acquired (Banfield 1974; Cohen and Hodges 1963; Leshan 1952; Lewis 1966; O'Rand and Ellis 1974). Not deferring gratification may be useful when the future is uncertain, suggesting that children raised in poor families may become more present-oriented adults, even if this results in suboptimal decision making.

2) Parenting requires attribution. Parents must motivate their children to engage in desirable behaviors and dissuade them from undesirable behaviors. Motivating another person requires understanding his or her preferences, thoughts, and feelings. Parents must also interpret and respond to the motivations behind the behavior of their children. A parent of a three-year-old who throws a tantrum is likely to respond differently whether she thinks that the child is just doing what any three-year-old does or if she thinks the child is being willfully defiant.

Inferring the cause of another person's behavior is perhaps one of the most difficult social judgments to perform accurately (Epley 2014). Ironically, this is especially true when one tries to adopt the perspective of a loved one (Savitsky et al. 2011). Married couples, for example, exhibit a remarkable inability to predict each other's preferences despite being quite confident in their ability to do so (Davis, Hoch, and Ragsdale 1986; Kruger and Gilovich 1999). For parents, the difficulty is compounded because children's preferences are often a moving target, and children sometimes lack the ability to articulate their motivations.

The need to interpret behavior and respond to preferences opens the door for attribution biases, which refer to systematic errors people make when they attempt to explain others' behaviors. Errors in attribution are due both to limitations in information processing and to individuals' own motivations (Gilbert and Malone 1995; Kunda 1990). Attribution bias arises from cognitive shortcuts that individuals use to process complex information. But people are also likely to favor attributions that are consistent with their own goals and sense of identity and to disfavor attributions that injure their self-esteem.

People's imperfect attribution processes create a number of different attribution biases. Among the most pervasive is self-serving attribution bias—the tendency to attribute our successes to our own internal traits and our failures to others or to the situation. A parent of a child who behaves well may attribute the child's behavior to his or her own good parenting. But when the child misbehaves the parent may attribute that behavior to the child being "bad" or having bad influences. Self-serving attributions arise from our desire to see ourselves positively (Mezulis et al. 2004). The magnitude of the self-serving bias varies across countries and is on average lower in Asian countries compared to the United States (Mezulis et al. 2004). It may also vary across groups in the United States, but we have no evidence on this possibility.

As another example, the "fundamental attribution error" is the tendency to overweight others' internal characteristics and personality and underweight external and situational circumstances when explaining others' behavior. For instance, parents may be more likely to attribute their child's failure to do her homework to a personality trait, such as laziness, rather than to a situational factor, such as lack of sufficient time. Although fundamental attribution error is present in every culture where it has been measured, the pervasiveness and depth of the bias differ across countries (Masuda and Nisbett 2001; Mezulis et al. 2004; Miller 1984; Hong et al. 2000). The magnitude of the biases also varies within countries by age and psychopathology. In addition, parents' attributions of child behavior and school success vary across countries (Bornstein, Putnick, and Lansford 2011).

We do not know why attribution biases vary across and within cultures. People may be culturally primed to invoke certain attributions (Shweder and Bourne 1982); people may have different needs to bolster their own self-esteem (Taylor and Brown 1988). However, the fact that attribution biases vary by cultural groups suggests that these biases may also vary by parental advantage.

A large research literature documents that parental attributions influence parent-child interactions. For example, parents who attribute hostile intent to their children's behavior are more likely to have interactions with the children that are characterized by conflict (MacKinnon-Lewis et al. 1992). Mothers with inaccurate expectations about their child's development tend to be harsher with their child (Azar et al. 1984; Twentyman and Plotkin 1982). Parent attributions are also implicated in child maltreatment and physical punishment of children (Dix, Ruble, and Zambarano 1989; Strassberg 1995).

We know little about why some parents are more prone to bias in the attributions they make about their child's behavior. Attribution bias is more likely to occur when information about the target of perspective taking is lacking. Indeed, studies indicate that mothers with greater knowledge of child development and therefore more accurate attributions of their child behavior demonstrate more effective parenting skills, at least as they are measured by researchers (Azar et al. 1984; Benasich and Brooks-Gunn 1996; Damast, Tamis-LeMonda, and Bornstein 1996; Fry 1985; Stevens 1984; Twentyman and Plotkin 1982). However, this evidence is from observational studies, so they do not imply that giving parents more information about child development would change parents' attributions and parenting decisions, especially if the source of the attribution bias is parents' own motivations.

As we have already noted, disadvantaged parents do not seem to lack information about the things they should do to improve their children's outcomes or how to do those things. Although information about child development may be a necessary first step to overcoming attribution bias with respect to one's child, it is unlikely to be sufficient to change parental behavior by much. Additional research is needed to understand how attribution bias influences parental decisions and the extent to which it varies by parental advantage.

3) Parenting decisions are often automatic rather than deliberate. Parenting often requires quick and on-the-spot decisions. When a child runs toward a busy street, a parent must react rather than contemplate. When a child screams in the checkout lane because the parent says no to his request for candy, the parent seldom has time to reflect on what to do. The need to act quickly and on the spot results in automaticity. Automaticity is a response done with minimal cognitive processing; it is useful in that it reduces cognitive load. An automatic response can be beneficial if it is efficacious but costly when it is not. Because automatic responses can be likened to habits, and habits are hard to break, ineffective automatic responses can lead to ineffective parenting.

Automaticity is the result of learning, repetition, and practice. Which automatic behaviors a parent adopts is likely to depend on the parent's own experiences. Behaviors that have been repeatedly observed or experienced as a child are likely to become the default behavior of the adult. An adult whose parents always spanked him when he misbehaved as a child is more likely to "automatically" spank his own children in response to their misbehavior, with little thought about alternative ways to discipline the child. We do not have a lot of evidence about how parents learn to parent. However, the little evidence that we do have (usually from small surveys) suggests that parenting behaviors are learned primarily from one's own parents, relatives, and friends (Berkule-Silberman et al. 2010; Koepke and Williams 1989; Shwalb et al. 1995).

Automaticity reduces cognitive demands, leads to rapid responses, and is useful for many parenting situations. But it can also create barriers to eliminating costly parental behaviors (e.g., yelling at a child, hitting a child, letting the child watch television before bed). Advantaged and disadvantaged parents may have the same goals for their children and even share the same information about how to achieve those goals, but because of differences in their own upbringings they might have different parenting habits. Any habit is hard to break, but if the automatic behavior is reinforced in the in-group where parents learn and practice parenting behaviors, it is even more difficult to change.

To the extent that spheres of parenting influence differ greatly for different groups and to the extent that they fail to intersect, different groups will develop distinctive parenting habits and behaviors. This is not a problem if the different parenting decisions have little impact on children's success; however, to the extent that they do, automaticity can result in very different child outcomes.

INTERVENTIONS TO MANAGE COGNITIVE BIASES IN PARENTING

Although the foregoing list of cognitive biases that influence parenting is far from exhaustive, it illustrates the potential of the behavioral perspective to improve parent decision making. Cognitive processes can prevent parents from "rationally" analyzing their decisions and force them instead to rely on biases. Adopting a behavioral approach can allow us to decompose parenting behaviors into a series of decisions and help researchers and practitioners identify and intervene when cognitive biases are likely to result in parenting decisions that are suboptimal from the parent's own point of view.

As an example of a way that a program could mitigate the effects of cognitive bias, consider the Parents and Children Together (PACT) study, a field experiment we conducted at the Behavioral Insights and Parenting Lab at the University of Chicago (Mayer et al. 2018). This field experiment was designed to test the ability of a behaviorally informed intervention to increase parent-child reading time among parents of children in the federally funded Head Start preschool program. This is an important outcome because reading to one's child at an early age is associated with improved literacy and social skills (Hale et al. 2011; Kloosterman et al. 2011; Mol and Bus 2011; Price and Kalil 2018; Raikes et al. 2006).

Extensive survey work conducted as part of this study revealed that parents in this population understood the importance of reading to children (in part this may be due to their attending Head Start, which strongly emphasizes parental reading to children); had access to reading materials (again, possibly due to Head Start's making books available to borrow); understood the "production function" of their time investment (i.e., they reported on surveys that the more time they invested reading to their children the greater would be the likelihood of their children's success in kindergarten); and reported that it was just as much if not more their responsibility (as opposed to the teacher's responsibility) to stimulate their child's development. Our other work, moreover, shows that low-income parents enjoy spending time in developmentally relevant activities with their children to the same extent as do high-income parents, and that low-income parents do not report feeling particularly stressed or unhappy engaging in learning and teaching activities with their children (Kalil et al. 2019).

What, then, leads to infrequent book reading among low-income families? We hypothesize that present bias may be key, so the PACT intervention was designed specifically to overcome this bias with a set of behavioral tools (goal setting, feedback, reminders, and social rewards) designed to "bring the future to the present" and help parents form a habit of regular book reading. On average, the PACT intervention had a very large treatment impact (~ 1 SD) on the amount of time parents spent reading with their children (the study measured time use objectively using digital tools). But even more important was the study's finding that the intervention was substantially more effective for those parents who were more present biased. In short, parents who suffer from present bias are the very ones who benefit from an intervention designed to overcome it. Those parents who were not present biased were already reading at higher levels to their children, and the intervention had little impact on them.

These findings suggest that parents' difficulty with making temporal trade-offs is partly responsible for their failure to read to their children. In addition, these findings provide a blueprint for reducing the effects of this cognitive bias. By using a set of known behavioral tools, parents are able to improve parental decision making. Moreover, the costs of the PACT program per family were relatively low, dwarfing the per-capita costs of current policy interventions designed to improve preschool children's educational outcomes, which suggests that behaviorally based interventions can feasibly be adapted for policy purposes.

As a second example, our research team implemented a behaviorally informed field experiment called Show Up to Grow Up, which was designed to increase attendance and diminish chronic absences at subsidized preschool programs in Chicago (Kalil, Mayer, and Gallegos

2021). Preschools serving low-income children in particular suffer from problems of chronic absenteeism and lateness on the part of the young children who attend them (Katz, Adams, and Johnson 2015). Because preschool children's attendance is governed by the decisions their parents make, the problem of chronic absenteeism from preschool offered us an opportunity to understand the decision-making processes that influence absenteeism and the extent to which these decisions arise from malleable factors.

One goal of our intervention was to help parents correct inaccurate beliefs. As noted by Robinson et al. (2018) and Rogers and Feller (2018), parents of grade-school children severely underestimate how many days their children have been absent from school and at the same time overestimate their children's attendance relative to that of other children. Limits on parental attention can interfere with parents' ability to accurately remember their children's absences for an entire school year (Chugh and Bazerman 2007; Simons and Chabris 1999). Parents may also be biased toward underestimating their own children's absences from school. Bringing this information to the top of parents' minds can reduce uncertainty, counteract this bias, and prompt behavior change.

A second type of inaccurate belief, which may be especially germane in preschool, is the belief that preschool experiences matter little for success in primary school. As Ehrlich et al. (2014) show, some parents may believe that preschool is simply "child care" and may not understand that children engage in a wide variety of school readiness activities during the day. Thus, they may not be aware of what their children are missing when they are absent from school.

Accordingly, we designed an intervention that sent personalized text messages to parents, targeting behavior driving children's absences from preschool. Messages designed to help parents correct inaccurate beliefs about learning opportunities in preschool told parents what their children were learning in preschool, framed to emphasize what children would miss out on if they were absent. We also sent feedback messages designed to correct misbeliefs about attendance, providing objective feedback on children's actual attendance at school in the prior month. The purpose of these messages is to help parents correct potentially inaccurate beliefs about the actual level of absenteeism of their child in the prior period (per Robinson et al. 2018) and Rogers and

Feller 2018). Parents in the treatment group also received goal setting messages that prompted parents to focus on meeting the goal of having the child attend school every day, and planning prompt messages that encouraged parents to identify and make a plan to address some of the impediments to attendance. The intervention lasted 18 weeks and included approximately four text messages per week. Using administrative records from preschools, we find that our intervention increased days attended by 2.5 (0.15 standard deviations) and decreased chronic absenteeism by 9.3 percentage points (20 percent) over the 18-week period. We found that parents who benefited the most were the ones who reported lower preferences for attendance in our baseline survey. These are the parents who are less likely than other parents to report that their child would be worse off in terms of their academic and social skills if they missed many days of preschool. In short, parents who have less strong beliefs in the importance of preschool benefit most from messages that emphasize its importance by prompting parents to focus on what their child is missing out on if they don't attend.

CONCLUSION

An important determinant of the intergenerational correlation in life outcomes is the decisions that parents make regarding how to raise their children. Rethinking the challenge of increasing economic and social mobility as requiring a change in the decisions that parents make allows us to reframe the challenge as one of overcoming cognitive biases that interfere with decision making. By conceiving of parenting as a series of decisions, researchers can identify and investigate specific constraints that prevent parents from following through on behaviors they believe can help their children. The behavioral approach to parenting holds substantial promise for improving the decisions of all parents, and especially of disadvantaged parents.

Behavioral science currently has many limitations. It often seems more like a classification system than a true theory. It is plagued by contradictions and inconsistencies in the classifications. But it still promises to be a powerful new way to understand parental behavior and especially differences in behavior by parental advantage. Though this field is still in its infancy, a number of studies have demonstrated how behavioral tools can help manage the cognitive biases that interfere with parent engagement (see, for example, Gennetian, Darling, and Aber 2016; Kalil 2014; Mayer et al. 2018; Robinson et al. 2018; Rogers and Feller 2018).

Despite our enthusiasm for this approach, it is important to raise some relevant cautions. For one, we do not yet know much about which parental decisions are driven by cognitive biases and which are due solely to economic and social deprivations or other social structural barriers. If parents cannot afford books, they will not read to their children no matter how many times they are "nudged." We also know little about behavioral spillovers, or whether subjecting parents to multiple behavioral tools to drive a single behavior will have synergistic or antagonistic effects on other behaviors. Most importantly, we do not yet know how to make a habit of new behaviors so that cognitive biases are overcome in the long run. A theory-driven approach to integrating behavioral tools into parenting interventions has the potential to answer these questions, thereby advancing science at the same time as it improves children's life chances.

Note

1. The cost of a wrong decision may also be greater for disadvantaged parents who have few resources to recover from such decisions than for advantaged parents. For example, a middle-class parent but not a low-income parent may be able to hire a tutor to make up for not spending enough time reading to her child.

References

Agee, Mark D., and Thomas D. Crocker. 1996. "Parental Altruism and Child Lead Exposure: Inferences from the Demand for Chelation Therapy." *Journal of Human Resources* 31(3): 677–691.

Akee, Randall, William E. Copeland, Gordon Keeler, Adrian Angold, and E. Jane Costello. 2010. "Parents' Incomes and Children's Outcomes: A Quasi-Experiment." *American Economic Journal: Applied Economics* 2(1): 86–115.

Altintas, Evrim. 2012. "Parents' Time with Children: Micro and Macro Perspectives." Doctoral diss., Nuffield College, University of Oxford, UK.

Attanasio, Orazio, Teodora Boneva, and Christopher Rauh. 2018. "Parental Beliefs about Returns to Different Types of Investments in School Children." Working Paper No. 2018-032. Chicago: Becker Friedman Institute for Economics at the University of Chicago.

Aud, Susan, William Hussar, Frank Johnson, Grace Kena, Erin Roth, Eileen Manning, Xiaolei Wang, and Jijun Zhang. 2012. *The Condition of Education 2012*. NCES 2012-045. Washington, DC: U.S. Department of Education, National Center for Education Statistics.

Azar, Sandra T., Denise R. Robinson, Elizabeth Hekimian, and Craig T. Twentyman. 1984. "Unrealistic Expectations and Problem-Solving Ability in Maltreating and Comparison Mothers." *Journal of Consulting and Clinical Psychology* 52(4): 687–691.

Banfield, Edward C. 1974. *The Unheavenly City Revisited*. Boston: Little, Brown and Company.

Baumrind, Diana. 1991. "The Influence of Parenting Style on Adolescent Competence and Substance Use." *Journal of Early Adolescence* 111(1): 56–95.

Becker, Gary S., and Casey B. Mulligan. 1997. "The Endogenous Determination of Time Preference." *Quarterly Journal of Economics* 112(3): 729–758.

Benasich, April Ann, and Jeanne Brooks-Gunn. 1996. "Maternal Attitudes and Knowledge of Child-Rearing: Associations with Family and Child Outcomes." *Child Development* 67(3): 1186–1205.

Berkule-Silberman, Samantha B., Benard P. Dreyer, Harris S. Huberman, Perry E. Klass, and Alan L. Mendelsohn. 2010. "Sources of Parenting Information in Low SES Mothers." *Clinical Pediatrics* 49(6): 560–568.

Bjorklund, Anders, Lena Lindahl, and Matthew J. Lindquist. 2010. "What More than Parental Income, Education and Occupation? An Exploration of What Swedish Siblings Get from Their Parents." *B.E. Journal of Economic Analysis and Policy* 10(1). https://doi.org/10.2202/1935-1682.2449 (accessed October 7, 2020).

Black, Sandra E., Paul J. Devereux, and Kjell G. Salvanes. 2005. "Why the Apple Doesn't Fall Far: Understanding Intergenerational Transmission of Human Capital." *American Economic Review* 95(1): 437–449.

Blau, David M. 1999. "The Effect of Income on Child Development." *Review of Economics and Statistics* 81(2): 261–276.

Boneva, Teodora, and Christopher Rauh. 2018. "Parental Beliefs about Returns to Educational Investments—The Later the Better?" *Journal of the European Economic Association* 16(6): 1669–1711.

Bornstein, Marc H., Diane L. Putnick, and Jennifer E. Lansford. 2011. "Parenting Attributions and Attitudes in Cross-Cultural Perspective." *Parenting: Science and Practice* 11(2–3): 214–237.

Buehler, Roger, Dale Griffin, and Michael Ross. 1994. "Exploring the 'Planning Fallacy': Why People Underestimate Their Task Completion Times." *Journal of Personality and Social Psychology* 67(3): 366–381.

Carneiro, Pedro, and James J. Heckman. 2003. "Human Capital Policy." NBER Working Paper No. 9495. Cambridge, MA: National Bureau of Economic Research.

Castillo, Mario, Paul J. Ferraro, P., Jeffrey L. Jordan, and Ragan Petrie. 2011. "The Today and Tomorrow of Kids: Time Preferences and Educational Outcomes of Children." *Journal of Public Economics* 95(11–12): 1377–1385.

Castleman, Benjamin L., and Lindsay Page. 2014. "Summer Nudging: Can Personalized Text Messages and Peer Mentor Outreach Increase College Going among Low-Income High School Graduates?" Working Paper No. 9. Charlottesville: University of Virginia Center for Education Policy and Workforce Competitiveness.

Ceballo, Rosario, and Vonnie C. McLoyd. 2002. "Social Support and Parenting in Poor, Dangerous Neighborhoods." *Child Development* 73(4): 1310–1321.

Chabris, Christopher F., David Laibson, Carrie L. Morris, Jonathon P. Schuldt, and Dmitry Taubinsky. 2008. "Individual Laboratory-Measured Discount Rates Predict Field Behavior." *Journal of Risk and Uncertainty* 37(2): 237–269.

Chugh, Dolly, and Max Bazerman. 2007. "Bounded Awareness: What You Fail to See Can Hurt You." *Mind and Society* 6(1): 1–18.

Cohen, Albert K., and Harold M. Hodges. 1963. "Characteristics of the Lower-Blue-Collar-Class." *Social Problems* 10(4): 303–334.

Cooper, Kerris, and Kitty Stewart. 2013. *Does Money Affect Children's Outcomes? A Systematic Review.* York, UK: Joseph Rowntree Foundation.

Cunha, Flávio, Irma Elo, and Jennifer Culhane. 2013. "Eliciting Maternal Expectations about the Technology of Cognitive Skill Formation." NBER Working Paper No. 19144. Cambridge, MA: National Bureau of Economic Research.

Cunha, Flávio, and James J. Heckman. 2007. "The Technology of Skill Formation." *American Economic Review* 97(2): 31–47.

Cunha, Flávio, James J. Heckman, and Lance Lochner. 2006. "Interpreting the Evidence on Life Cycle Skill Formation." In *Handbook of the Economics of Education*, Erik A. Hanushek and Finis Welch, eds. Amsterdam: North-Holland, pp. 698–812.

Dahl, Gordon B., and Lance Lochner. 2012. "The Impact of Family Income on Child Achievement: Evidence from the Earned Income Tax Credit." *American Economic Review* 102(5): 1927–1956.

Damast, Amy Melstein, Catherine S. Tamis-LeMonda, and Marc H. Bornstein. 1996. "Mother-Child Play: Sequential Interactions and the Relation between Maternal Beliefs and Behaviors." *Child Development* 67(4): 1752–1766.

Darling, Nancy, and Laurence Steinberg. 1993. "Parenting Style as Context: An Integrative Model." *Psychological Bulletin* 113(3): 487–496.

Davis, Harry L., Stephen J. Hoch, and E.K. Easton Ragsdale. 1986. "An Anchoring and Adjustment Model of Spousal Predictions." *Journal of Consumer Research* 13(1): 25–37.

Dix, Theodore, Diane N. Ruble, and Robert J. Zambarano. 1989. "Mothers' Implicit Theories of Discipline: Child Effects, Parent Effects, and the Attribution Process." *Child Development* 60(6): 1373–1391.

Dohmen, Thomas, Armin Falk, David Huffman, and Uwe Sunde. 2010. "Are Risk Aversion and Impatience Related to Cognitive Ability?" *American Economic Review* 100(3): 1238–1260.

Eckel, Robert H., Scott M. Grundy, and Paul Z. Zimmet. 2005. "The Metabolic Syndrome." *Lancet* 365(9468): 1415–1428.

Ehrlich, Stacy B., Julia A. Gwynne, Amber Stitziel Pareja, and Elaine M. Allensworth. 2014. *Preschool Attendance in Chicago Public Schools: Relationships with Learning Outcomes and Reasons for Absences.* Chicago: University of Chicago Consortium on Chicago School Research.

Epley, Nicholas. 2014. *Mindwise: How We Understand What Others Think, Believe, Feel, and Want.* New York: Knopf.

Fiorini, Mario, and Michael P. Keane. 2014. "How the Allocation of Children's Time Affects Cognitive and Noncognitive Development." *Journal of Labor Economics* 32(4): 787–836.

Frederick, Shane, George Loewenstein, and Ted O'Donoghue. 2002. "Time Discounting and Time Preference: A Critical Review." *Journal of Economic Literature* 40(2): 351–401.

Fry, P.S. 1985. "Relations between Teenagers' Age, Knowledge, Expectations and Maternal Behaviour." *British Journal of Developmental Psychology* 3(1): 47–55.

Gennetian, Lisa, Matthew Darling, and J. Lawrence Aber. 2016. "Behavioral Economics and Developmental Science: A New Framework to Support Early Childhood Interventions." *Journal of Applied Research on Children: Informing Policy for Children at Risk* 7(2): Article 2.

Gigerenzer, Gerd, and Reinhard Selten. 2001. "Rethinking Rationality." In *Bounded Rationality: The Adaptive Toolbox*, Gerd Gigerenzer and Reinhard Selten, eds. Cambridge, MA: MIT Press, pp. 1–12.

Gilbert, Daniel T., and Patrick S. Malone. 1995. "The Correspondence Bias." *Psychological Bulletin* 117(1): 21–38.

Gilovich, Thomas, Dale Griffin, and Daniel Kahneman, eds. 2002. *Heuristics and Biases: The Psychology of Intuitive Judgment.* Cambridge: Cambridge University Press.

Golsteyn, Bart, Hans Grönqvist, and Lena Lindahl. 2014. "Time Preferences and Lifetime Outcomes." *Economic Journal* 124(580): F739–F761.

Guryan, Jonathan, Erik Hurst, and Melissa Kearney. 2008. "Parental Education and Parental Time with Children." *Journal of Economic Perspectives* 22(3): 23–46.

Hale, Lauren, Lawrence M. Berger, Monique K. LeBourgeois, and Jeanne Brooks-Gunn. 2011. "A Longitudinal Study of Preschoolers' Language-Based Bedtime Routines, Sleep Duration, and Well-Being." *Journal of Family Psychology* 25(3): 423–433.

Harris, Yvette R., Denise Terrel, and Gordon Allen. 1999. "The Influence of Education Context and Beliefs on the Teaching Behavior of African American Mothers." *Journal of Black Psychology* 25(4): 490–503.

Harrison, Glenn W., Morten I. Lau, and Melonie B. Williams. 2002. "Estimating Individual Discount Rates in Denmark: A Field Experiment." *American Economic Review* 92(5): 1606–1617.

Hausman, Jerry A. 1979. "Individual Discount Rates and the Purchase and Utilization of Energy-Using Durables." *Bell Journal of Economics* 10(1): 33–54.

Heckman, James J., and Tim D. Kautz. 2012. "Hard Evidence on Soft Skills." *Labour Economics* 19(4): 451–464.

Heckman, James J., and Dimitriy Masterov. 2004. "The Productivity Argument for Investing in Young Children." *Review of Agricultural Economics* 29(3): 446–493.

Hong, Ying-Yi, Michael W. Morris, Chi-Yue Chiu, and Verónica Benet-Martínez. 2000. "Multicultural Minds: A Dynamic Constructivist Approach to Culture and Cognition." *American Psychologist* 55(7): 709–720.

Hurst, Erik. 2010. *Comments and Discussion for* The Rug Rat Race. Washington, DC: Brookings Institution Press.

John, Leslie K., George Loewenstein, and Kevin Volpp. 2012. "Empirical Observations on Longer-Term Use of Incentives for Weight Loss." *Preventive Medicine* 55: S68–S74.

Kahneman, Daniel, and Amos Tversky. 1979. "Prospect Theory: An Analysis of Decision under Risk." *Econometrica* 47(2): 263–291.

Kalil, Ariel. 2014. "Addressing the Parenting Divide and Children's Life Chances." The Hamilton Project Discussion Paper. Washington, DC: Brookings Institution.

Kalil, Ariel, Susan Mayer, William Delgado, and Lisa Gennetian. 2019. "The Education Gradient in Parental Time Use: Investment or Enjoyment?" Unpublished manuscript.

Kalil, Ariel, Susan Mayer, and Sebastian Gallegos. 2021. "Using Behavioral Insights to Increase Attendance at Subsidized Preschool Programs: The Show Up to Grow Up Intervention." *Organizational Behavior and Human Decision Processes* 163: 65–79.

Kalil, Ariel, Rebecca Ryan, and Michael Corey. 2012. "Diverging Destinies: Maternal Education and the Developmental Gradient in Time with Children." *Demography* 49(4): 1361–1383.

Katz, Michael, Gina Adams, and Martha C. Johnson. 2015. *Insight into Absenteeism into DPCS Early Childhood Program: Contributing Factors and Promising Strategies.* Washington, DC: Urban Institute.

Kloosterman, Rianne, Natascha Notten, Jochem Tolsma, and Gerbert Kraaykamp. 2011. "The Effects of Parental Reading Socialization and Early School Involvement on Children's Academic Performance: A Panel Study of Primary School Pupils in the Netherlands." *European Sociological Review* 27(3): 291–306.

Koepke, Jean E., and Cheri Williams. 1989. "Child-Rearing Information: Resources Parents Use." *Family Relations* 38(4): 462–465.

Kruger, Justin, and Thomas Gilovich. 1999. "'Naive Cynicism' in Everyday Theories of Responsibility Assessment: On Biased Assumptions of Bias." *Journal of Personality and Social Psychology* 76(5): 743–753.

Kunda, Ziva. 1990. "The Case for Motivated Reasoning." *Psychological Bulletin* 108(3): 480–498.

Lawrance, Emily C. 1991. "Poverty and the Rate of Time Preference: Evidence from Panel Data." *Journal of Political Economy* 99(1): 54–77.

Lazarides, Rebecca, Judith Harackiewicz, Elizabeth Canning, Laura Pesu, and Jaana Viljaranta. 2015. "The Role of Parents in Students' Motivational Beliefs and Values." In *The Routledge International Handbook of Social Psychology of the Classroom*, Christine M. Rubie-Davies, Jason M. Stephens, and Penelope Watson, eds. Abingdon, UK: Routledge, pp. 81–94.

Leshan, Lawrence. 1952. "Time Orientation and Social Class." *Journal of Abnormal and Social Psychology* 47(3): 589–592.

Lewis, Oscar. 1966. "The Culture of Poverty." *Scientific American* 215(4): 19–25.

MacKinnon-Lewis, Carol, Michael E. Lamb, Barry Arbuckle, Laila Baradaran, and Brenda L. Volling. 1992. "The Relationship of Biased Maternal and Filial Attributions and the Aggressiveness of Their Interactions." *Development and Psychopathology* 4(3): 403–415.

Masuda, Takahiko, and Richard E. Nisbett. 2001. "Attending Holistically versus Analytically: Comparing the Context Sensitivity of Japanese and Americans." *Journal of Personality and Social Psychology* 81(5): 922–934.

Mayer, Susan E. 2010. "The Relationship between Income Inequality and Inequality in Schooling." *Theory and Research in Education* 8(1): 5–20.

Mayer, Susan E., Ariel Kalil, Philip Oreopoulos, and Sebastian Gallegos. 2018. "Using Behavioral Insights to Increase Parental Engagement: The Parents and Children Together Intervention." *Journal of Human Resources* 54(4): 900–925.

Meier, Stephan, and Charles Sprenger. 2010. "Present-Biased Preferences and Credit Card Borrowing." *American Economic Journal: Applied Economics* 2(1): 193–210.

Mezulis, Amy H., Lyn Y. Abramson, Janet S. Hyde, and Benjamin L. Hankin. 2004. "Is There a Universal Positivity Bias in Attributions? A Meta-Analytic Review of Individual, Developmental, and Cultural Differences in the Self-Serving Attributional Bias." *Psychological Bulletin* 130(5): 711–747.

Miller, John G. 1984. "Culture and the Development of Everyday Social Explanation." *Journal of Personality and Social Psychology* 46(5): 961–978.

Mol, Suzanne E., and Adriana G. Bus. 2011. "To Read or Not to Read: A Meta-Analysis of Print Exposure from Infancy to Early Adulthood." *Psychological Bulletin* 13(72): 267–296.

Noel, Amber, Patrick Stark, and Jeremy Redford. 2015. "Parent and Family Involvement in Education, from the National Household Education Surveys Program of 2012." NCES 2013-028.REV2. Washington, DC: U.S. Department of Education, National Center for Education Statistics.

Nord, Winquist, Christine Jean Lennon, Baiming Liu, and Kathryn Chandler. 1999. *Home Literacy Activities and Signs of Children's Emerging Literacy, 1993 and 1999.* NCES 2000-026rev. Washington, DC: U.S. Department of Education, National Center for Education Statistics.

O'Rand, Angela, and Robert A. Ellis. 1974. "Social Class and Social Time Perspective." *Social Forces* 53(1): 53–62.

Pabilonia, Sabrina Wulff, and Younghwan Song. 2013. "Single Mothers' Time Preference, Smoking, and Enriching Childcare: Evidence from Time Diaries." *Eastern Economic Journal* 39(2): 227–255.

Pew Charitable Trusts. 2012. *Pursuing the American Dream: Economic Mobility across Generations.* Washington, DC: Pew Charitable Trusts. https://www.pewtrusts.org/~/media/legacy/uploadedfiles/pcs_assets/2012/pursuingamericandreampdf.pdf (accessed October 8, 2020).

Price, James, and Ariel Kalil. 2018. "The Effect of Mother-Child Reading Time on Children's Reading Skills: Evidence from Natural Within-Family Variation." *Child Development* 90(6): e688–e702.

Raikes, Helen, Barbara Alexander Pan, Gayle Luze, Catherine S. Tamis-LeMonda, Jean Brooks-Gunn, Jill Constantine, . . . Eileen T. Rodriguez. 2006. "Mother-Child Book Reading in Low-Income Families: Correlates and Outcomes during the First Three Years of Life." *Child Development* 77(4): 924–953.

Ramey, Garey, and Valerie A. Ramey. 2010. "The Rug Rat Race." *Brookings Papers on Economic Activity* 41(1): 129–176.

Robinson, Carly D., Monica G. Lee, Eric Dearing, and Todd Rogers. 2018.

"Reducing Student Absenteeism in the Early Grades by Targeting Parental Beliefs." *American Educational Research Journal* 26(3): 353–383.

Rodgers, Anthony, Tim Corbett, Dale M. Bramley, Tania Riddell, Mary Willis, Ruey-Bin Lin, and Mark Jones. 2005. "Do U Smoke after Txt? Results of a Randomised Trial of Smoking Cessation Using Mobile Phone Text Messaging." *Tobacco Control* 14(4): 255–261.

Rogers, Todd, and Avi Feller. 2018. "Reducing Student Absences at Scale by Targeting Parents' Misbeliefs." *Nature Human Behavior* 2(5): 335–342.

Savitsky, Kenneth, Boaz Keysar, Nicholas Epley, Travis Carter, and Ashley Swanson. 2011. "The Closeness-Communication Bias: Increased Egocentrism among Friends versus Strangers." *Journal of Experimental Social Psychology* 47(1): 269–273.

Sharek, Zachariah, Robert E. Schoen, and George Loewenstein. 2012. "Bias in the Evaluation of Conflict of Interest Policies." *Journal of Law, Medicine, and Ethics* 40(2): 368–382.

Shea, John. 2000. "Does Parents' Money Matter?" *Journal of Public Economics* 77(2): 155–184.

Shwalb, David W., Hisashi Kawai, Junichi Shoji, and Kinya Tsunetsugu. 1995. "The Place of Advice: Japanese Parents' Sources of Information about Childrearing and Child Health." *Journal of Applied Developmental Psychology* 16(4): 629–644.

Shweder, Richard A., and Edmund J. Bourne. 1982. "Does the Concept of the Person Vary Cross-Culturally?" In *Cultural Conceptions of Mental Health and Therapy*, Anthony J. Marsella and Geoffrey M. White, eds. Dordrecht: D. Reidel Publishing Company, pp. 97–137.

Simons, Daniel J., and Christopher F. Chabris. 1999. "Gorillas in Our Midst: Sustained Inattentional Blindness for Dynamic Events." *Perception* 28(9): 1059–1074.

Stevens, Joseph H., Jr. 1984. "Child Development Knowledge and Parenting Skills." *Family Relations* 33(2): 237–244.

Strassberg, Zvi. 1995. "Social Information Processing in Compliance Situations by Mothers of Behavior-Problem Boys." *Child Development* 66(2): 376–389.

Sutter, Matthias, Martin G. Kocher, Daniela Glätzle-Rützler, and Stefan T. Trautmann. 2013. "Impatience and Uncertainty: Experimental Decisions Predict Adolescents' Field Behavior." *American Economic Review* 103(1): 510–531.

Taylor, Shelley E., and Jonathon D. Brown. 1988. "Illusion and Well-Being: A Social Psychological Perspective on Mental Health." *Psychological Bulletin* 103(2): 193–210.

Twentyman, Craig T., and Ron C. Plotkin. 1982. "Unrealistic Expectations of

Parents Who Maltreat Their Children: An Educational Deficit That Pertains to Child Development." *Journal of Clinical Psychology* 38(3): 497–503.

Villena-Rodán, Benjamin, and Cecilia Ríos-Aguilar. 2011. "Causal Effects of Maternal Time-Investment on Children's Cognitive Outcomes." Working Paper No. 285. Santiago, Chile: Center for Applied Economics.

Wan, Mei, Marc Oliver Rieger, and Thorsten Hens. 2016. "How Time Preferences Differ: Evidence from 53 Countries." *Journal of Economic Psychology* 52: 115–135.

Washbrook, Elizabeth V., and Jane Waldfogel. 2011. *On Your Marks: Measuring the School Readiness of Children in Low-to-Middle Income Families.* London: Resolution Foundation.

4

Gender Differences in (Some) Formative Inputs to Child Development

Michael Baker
University of Toronto

It is well documented that females and males face different socio-economic trajectories over the life cycle, such as jobs, income, health, living arrangements, and human capital investments. The reasons for these differences include discrimination, individual choice, environmental factors, and biology, among many others.

In studies of the specific factors that contribute to particular outcomes in a person's life, researchers typically focus on a part of the life cycle that is believed to be critical to lifetime outcomes. The fetal origins hypothesis (Barker 1990) directs attention to the early years of life and the prenatal period, and much of social science research on inequality is now focused on this interval.[1] However, for the study of gender differences, research also reveals that later life events, such as the birth of a first child (Angelov, Johansson, and Lindahl 2016; Kleven, Landais, and Egholt Søgaard 2018), can significantly change important economic and social choices.

Much of the previous research on early life environmental factors, thought to be important to child development and adult outcomes, stratifies the data by socioeconomic status. In turn, this research has revealed that changes in the early life circumstances—that is, these inputs—can have significant effects on lifetime outcomes, especially for disadvantaged children. One prominent example is the Perry Preschool Project, a randomized control trial (RCT) with a sample of 128 three- and four-year-old African American children living in poverty and assessed to be at high risk of school failure (Heckman and Karapakula 2019).

Although there is now a sizable literature on how these inputs vary by gender in certain developing countries,[2] there is less direct evidence on any corresponding differences in developed countries.[3] Previous studies have shown that males receive more total time from their parents as a result of extra inputs from their fathers (Lundberg, Pabilonia, and Ward-Batts 2007; Yeung et al. 2001), and that family structure might vary by the gender of children (Lundberg and Rose 2003). Lundberg (2005) and Raley and Bianchi (2006) provide reviews of the literature.

In this chapter I investigate differences in several inputs by gender: medical care after birth, breastfeeding, maternal mental health postbirth, and parenting. The circumstances of birth—for example, low birth weight—are known correlates of adult outcomes. While the claimed benefits of breastfeeding probably exceed those rigorously documented, evidence from RCT investigation indicates there are advantages to children from this source of nutrition. Finally, parenting and parental time inputs are widely cited as an important developmental input. For example, some of the benefits of the Perry Preschool intervention have been attributed to its effects on home environment and parent/child attachments (e.g., Heckman and Karapakula 2019).

The analysis in this chapter reveals differences in both maternal mental health postbirth and early parent/child interactions, depending on whether the first-born child is a boy or a girl; these differences are consistent with boys experiencing a less nurturing and more aversive home life. There are small gender differences in the periods in which first-born children are breastfed, but previous evidence on the impact of breastfeeding suggests these would have little consequence. Finally, while boys with lower birth weights receive more hospital care than girls, the impact of variation in this care around the very low birth weight (VLBW) threshold by sex suggests that the survival and development of low birth weight (LBW) children might be improved by reallocating even more care to boys.

DO FEMALES AND MALES ENTER THE LABOR
MARKET EQUALLY SKILLED?

Individuals' lifetime income trajectories depend in part on the skills and aptitudes they bring to the labor market. There is now a large literature, much of it outside economics, that has investigated gender differences in these skills. This research has generated both popular (Fine 2010; Gray 1992) and academic (Hyde 2014; Spelke 2005) debate.

Economics research has focused on gender differences in competitiveness (e.g., Niederle and Vesterlund 2007), people skills (e.g., Lordan and Pischke 2018) or more generally interpersonal skills (e.g., Cortes, Jaimovich, and Siu 2018), risk preferences (e.g., Borghans et al. 2009), and willingness to work long hours (e.g., Goldin 2014). These are thought to help account for the considerable gender-based occupational segregation in the labor market (e.g., Blau, Brummund, and Yung-Hsu Liu 2013) and gender differences in within-occupation success. However, direct evaluations of the relationship between the degree of occupational segregation and gender differences in these or other skills are relatively rare (e.g., Baker and Cornelson 2018).

If the gender differences in these skills are important for labor market success, then it is more than an academic question to discover their source. Often this inquiry is cast as a duel between biology and the environment, although research on genetics tells us that this dichotomy is problematic due to the impact of environment on gene expression. However, it likely retains its allure because it appears to present a division between factors thought to be immutable or hardwired (biology) and those that can be remediated if necessary (environmental).

The focus here is on differences in environmental factors that girls and boys experience as they grow up. The analysis neither presumes that these factors are the most important nor definitively connects any environmental differences to specific adult outcomes. Rather, the objective is to fill in missing evidence to help target future investigation.

SHOULD GENDER DIFFERENCES IN ENVIRONMENTAL INPUTS MATTER?

Whether to expect that any found gender difference in an environmental developmental input is consequential is complicated by the fact that males and females simultaneously differ in other ways that may mediate the effect of that input. For example, first-born females in Canada, the United Kingdom, and the United States receive more reading time with their parents than first-born males starting at very young ages (e.g., Baker and Milligan 2016). This might be consequential and contribute to the sometimes cited, but also disputed, female advantage in verbal skills (Hyde 2014), if a "unit" of reading has the same developmental effect on boys and girls. But, for example, if boys are more receptive to reading than females, then the gender difference in this input might not matter.

One reason the impact of an input might differ by gender is genetics. For example, some research argues that the relationship between stress and consequent depression is in part mediated by genetic vulnerability that in turn appears to differ by gender (Salk and Hyde 2012). Therefore, a given amount of stress might create a different level of depression in females and males, or alternatively, different amounts of stress would be required to result in the same level of depression.

As a result, without additional assumptions or evidence, it is impossible to interpret the gender differences documented here as important to gender differences in the skills and aptitudes that males and females develop in their lives.

DATA

The following analysis uses several data sources that survey the conditions of young children in the United States and Canada. For the investigation of medical care after birth, I use the U.S. National Center for Health Statistics (NCHS) public use birth cohort–linked birth/infant death files for the years 1983–1991 and 1995–2010.[4] These data for the population of births provide a variety of measures of mortality and the cause of death for infants who die within the first year, as well as birth certificate information such as birth weight and characteristics of the mother. I also use hospital discharge data for 1995–2005 for Arizona, Maryland, New York, and New Jersey, distributed by the Healthcare Cost and Utilization Project (HCUP).[5] Information provided for each recorded birth includes birth weight, length of hospital stay, and hospital charges.

The study of sex differences in breastfeeding uses the National Immunization Survey (NIS) for the years 2010–2018. The NIS is nationally representative of the American public and is conducted annually, primarily to survey the vaccination of young children and teenagers in the United States. I use survey data of children aged 19–35 months (NIS-Child). The survey includes questions about whether, and how long, each child was breastfed. Due to the ages of the surveyed children, breastfeeding may still be ongoing. To address this issue, I examine milestones of breastfeeding in the first year, such as initiation, breastfed at least three months, and the number of days of the first year of life the child was breastfed, which is coded 365 for those breastfed 12 months or longer.

Finally, estimates of sex differences in mothers' mental health postbirth and parenting behavior are based on the Canadian National Longitudinal Survey of Children and Youth (NLSCY) and the U.S. Early Childhood Longitudinal Survey-Birth Cohort (ECLS-B). The NLSCY is a nationally representative survey of Canadian children conducted biennially between 1994–1995 and 2008–2009. A new cohort of children aged 0 and 1 entered the survey each wave and were followed until age 4–5.[6] The ECLS-B is a nationally representative survey of children born in 2001, and followed subsequently through multiple waves (e.g., age 9 months, 2 years, etc.).

In much of the analysis I sample first-born children if possible. The assumption that the sex of the child is randomly assigned is most tenable for first-born children. The sex of subsequent children may not be random if the probability of higher-order births is related to the sex of realized births. Furthermore, the parity of the birth may affect the parental inputs a child receives (e.g., Price 2008), so holding parity constant in any gender comparisons is important. However, the sex of the first-born child may be related to some important environmental factors, such as whether the father of the child is present in the household.[7] That said, in some analyses I consider the sample of all children or explicitly compare the results for the first-born and all children samples, where the behavior under study is likely to be less sensitive to parity (e.g., hospital provided care directly postbirth), or the comparison reveals interesting differences.

MEDICAL CARE AFTER BIRTH

Girls and boys face different medical challenges immediately post-birth. I document a number of these differences. Figure 4.1 shows evidence of sex differences in one-year mortality rates from the NCHS data for the years 1983–1991 and 1995–2010. In the top panel I present the one-year mortality rates for all girls and boys. The rates for both sexes have been trending downward over time, with more pronounced declines in the 1980s. There also is a persistent gap between the rates for males and females, which has narrowed somewhat over the period. The bottom panel shows the corresponding statistics for the sample of LBW births defined by birth weight less than 2,500 grams (5.5 pounds). The same patterns are present here with the gender gap declining from over 4 deaths per 100 in the 1980s to under 2 by 2010. In both graphs girls have lower mortality rates than males in all years.[8]

Table 4.1 presents the causes of death in the first year, by sex, for the full (first three columns) and LBW (last three columns) samples, conditioning on death in this period. The causes of death classifications were changed starting in 1990, so here I restrict the sample to 1990–1991 and 1995–2010. In the full sample, the larger gender differences are for congenital malformations (higher for females), sudden infant death syndrome (higher for males), and deaths associated with the respiratory system (again higher for males). In the LBW sample, there are also larger gender differences in conditions from the perinatal period and deaths associated with the circulatory system.

At least some of these sex differences in morbidities may be responsive to more intensive medical care. A reason why there may be an interaction between sex differences in early life ailments and corresponding differences in medical care is that some of the important indicators for more intensive medical care—low and very low birth weight—do not

Figure 4.1 Trends in One-Year Mortality of Children, by Sex, United States, 1983–2010

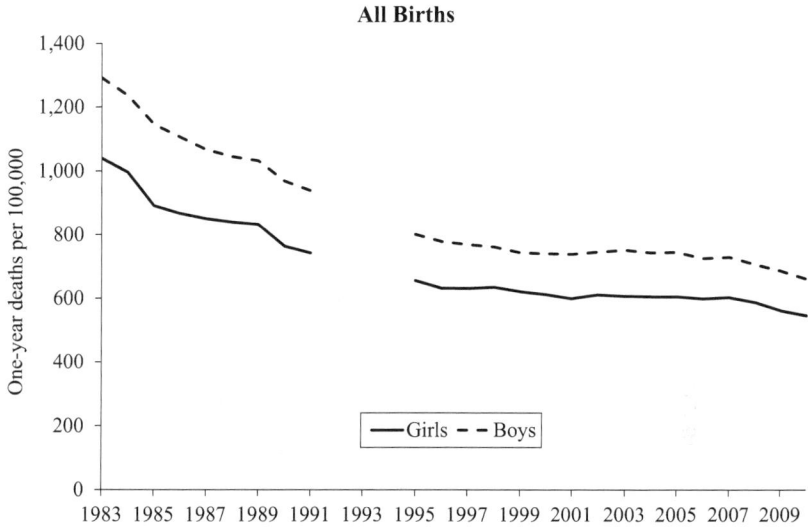

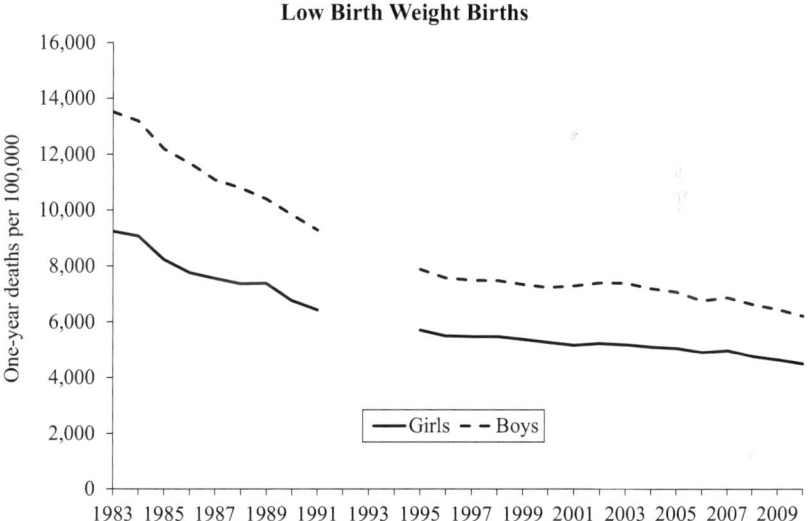

SOURCE: Author's calculations from NCHS public use birth cohort–linked birth/infant death files.

Table 4.1 Causes of Death in the First Year of Life, 1990–1991 and 1995–2010, United States

	All births (N = 575,173)			Low birth weight births (N = 383,445)		
	Girls	Boys	Difference	Girls	Boys	Difference
Infectious and parasitic	0.0259	0.0260	-0.0001 (0.0004)	0.0220	0.0221	-0.0001 (0.0005)
Neoplasms	0.0082	0.0067	0.0016*** (0.0002)	0.0058	0.0041	0.0016*** (0.0002)
Diseases of the blood	0.0162	0.0169	-0.0007** (0.0003)	0.0099	0.0102	-0.0003 (0.0003)
Endocrine	0.0149	0.0144	0.0005 (0.0003)	0.0130	0.0123	0.0007** (0.0004)
Nervous system	0.0323	0.0318	0.0005 (0.0005)	0.0367	0.0368	-0.0000 (0.0006)
Ear and mastoid process	0.0001	0.0001	-0.0000 (0.0000)	0.0000	0.0000	-0.0000 (0.0000)
Circulatory system	0.0383	0.0401	-0.0018*** (0.0005)	0.0397	0.0442	-0.0046*** (0.0007)
Respiratory system	0.0433	0.0492	-0.0058*** (0.0006)	0.0301	0.0319	-0.0017*** (0.0006)
Digestive system	0.0136	0.0148	-0.0012*** (0.0003)	0.0122	0.0140	-0.0018*** (0.0004)
Genitourinary system	0.0099	0.0102	-0.0003 (0.0003)	0.0087	0.0090	-0.0003 (0.0003)
Conditions from perinatal period	0.3432	0.3447	-0.0015 (0.0013)	0.4619	0.4818	-0.0199*** (0.0016)

Congenital malformations	0.1525	0.1327	0.0197*** (0.0009)	0.1405	0.1155	0.0250*** (0.0011)
SIDS	0.0797	0.0887	−0.0091*** (0.0007)	0.0280	0.0283	−0.0002 (0.00005)
All other diseases	0.0004	0.0006	−0.0001** (0.0001)	0.0003	0.0005	−0.0002*** (0.0001)
External causes	0.2216	0.2233	−0.0017 (0.0011)	0.1912	0.1894	0.0018 (0.0013)

NOTE: * significant at the 0.10 level; ** significant at the 0.05 level; *** significant at the 0.01 level.
SOURCE: Author's calculations from NCHS public use birth cohort–linked birth/infant death files. Reported statistics are conditional on death in the first year for the indicated samples.

distinguish by sex. This is perhaps surprising because females are, on average, of smaller stature than males throughout their lives. In the United States, females are of lower average birth weight and attain an adult height almost four inches lower than males (Baker and Cornelson 2019). There is, therefore, some intuition for using different cutoffs to indicate birth weights of concern for girls and boys.

Figure 4.2 provides information on gender differences in average birth weights. It shows the average birth weight by birth percentile for girls and boys. Boys' average birth weight is higher than girls' starting at roughly the third percentile. Interestingly, the first and second percentiles of birth weight, and the average birth weights within these percentiles, are almost identical for boys and girls in these data. However, the outcomes of children in these lower percentiles differ markedly by sex. Figure 4.3 graphs the one-year mortality rate of girls and boys in their respective first 10 percentiles of birth weight. The mortality rate for boys is elevated relative to the rate for girls over the first 3–4 per-

Figure 4.2 Average Birth Weight by Sex, by Percentile, United States, 1983–2010

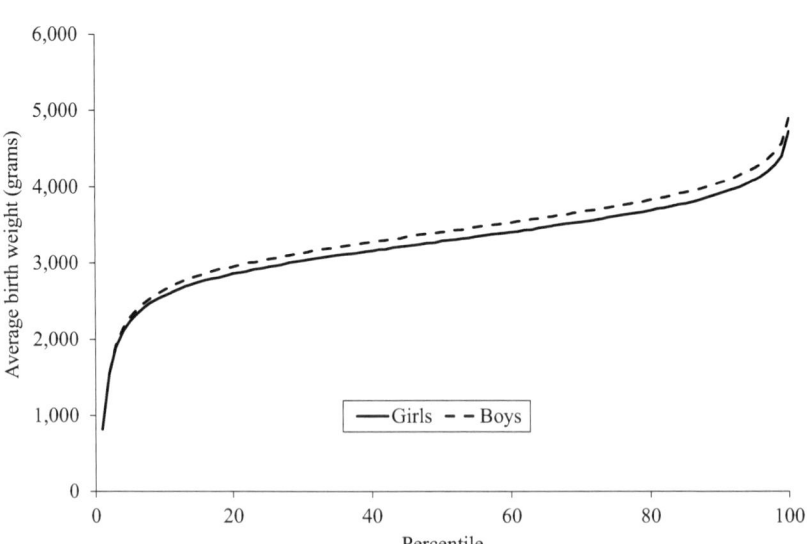

SOURCE: Author's calculations from NCHS public use birth cohort–linked birth/ infant death files.

Figure 4.3 One-Year Infant Mortality by Sex, by Percentile, Bottom 10 Percentiles, United States, 1983–2010

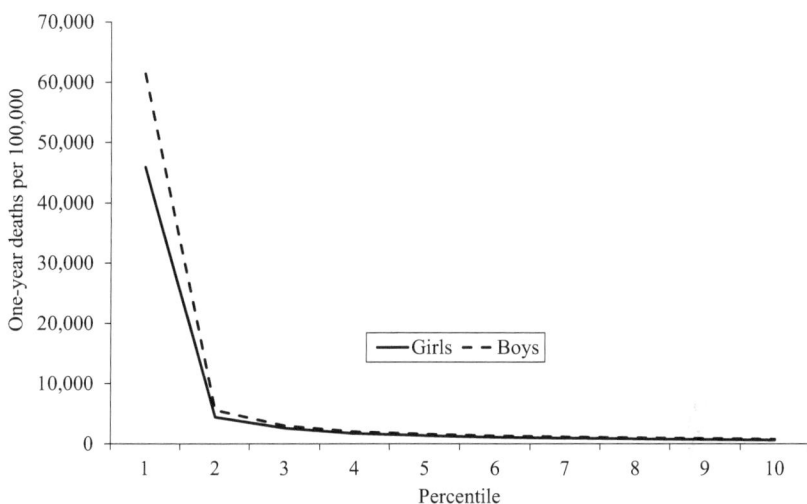

SOURCE: Author's calculations from National Center for Health Statistics public use birth cohort–linked birth/infant death files.

centiles. The fourth percentile of birth weight is 2,211 g (4.9 pounds) for boys and 2,170 g (4.8 pounds) for girls. Therefore, it is at the percentiles of birth weight in which girls' and boys' average birth weights are roughly similar that we observe the excess mortality for males. The graph for 28-day mortality (not shown) tells a very similar story.

Low birth weight can have both health and socioeconomic repercussions. While the research on the associations of low birth weight is extensive, few studies of either of these classes of outcomes make a distinction by sex. An exception is Stevenson et al. (2000), who report that boys who are VLBW face higher rates of mortality and a number of morbidities.[9]

The preceding evidence suggests that VLBW boys should receive higher levels of critical care than their VLBW female counterparts. This is easily checked in the data. The excess mortality of boys at these weights also suggests that this care might be more consequential to their survival. To investigate this possibility, I examine how gender differences in mortality in the lower birth weight percentiles interact with the

VLBW threshold (birth weight <1,500 grams) as an indicator for more intensive medical care. Almond et al. (2010) take this methodological tack to demonstrate the returns to marginal medical care, comparing the mortality of babies with birth weights just above and just below the VLBW cutoff.[10] They find an increase in mortality for babies marginally heavier than the cutoff, which they interpret as a result of specialized care that is withdrawn as birth weight passes through the VLBW cutoff. They also demonstrate that care—captured by data on hospital costs and length of stay in the hospital—changes discontinuously at the VLBW cutoff supporting this interpretation of the results.

The intuition for the investigation here is that because the VLBW cutoff does not vary by sex but the underlying risk of mortality of low birth weight children does, there should be corresponding differences in the impact of the variation in medical care across the VLBW threshold. A difference in the impact of this care by sex might indicate a misallocation of resources through which care is provided to children who do not need it at the expense of children who do or children who need it more.

There has been some debate in this literature over the robustness of the main results in Almond et al. (2010) to the treatment of births exactly at the VLBW cutoff (Almond et al. 2011; Barreca et al. 2011). I report results both including and omitting these births to investigate whether this issue has implications for any gender gap in this specialized care.

Following the lead of that literature, I use ordinary least squares to estimate Equation (4.1):

$$y_{it} = \alpha + \beta VLBW_i + y VLBW_i \cdot (1500 - w_i) + \eta(1 - VLBW_i) \cdot (1500 - w_i) + X\mu + \varepsilon_i$$

where y is some outcome for child i born in year t, VLBW is a 0/1 indicator that the child's weight is less than 1,500 grams (3.3 pounds), w_i is the child's weight in grams, and X is a set of control variables, which for the analysis of mortality in the first year include fixed effects for year of birth, mother's and father's five-year age groups, race, whether the mother was born out of state, and controls for the child's gestational age and plurality.[11] I restrict the sample to children with weight within 85 grams of the 1,500-gram cutoff. Following developments in this research, I estimate models that retain children with weights equal to 1,500 grams in the sample, and also so-called donut estimators that omit these and surrounding observations. I present both robust standard errors and standard errors clustered at the gram level.

Figures 4.4 and 4.5 report the one-year and 28-day mortality rates of boys and girls, by one-ounce (28 grams) weight bins in the vicinity of the VLBW threshold. In the top panel of each figure I include 1,500-gram birth weights in the first bin above the threshold, while in the lower panel I omit these births to provide some intuition for how the donut estimates might differ from the full sample estimates.

The top panels of Figures 4.4 and 4.5 show evidence of elevated mortality rates in the first bin above the threshold, potentially signaling that the withdrawal of care at the threshold is affecting the survival of these marginally heavier births. There is also a distinct difference between boys and girls, as the uptick for boys is larger in both absolute and proportional terms, especially for one-year mortality. This is consistent with the intuition that the withdrawal of care at the threshold may be more consequential for boys than for girls. In the bottom panels of both figures the upticks are smaller for boys and they disappear for girls, removing the 1,500-gram births from the sample. The diminution of the upticks is expected, given the evidence in Barreca et al. (2011) that mortality at exactly 1,500 grams is elevated compared to mortality at surrounding birth weights. The difference in the effect of this change in sample by sex suggests that the donut estimators are less likely to provide evidence that the cutoff of critical care at the 1,500-gram threshold has an effect on the mortality of females.

This inference is formalized in Table 4.2, where I present estimates for VLBW of β from Equation (4.1) for one-year mortality rates. The first row shows the estimate retaining babies weighing 1,500 grams in the sample, to match the sample selection in Almond et al. (2010).[12] Note, however, that the sample here is not strictly comparable to the one in this previous study, as I use data from an additional eight years (2003–2010). The pooled estimate in the first column for this longer period is marginally smaller than the estimate in Almond et al. (2010). The estimates in the succeeding columns indicate that once the sample is split by gender, it is males who drive the pooled result. The estimate for males is more than twice as large as the estimate for females—it is almost 18 percent of the mean mortality rate for boys in the sample bins above the threshold. The estimate for girls is 8 percent of the mortal-

**Figure 4.4 One-Year Mortality by Sex around the Very Low Birth Weight
Threshold, United States, 1983–2010**

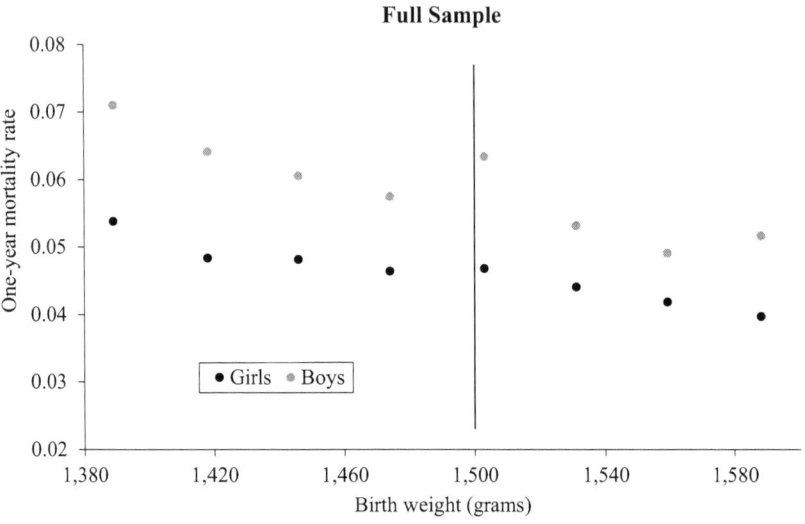

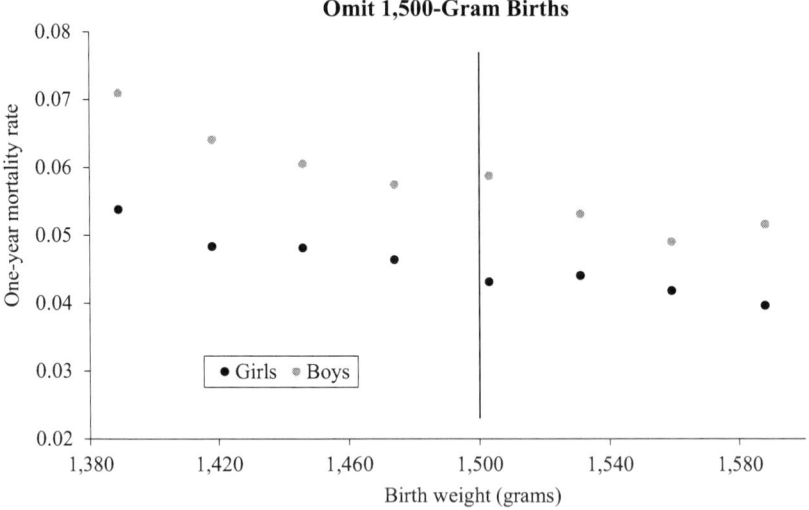

NOTE: Median birth weight by one-ounce (28g) bins radiating away from the 1,500g
threshold. Top panel—1,500g births included in the first bin above threshold. Bottom
panel—1,500g births omitted. Plotted at median birth weight in each bin.
SOURCE: Author's calculations from NCHS public use birth cohort-linked birth/infant
death files.

**Figure 4.5 28-Day Mortality by Sex around the Very Low Birth Weight
Threshold, United States, 1983–2010**

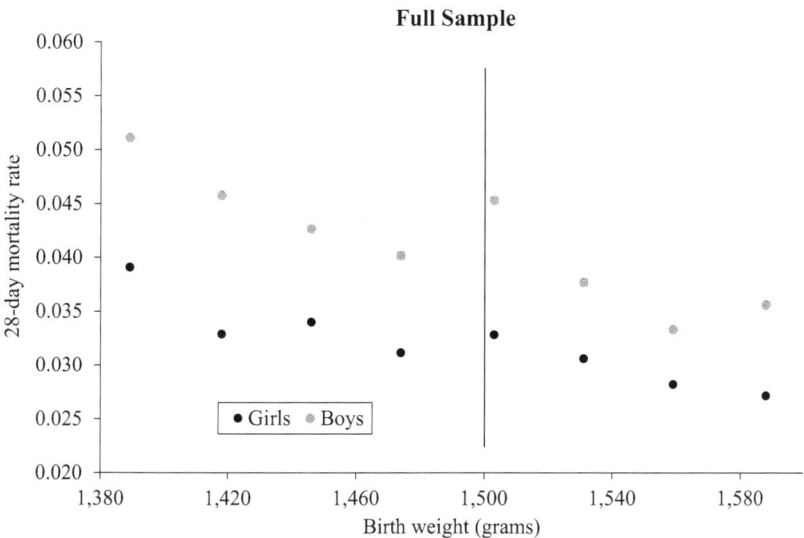

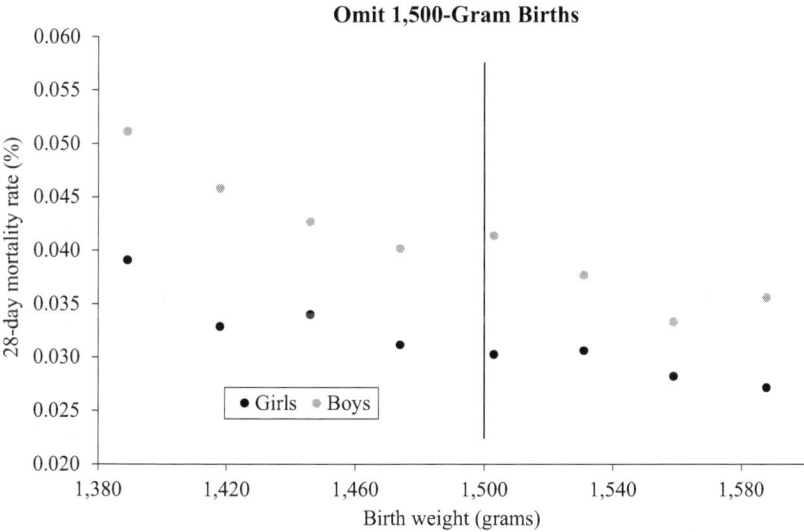

NOTE: Median birth weight by one-ounce (28g) bins radiating away from the 1,500g
threshold. Top panel—1,500g births included in the first bin above threshold. Bottom
panel—1,500g births omitted. Plotted at median birth weight in each bin.
SOURCE: Author's calculations from NCHS public use birth cohort–linked birth/
infant death files.

Table 4.2 Changes in One-Year Mortality at the VLBW Threshold, by Sex, 1983–2010, United States

Sample omission	Pooled	Girls	Boys	Difference
None	−0.0057	−0.0032	−0.0081	0.0049
	(0.0015)***	(0.0020)	(0.0023)***	(0.0030)
	[0.0033]*	[0.0031]	[0.0040]**	(0.0025)*
1,500g	−0.0026	−0.0007	−0.0044	0.0037
	(0.0015)*	(0.0020)	(0.0023)*	(0.0031)
	[0.0013]**	[0.0018]	[0.0017]**	(0.0024)
1,500g +/−1g	−0.0028	−0.0009	−0.0047	0.0038
	(0.0015)*	(0.0020)	(0.0023)**	(0.0031)
	[0.0013]**	[0.0018]	[0.0017]***	(0.0024)
1,500g +/−2g	−0.0021	−0.0002	−0.0040	0.0038
	(0.0016)	(0.0021)	(0.0023)*	(0.0031)
	[0.0013]	[0.0017]	[0.0018]**	(0.0024)
1,500g +/−3g	−0.0008	0.0006	−0.0022	0.0028
	(0.0018)	(0.0025)	(0.0027)	(0.0037)
	[0.0015]	[0.0025]	[0.0019]	(0.0033)

NOTE: * significant at the 0.10 level; ** significant at the 0.05 level; *** significant at the 0.01 level. In the first row that sample sizes are 344,793 for the pooled sample, 17,2103 for the sample of girls, and 172,690 for the sample of boys. In subsequent rows births with the indicated weight are omitted from the sample. The reported statistics in the first three rows are estimates of a dummy variable for birth weight below the VLBW threshold following Equation (4.1). The statistic reported in the fourth row is the estimate of the interaction between sex and VLBW from a pooled regression with a full set of interactions between the control variables and sex. Control variables include fixed effects for year of birth, mother's and father's five-year age groups, race, and whether the mother was born out of state, and controls for the child's gestational age and plurality, as well as separate linear trends in birth weight above and below the threshold. Robust standard errors in parentheses. Standard errors clustered at the gram level in square brackets.

SOURCE: Author's calculations from NCHS public use birth cohort–linked birth/infant death files.

ity rate above the threshold. Also, the estimate for boys is statistically significant at conventional levels, while the estimate for girls is not. Finally, the estimate in the fourth column reveals that this sex difference is marginally statistically significant at conventional levels.[13]

The subsequent rows present estimates from the donut estimator following the sample deletions in Barreca et al. (2011). Omitting observations at 1,500 grams, the estimates of VLBW fall by roughly 50 percent. This is consistent with the findings in Barreca et al. (2011). Only the estimate for males is statistically significant, and the estimate for females is now quite small. Additional omissions of births within 1 or 2 grams of 1,500 grams from the sample lead to the same conclusion. Given the standard errors, the sex differences in these samples are no longer statistically significant, although this conclusion is tempered by both the individual estimates by sex and the evidence in Figure 4.4. Note that when births within 3 grams of 1,500 grams are omitted, the estimate for males is halved again and is no longer statistically significant. As noted by both Barreca et al. (2011) and Almond et al. (2011), this donut omits births at 1,503 grams, which is at a spike in reported weights, as it corresponds to 53 ounces.

A corresponding analysis of the 28-day mortality rate is presented in Table 4.3. The message here is very similar to that in the preceding table, with some important exceptions. First, even when the sample omission is extended to births of weights 1,497 grams through 1,503 grams, the estimate of VLBW for males remains statistically significant and is 10 percent of the sample mean mortality rate. Second, the gender differences are more consistently statistically significant.

This evidence supports the initial intuition to investigate the impact of the VLBW cutoff on mortality by gender. The VLBW cutoff is far more meaningful for males than for females, as judged by their mortality in the first year. While this is interesting, it does not necessarily imply a misallocation of hospital critical care resources. It may be that medical staff already know the more critical consequences of the VLBW cutoff for males and therefore the threshold has less impact on the medical care for females. Alternatively, the threshold may lead to a discrete increase in the care of females that consumes resources that might otherwise be devoted to LBW males.

Figures 4.6 and 4.7 present the birth weight profiles of two measures of care from the HCUP data, total hospital charges and length of stay. Again, the top panel includes 1,500-gram births in the first bin above the threshold, while the lower panel omits these births from the sample. Both figures show evidence that boys receive more care than girls by these measures, conditional on birth weight, likely reflective of the greater risks of mortality boys face at lighter weights. The top panels show a clear, discrete decline in these two measures of care at the threshold, which is modestly larger for males. Omitting the 1,500-gram

**Table 4.3 Changes in 28-Day Mortality at the VLBW Threshold, by Sex,
1983–2010, United States**

Sample omission	Pooled	Girls	Boys	Difference
None	−0.0057	−0.0036	−0.0078	0.0042
	(0.0013)***	(0.0017)**	(0.0019)***	(0.0026)*
	[0.0027]**	[0.0023]	[0.0035]**	(0.0021)**
1,500g	−0.0033	−0.0017	−0.0047	0.0030
	(0.0013)**	(0.0017)	(0.0019)**	(0.0026)
	[0.0011]***	[0.0014]	[0.0013]***	(0.0015)*
1,500g +/−1g	−0.0034	−0.0018	−0.0049	0.0032
	(0.0013)***	(0.0017)	(0.0019)**	(0.0026)
	[0.0011]***	[0.0014]	[0.0013]***	(0.0016)**
1,500g +/−2g	−0.0028	−0.0013	−0.0043	0.0030
	(0.0013)**	(0.0017)	(0.0020)**	(0.0026)
	[0.0010]***	[0.0014]	[0.0012]***	(0.0016)*
1,500g +/−3g	−0.0021	−0.0003	−0.0039	0.0036
	(0.0016)	(0.0021)	(0.0023)*	(0.0031)
	[0.0013]	[0.0021]	[0.0016]**	(0.0026)

NOTE: * significant at the 0.10 level; ** significant at the 0.05 level; *** significant
at the 0.01 level. In the first row the sample sizes are 344,793 for the pooled sample,
172,103 for the girls' sample, and 172,690 for the boys' sample. In subsequent rows
births with the indicated weight are omitted from the sample. The reported statistics
are estimates of a dummy variable for birth weight below the VLBW threshold following Equation (4.1). The statistic reported in the fourth row is the estimate of the
interaction between sex and VLBW from a pooled regression with a full set of interactions between the control variables and sex. Control variables include fixed effects
for year of birth, mother's and father's five-year age groups, race, and whether the
mother was born out of state, and controls for the child's gestational age and plurality, as well as separate linear trends in birth weight above and below the threshold.
Robust standard errors in parentheses. Standard errors clustered at the gram level in
square brackets.
SOURCE: Author's calculations from NCHS public use birth cohort–linked birth/
infant death files.

births does not materially affect this inference—the drop-offs in care for
both girls and boys remain. The omission of the 1,500-gram births has
less consequence here because, as noted by Almond et al. (2011), the
provision of care to 1,500-gram and marginally heavier babies does not
differ substantially.

Tables 4.4 and 4.5 present the corresponding regression estimates.
The standard errors are relatively large for this analysis, reflecting in

**Figure 4.6 Hospital Charges by Sex around the Very Low Birth
            Weight Threshold**

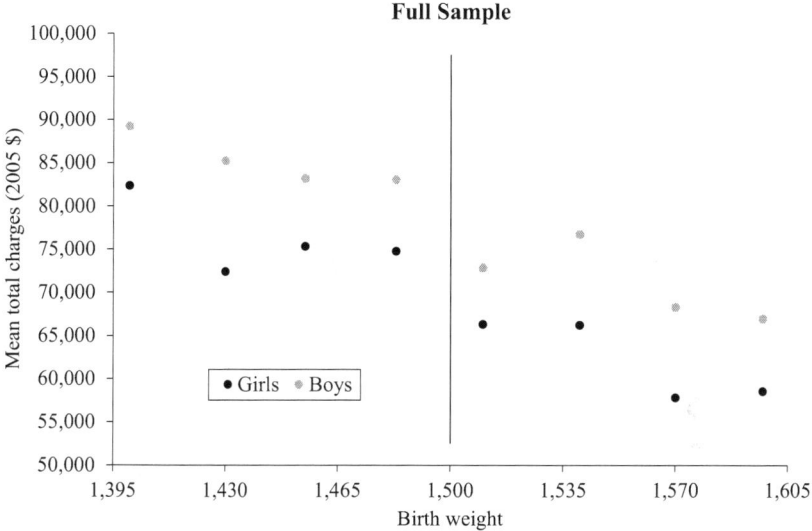

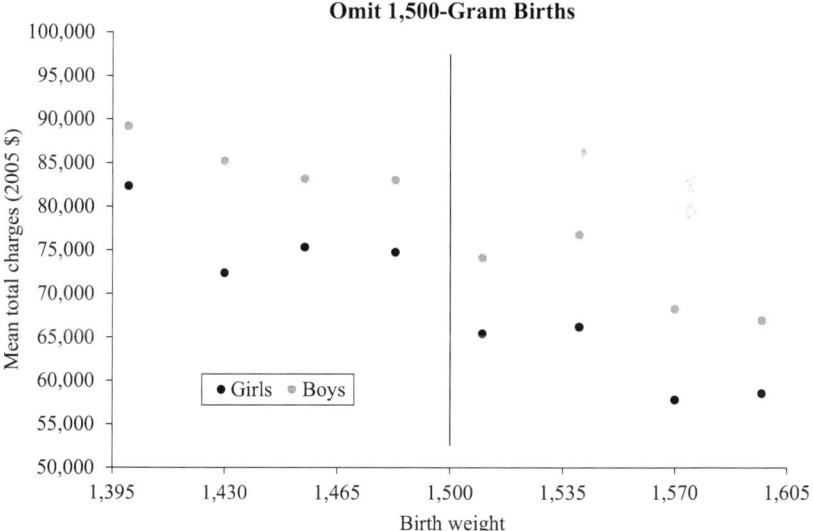

NOTE: Median birth weight by one-ounce (28g) bins radiating away from the 1,500g
    threshold. Top panel—1,500g births included in the first bin above threshold. Bottom
    panel—1,500g births omitted. Plotted at median birth weight in each bin.
SOURCE: Author's calculations from HCUP data for births in Arizona, Maryland, New
    York, and New Jersey, 1995–2005.

**Figure 4.7 Hospital Length of Stay by Sex around the Very Low Birth
Weight Threshold**

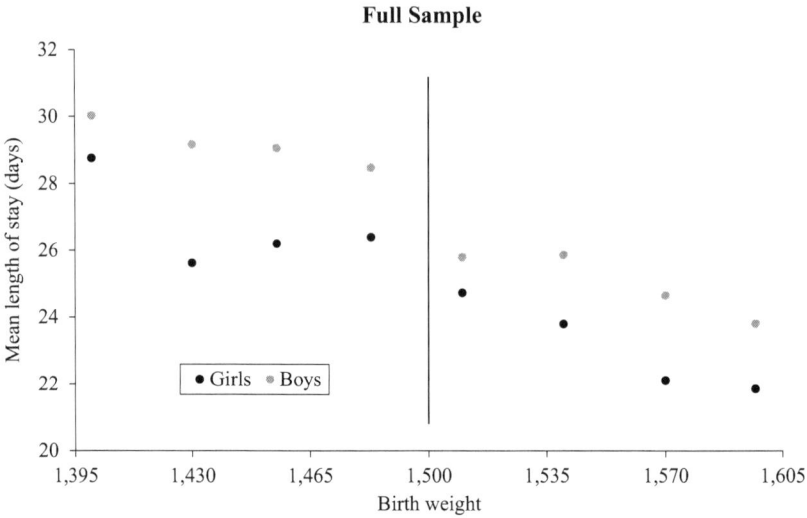

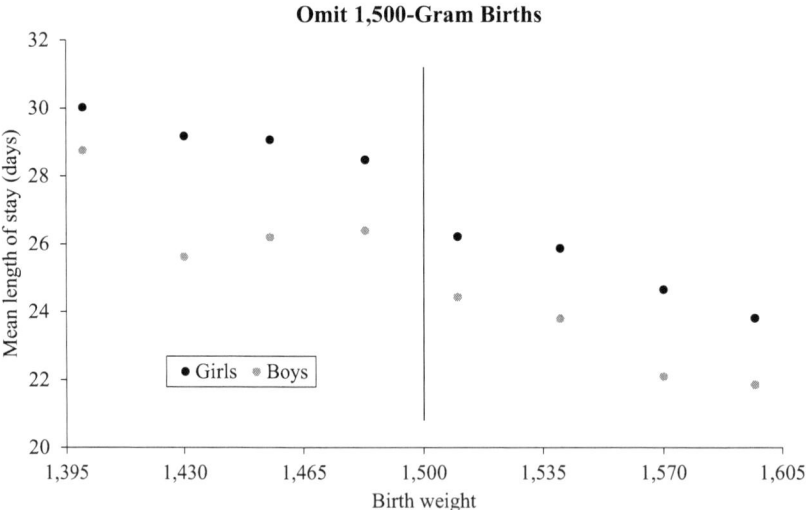

NOTE: Birth weight grouped into one-ounce (28g) bins radiating away from the 1,500g
threshold. Top panel—1,500g births included in the first bin above threshold. Bottom
panel—1,500g births omitted. Plotted at median birth weight in each bin.
SOURCE: Author's calculations from HCUP data for births in Arizona, Maryland, New
York, and New Jersey, 1995–2005.

Table 4.4 Changes in Hospital Costs at the VLBW Threshold, by Sex, 1995–2005, United States

Sample omission	Pooled	Girls	Boys	Difference
None	5,353	6,224	4,258	1,966
	(2,114)**	(2,769)**	(3,204)	(4,230)
	[3,527]	[3,919]	[4,578]	[4,829]
1,500g	4,736	7,161	2,044	5,117
	(2,185)**	(2,805)**	(3,367)	(4,377)
	[3,930]	[4,271]*	[4,833]	[4,683]
1,500g +/−1g	4,243	6,730	1,455	5,275
	(2,224)*	(2,859)**	(3,421)	(4,453)
	[3,996]	[4,333]	[4,923]	[4,782]
1,500g +/−2g	3,206	6,824	−807.3	7,631
	(2,217)	(2,927)**	(3,338)	(4,435)*
	[4,088]	[4,480]	[4,871]	[4,673]
1,500g +/−3g	611	4,364	−3,428	7,792
	(2,326)	(3,060)	(3,510)	(4,651)*
	[3,497]	[4,036]	[4,588]	[5,090]

NOTE: * significant at the 0.10 level; ** significant at the 0.05 level; *** significant at the 0.01 level. In the first row the sample sizes are 20,423 for the pooled sample, 10,199 for the sample of girls, and 10,224 for the sample of boys. In subsequent rows births with the indicated weight are omitted from the sample. The reported statistics are estimates of a dummy variable for birth weight below the VLBW threshold following Equation (4.1). The statistic reported in the fourth row is the estimate of the interaction between sex and VLBW from a pooled regression with a full set of interactions between the control variables and sex. Control variables include fixed effects for year of birth, state, controls for mothers' race, twin and multiple births, C-sections, and preterm births, as well as separate linear trends in birth weight above and below the threshold. Robust standard errors in parentheses. Standard errors clustered at the gram level in square brackets.
SOURCE: Author's calculations from HCUP data.

part the restricted sample of states. For hospital costs (Table 4.4) there is discrete increase in costs for both girls and boys at the VLBW threshold, congruent with the evidence in Figure 4.6. Only the estimate for girls is statistically significant, however, and it is almost 50 percent larger than the estimate for boys.[14] Omitting observations at and around the threshold, the estimate for girls mostly maintains its magnitude, and to a lesser extent its statistical significance, while the estimate for boys attenuates. The corresponding estimates for hospital length of stay are reported in Table 4.5. In the full sample the estimates indicate a discrete

Table 4.5 Changes in Hospital Length of Stay at the Very Low Birth Weight Threshold, by Sex, 1995–2005, United States

Sample omission	Pooled	Girls	Boys	Difference
None	1.083	0.772	1.345	−0.572
	(0.506)**	(0.688)	(0.744)*	(1.012)
	[0.747]	[0.788]	[1.047]	[1.119]
1,500g	0.979	1.098	0.827	0.271
	(0.524)*	(0.696)	(0.787)	(1.049)
	[0.840]	[0.825]	[1.078]	[0.951]
1,500g +/−1g	0.703	0.829	0.536	0.293
	(0.553)	(0.709)	(0.798)	(1.066)
	[0.811]	[0.771]	[1.074]	[0.956]
1,500g +/−2g	0.434	0.804	0.003	0.801
	(0.533)	(0.722)	(0.785)	(1.066)
	[0.825]	[0.795]	[1.048]	[0.904]
1,500g +/−3g	−0.085	0.397	−0.601	0.997
	(0.556)	(0.753)	(0.818)	(1.110)
	[0.723]	[0.755]	[0.943]	[0.929]

NOTE: * significant at the 0.10 level; ** significant at the 0.05 level; *** significant at the 0.01 level. In the first row the sample sizes are 20,502 for the pooled sample, 10,234 for the sample of girls, and 10,268 for the sample of boys. In subsequent rows births with the indicated weight are omitted from the sample. The reported statistics are estimates of a dummy variable for birth weight below the VLBW threshold following Equation (4.1). The statistic reported in the fourth row is the estimate of the interaction between sex and VLBW from a pooled regression with a full set of interactions between the control variables and sex. Control variables include fixed effects for year of birth, state, controls for mothers' race, twin and multiple births, C-sections, and preterm births, as well as separate linear trends in birth weight above and below the threshold. Robust standard errors in parentheses. Standard errors clustered at the gram level in square brackets.
SOURCE: Author's calculations from HCUP data.

increase in stay for both sexes at the threshold, but here it is the estimate for boys that is larger and statistically significant. Again, in the donut estimators the estimates for girls mostly maintain their magnitude while the estimates for boys attenuate. The estimates for these measures of care appear more sensitive to the sample omissions of the donut estimators than the estimates for mortality.

The preceding evidence supports the intuitive hypothesis that the impact of variation in critical care around the VLBW threshold differs by sex. Boys exhibit higher mortality rates than girls in the first percentiles of birth weight and are more affected by this variation in care than girls. However, the VLBW threshold makes no accommodation by sex, and the HCUP data suggest that critical care varies around the threshold for both girls and boys. While lower birth weight boys receive more care conditional on birth weight than girls, the efficacy of the care provided to girls is challenged, at least by the measures of first-year mortality. If hospital care is a scarce resource, these results suggest that there may be overall improvement in child survival and health if a lower VLBW threshold for females freed up care for boys marginally above the current unisex threshold. Furthermore, the evidence in Bharawaj, Loken, and Neilson (2013); Chyn, Gold, and Hastings (2021); and Daysal et al. (forthcoming) suggests that a reallocation of this care may have longer-term payoffs for the educational attainment of these children, and positive spillover effects for their siblings and their parents. These findings underline gender differences in the contemporaneous consequences of being born with LBW, which may in turn lead to corresponding differences in the long-run outcomes. As noted above, few studies of the long-run consequences of LBW have made a distinction by sex.

BREASTFEEDING

Breastfeeding newborns is widely encouraged.[15] Some of the best evidence of positive impacts of breastfeeding come from the Promotion of Breastfeeding Intervention Trial (PROBIT) RCT in Belarus, which randomly allocated lactation support across hospitals. This support had a positive impact on breastfeeding incidence and duration and therefore provides a basis to examine the possible impacts of breastfeeding free of confounding factors. The children who were treated by this RCT have been followed over time (Yang et al. 2018) and have revealed that the treatment led to lower rates of gastrointestinal infections and eczema (up to the teenage years) and a modest positive impact on IQ at age six, which appears to have diminished by the teenage years. Many of the other claimed positive impacts of breastfeeding have been harder to substantiate outside correlational analysis (Baker and Milligan 2008).

To investigate any differences in breastfeeding practices by child gender, I select cases in the NIS-Child in which the mother is the respondent and the child is the first born. Table 4.6 reports summary statistics for this sample, as well as the statistics for the larger sample of all children and the marginally smaller sample, which has nonmissing values for the regression analysis, to make clear any impact of sample restrictions. The incidence of breastfeeding is very similar for girls and boys in each sample, at 81 percent. There are sex differences in the unconditional duration of breastfeeding in the first year favoring girls of one to two days across samples, smallest in the sample for the regression analysis. While girls are more likely to reach each breastfeeding milestone in each sample, it is the difference in the proportions reaching at least 12 months that is largest in both absolute and relative value. It is roughly 1.3 percentage points and statistically significant at the 0.01 level in each sample.

To refine this inference, Table 4.7 presents estimates for a dummy variable for boys from a linear regression of the various measures of breastfeeding indicated in the top row of the table, and additional controls for household income below the poverty line, whether the mother is married, whether the household has ever received WIC benefits, and fixed effects for the child's and mother's ages, the mother's education, the child's race, and the number of children in the household. The con-

Table 4.6 Sample Characteristics of the NIS-Child Breastfeeding Survey, 2010–2018, United States

	Mother respondent		Mother respondent-first born		Mother respondent-first born-regression sample	
	Girls	Boys	Girls	Boys	Girls	Boys
Ever breastfed	0.811	0.814	0.818	0.817	0.818	0.819
Duration in first year (days)	180.13	178.11	172.70	170.55	172.05	170.83
Breastfed >3 months	0.656	0.652	0.636	0.632	0.636	0.632
Breastfed >6 months	0.430	0.423	0.402	0.401	0.403	0.402
Breastfed >12 months	0.292	0.279	0.267	0.254	0.267	0.254
N	159,169		60,308		56,574	

SOURCE: Author's calculations from NIS-Child. All statistics calculated using sample weights.

Table 4.7 Sex Differences in Breastfeeding Milestones, First-Born Children, 2010–2018, United States

	Ever breastfed	Duration first year	Breastfed >3 months	Breastfed >6 months	Breastfed >12 months
Boy	−0.003	−2.908	−0.009	−0.006	−0.017**
	(0.006)	(2.104)	(0.007)	(0.007)	(0.007)
Poverty cutoff	−0.036***	−2.067	−0.017	−0.004	−0.016*
	(0.009)	(3.190)	(0.011)	(0.011)	(0.010)
Married	0.070***	35.580***	0.106***	0.102***	0.084***
	(0.008)	(3.886)	(0.010)	(0.010)	(0.009)
WIC benefits	−0.056***	−39.440***	−0.101***	−0.129***	−0.087***
	(0.008)	(3.088)	(0.010)	(0.011)	(0.010)

NOTE: * significant at the 0.10 level; ** significant at the 0.05 level; *** significant at the 0.01 level. N = 56,574. Each column is from a separate linear regression of the indicated dependent variable, on the reported independent variables plus controls for mother's and child's age, mother's education, child's race, and number of children in the household. Robust standard errors in parentheses.
SOURCE: Author's calculation from NIS-Child using sample weights.

trol factors could vary systematically between boys and girls if, for example, the sex of the first born has an impact on family structure.

The estimates are slightly greater than the differences in the table of means but largely confirm the inference. The difference in incidence between the sexes is very small. Over the first year boys are breastfed less than girls, the difference here approaching three days, although not statistically significant at conventional levels. Again, the most substantial gender difference in milestones is at 12 months. It should be noted that the estimates from the larger sample of all children (not reported) are very similar to the ones reported in Table 4.7, except all gender differences in duration are statistically significant at the 5 percent level. For example, the difference in breastfeeding duration in the first year favors girls by 3.34 days (standard error 1.318).

The message of this analysis is that while there are differences in breastfeeding duration among girls and boys in the United States favoring girls, they are quite small. As a point of reference, in the PROBIT study the differences in breastfeeding between the treatment and control groups, which underly the reported positive impacts of this practice, are of an order of magnitude greater than the gender differences reported here. For example, the treatment/control difference in reporting six or more months of breastfeeding is 11.2 percentage points, or 31 percent of the control group mean (Yang et al. 2018).

PARENTING AND PARENTAL TIME INPUTS

The quality and type of parental/child interactions are thought to be key inputs to child development (Heckman and Mosso 2014). More authoritative (versus authoritarian), sensitive, and interactive parenting practices promote development and vary across families stratified by socioeconomic status. This latter point may account for the evidence that the benefits of early childhood education appear to accumulate to disadvantaged children, and the universal early childhood education is sometimes found to have negative impacts on children from more affluent families (Baker, Gruber, and Milligan 2008, 2019; Fort, Ichino, and Zanella 2020).

Any sex differences in parenting might result from factors on either the child or parent side. For example, boys might be more difficult to parent, leading to different discipline and control strategies. However, it is also possible that the birth of a boy or girl differently affects the mental state of a parent, perhaps due to preferences for a child of a particular sex, which in turn affects parent/child interactions.

The analysis begins with an examination of mothers' mental state after the birth of a child. Two studies of small samples of mothers in France and the UK find associations between postpartum depression and the birth of a male child (de Tychey et al. 2007; Myers and Johns 2019). The suspected mechanisms in these studies are cultural preferences for babies of a specific gender and mothers' greater inflammatory response to the male fetus. Perhaps supportive of the former hypothesis are studies reporting that postpartum depression is related to the birth of a female child in India, Nigeria, Turkey, and China, countries where son preference arguably is more common.[16]

Regarding sex preference in North America, it is generally maintained that couples prefer a child of each gender (Angrist and Evans 1998 for the United States and McDougall, DeWit, and Ebanks 1999 for Canada), although there is some evidence for son preference in certain immigrant communities.[17] Sex preference in this research is typically investigated by relating fertility decisions to the sex composition of previously born children (e.g., a second child is more likely if the first born is male versus female). Baker and Milligan (2016) take a different approach. They examine data in which, after their child is born, mothers are asked to think back to the time of conception and report whether they, or the father, at that time viewed the pregnancy as wanted or at the right time.[18] Analyzing the responses, they report that in the United States mothers are more likely to report the pregnancy as unwanted when their child is a male.[19]

Maternal depression is potentially important for the quality of child/parent interactions. Depressed mothers can be either more withdrawn or more hostile and intrusive, either of which can undermine the preferred "serve and return" interaction thought important to brain development. Exposure to depressed caregivers has been associated with higher levels of stress and lower cognition in children (Liu et al. 2017; Madigan et al. 2018). Finally, there is evidence that postbirth maternal stress transmitted to the child through breast milk can negatively impact behavior (Glynn et al. 2007).

I begin by examining the relationship between the incidence of postpartum depression and postpartum problems and the sex of the first born in nationally representative samples of U.S. (the ECLS-B) and Canadian (the NLSCY) children. I estimate linear regressions of indicators of maternal depression on a dummy variable for males and controls for geography, child's age, mother's age, education, and foreign birth and ethnicity, which differ marginally by sample.[20] The estimates of the dummy variable for boys are presented in Table 4.8.[21]

The results from the ECLS-B are in the first panel and are from the wave when the child is nine months old. The first three rows show the estimates for 0/1 indicators of whether the mothers reported being depressed, sad, or blue either moderately or most of the time over the past week.[22] The fourth row shows the result for a 0/1 indicator that the mother had consulted with a health care professional about her emotional or psychological state. For each outcome the mean is higher if the first-born child is male. For depression, the difference at 2.5 percentage points is statistically significant and just over 40 percent of the mean for a female child. The last column shows the estimate conditional on the controls, which make little difference to the estimated gender differences or their statistical significance.

Table 4.8 Child Mother's Health Postbirth by the Sex of Their First Born Child, United States and Canada

	N	Males	Females	Difference	Conditional difference
ECLS-B: 9 months					
Depressed	3,450	0.087	0.062	0.025***	0.024**
				(0.009)	(0.011)
Sad	3,450	0.083	0.072	0.011	0.008
				(0.009)	(0.012)
Blue	3,450	0.069	0.063	0.007	0.007
				(0.008)	(0.011)
Talked to doctor about emotional/psycho-logical state	3,500	0.115	0.107	0.008	0.007
				(0.011)	(0.014)
NLSCY Ages 0 and 1					
Postpartum depression	4,754	0.139	0.115	0.024*	0.028**
				(0.013)	(0.013)
Postpartum problems	4,723	0.280	0.216	0.064***	0.067***
				(0.022)	(0.021)
Mother's self-reported depression	7,016	0.180	0.165	0.015	0.016
				(0.012)	(0.012)

NOTE: * significant at the 0.10 level; ** significant at the 0.05 level; *** significant at the 0.01 level. Sample sizes from the ECLS-B are rounded to the nearest 50 observations. The reported regression estimates are the estimated parameter on a 0/1 indicator that the child is male. Control variables for the ECLS-B regressions are age (single month), birth state, mother's age (single year), education, foreign birth and indicators for whether the mother is Black or Hispanic. Control variables for the NLSCY regressions are child's age effects (single month), mother's age effects (single year), mother's education (4 categories), mother's foreign birth, dummy variables for province, urban size (5 categories), and year of birth. Robust standard errors in parentheses.
SOURCE: Author's calculations from ECLS-B and NLSCY.

The second panel of Table 4.8 presents results for mothers in Canada. This switch in country helps calibrate some subsequent analysis of gender differences in parenting, which is possible with the NLSCY. While clearly cross-country institutional and cultural differences can confound the U.S./Canada comparisons, Canada and the United States are generally considered reasonably similar for these purposes compared to other possible comparisons.

There is clear evidence that mothers of first-born boys in Canada are also more likely to experience postpartum depression and postpartum problems.[23] The differences are quite substantial—2.5 percentage points for postpartum depression and over 6 percentage points for postpartum problems. Again, the inference from conditional differences is very similar to that from unconditional differences.

The results in Table 4.8 support the previous research, based on more select samples, that mothers face a heightened risk of postbirth depression when their child is a boy. Below I examine how childhood parenting practices vary by gender. While I cannot causally connect any differences in parenting to the preceding results on depression, previous research suggests that maternal depression can spill over into parent/child interactions.

The NLSCY provides parenting scales based on the responses of the person most knowledgeable about the child (in the vast majority of cases the child's mother) to a series of questions about how they relate with their child. The scales attempt to capture positivity, hostility, consistency, and adversity in the parent/child relationship. In each case a higher score means more of the indicated parenting dimension. Each scale is built up from the responses to a series of questions tailored to the age of the child.[24] I also examine the responses to a question of whether the respondent considers the child "difficult" for his or her age; a higher score indicates more difficult.[25]

The estimates for first-born children aged 0–1 in Table 4.9 indicate that boys receive more hostile parenting, and that boys of this age are also more likely to be viewed as difficult by their parent. At ages 3–5, the largest estimates suggest boys receive more hostile and aversive parenting, although only the estimate for aversive parenting is statistically significant. Overall, the message here is that the interactions between the parent and the first-born boy are more confrontational.

These results suggest that first-born males in Canada spend their first years in a somewhat different parental environment than their female counterparts. The results are consistent with the belief that boys are harder to parent, and so require different parenting strategies. However, the results are also consistent with boys' and girls' posing similar challenges, but some mothers meeting these challenges differently according to the sex of their child due to the association of a male birth with their mental health.

Table 4.9 Parenting/Child Interactions by the Sex of the First-Born Child, Canada

	N	Males	Females	Difference	Conditional difference
Positive: age 0–1	4,900	18.072	18.123	−0.050 (0.090)	−0.056 (0.084)
Hostile: age 0–1	4,904	2.177	2.011	0.166** (0.068)	0.188*** (0.060)
Child is difficult for age: age 0–2	6,024	2.226	2.080	0.146*** (0.049)	0.140*** (0.046)
Positive: age 3–5	6,847	16.425	16.355	0.070 (0.093)	0.062 (0.082)
Hostile: age 3–5	6,692	8.706	8.500	0.206 (0.141)	0.217 (0.135)
Consistent: age 3–5	6,565	15.502	15.397	0.105 (0.122)	0.080 (0.113)
Averse: age 3–5	6,812	4.062	3.912	0.150* (0.083)	0.162** (0.080)

NOTE: * significant at the 0.10 level; ** significant at the 0.05 level; *** significant at the 0.01 level. In the regression results the reported statistics are the estimated parameter on a 0/1 indicator that the child is male. Control variables for the conditional difference are child's age effects (single month), mother's age effects (single year), mother's education (4 categories), mother's foreign birth, dummy variables for province, urban size (5 categories), and year of birth. Robust standard errors in parentheses.
SOURCE: Author's calculations from NLSCY data.

CONCLUSION

Childhood environmental influences are viewed as an important, but not the sole, determinant of adult social and economic outcomes. Much of the previous research on childhood environment in developed countries has looked for differences in childhood environments by socioeconomic indicators. This is an important distinction in the data, as any intergenerational persistence in childhood environments can feed directly into corresponding persistence in adult outcomes and thereby undermine social mobility and opportunity.

Relatively understudied in this research is another dimension of inequality—gender. While gender differences in socioeconomic outcomes are persistent over time, much of the research on its causes focuses on adulthood factors such as discrimination, family/work balance, and employment decisions. However, there is intuition for gender differences in childhood environment to matter to adult outcomes, given that research has documented that corresponding differences in environment by family income or parents' educations have such effects.

Previous research has shown that there are gender differences in the amount of time children spend with their parents. For example, Baker and Milligan (2016) show that parents spend more time teaching activities with their first-born daughters than their first-born sons, starting at very young ages, in Canada, the United Kingdom, and the United States. In the chapter I extend this evidence to environmental factors, including medical care after birth, breastfeeding, mothers' mental health, and parenting practices.

Lower birth weight boys in the United States receive more care immediately after birth than their female counterparts, as measured by hospital costs and hospital length of stay. This likely reflects the higher risk of mortality these boys face relative to girls. However, variation in this care around the VLBW threshold reveals that while it has a consequential impact on the one-year and 28-day mortality of boys, it has a much smaller to no effect on the mortality of girls. This suggests a possible misallocation of resources. Sex-specific thresholds for VLBW might result in greater aggregate return to critical care for these children. These findings also suggest that the consequences of LBW for longer-term outcomes may differ by sex, a topic that has received little attention in the literature.

Breastfeeding is widely encouraged for children as a source of nutrition in the first year of life. I find that sex differences in this nutritional input in the United States favor girls. However, the differences are small, and, based on the guidance of previous research on the benefits of breastfeeding, unlikely to have a substantive impact on longer-run gender differences in outcomes.

I also examine measures of the interactions between parents and their young children in Canada. Measures of parenting practice reveal that, on average, first-born boys experience more confrontational, hostile, and aversive parenting than first-born girls. Perhaps connected is that mothers in the United States and Canada are more likely to report postpartum depression after the (first) birth of a boy. This latter result, from nationally representative data, supports previous findings from small selected samples.

The results in this chapter paint a picture of male disadvantage in these selected outcomes. They are consistent with a social extension of the "fragile male" hypothesis (Kraemer 2000), which is more typically posed as a conjecture about males' relative genetic fragility.

This analysis covers a small selection of the wide array of environmental factors that previous research indicates are important to adult outcomes. Clearly, taking a gender lens to the study of these inputs is needed to understand if sex differences in childhood environmental inputs are potentially important. However, equally essential is applying this same lens to the causal study of the relationship between these inputs and adult socioeconomic status.

Notes

I thank Boriana Miloucheva for outstanding research assistance, and Doug Almond and Janet Currie for useful suggestions. The analysis of mother's health and parenting postbirth reported in the paper is a by-product of previous research collaborations with Kevin Milligan. I thank him for his permission to present these results here. I gratefully acknowledge the research support of a Canada Research Chair at the University of Toronto. Some of the analysis for this paper was conducted at the Toronto Region Statistics Canada Research Data Centre, which is part of the Canadian Research Data Centre Network (CRDCN). The services and activities provided by the CRDCN are made possible by the financial or in-kind support of the SSHRC, the CIHR, the CFI, Statistics Canada, and participating universities, whose support is gratefully acknowledged. The views expressed in this chapter do not necessarily represent the CRDCN's or its partners.

1. See Almond, Currie, and Duque (2018) for a recent review of the economic literature.
2. Much of this research investigates these differences within populations in which there is preference for male offspring. See, for example, Barcellos, Carvalho, and Lleras-Muney (2014); Das Gupta (1987); and Pande (2003) on nutrition; and Borooah (2004) and Ganatra and Hirve (1994) on health care and vaccination rates.
3. There is a distinction here between gender differences in the provision of an input and gender differences in the effect of a given input. A developing literature investigates this latter issue (e.g., Bertrand and Pan 2013).
4. These files are not available for the years 1992–1994.
5. The data from 1997 for Arizona is omitted from the analysis. Average birth weight calculated from these data for this state displays a sharp downward spike of over

400 grams in this year. This is because of a spike in the proportion of births with recorded birth weight of zero and roughly 200 grams.

6. An "original" cohort of children surveyed in the first wave and followed throughout the waves.

7. Both Lundberg and Rose (2002) and Dahl and Moretti (2008) present evidence that a first-born female raises the probability of an absent father. Baker and Milligan (2016) find no evidence of this effect in some of the data sets examined here.

8. The corresponding graphs for 28-day mortality (not shown) exhibit very similar patterns.

9. See also Ernst et al. (2020).

10. See also Almond et al. (2011); Barreca et al. (2011); Bharawaj, Loken, and Neilson (2013); and Daysal et al. (forthcoming).

11. Here I use births of all pluralities to maximize sample size. Also, I am not aware of evidence that hospital personnel administer care differently according to the plurality of the birth.

12. The corresponding estimate in Almond et al. (2010) is −0.0072 (0.0022).

13. The estimate of the difference is from the pooled regression with a full set of interactions between a dummy variable for sex and all other control variables. The reported statistic is for the estimate of the interaction with the VLBW dummy variable.

14. The pooled estimate of 5,353 (2,114) is smaller than the comparable estimate in Almond et al. (2010), which is 9,065 (2,297). Different here is the inclusion for all years between 1995 and 2005 for the four states (except 1997 for AZ), the omission of 2006, and the omission of the 1991–2002 data for California. One consequence of these differences is that the pooled sample used here is roughly one-third smaller than the sample in Almond et al. (2010).

15. See, for example, https://www.who.int/health-topics/breastfeeding#tab=tab_1 (accessed March 2, 2020).

16. See Adewuya et al. (2005); Ekuklu et al. (2004); Patel, Rodrigues, and DeSouza (2014); and Xie et al. (2007).

17. See, for example, Abrevaya (2009) and Almond, Edlund, and Milligan (2013).

18. The respondent is asked to think back to the time just before the pregnancy in answering, but the question is asked after the child has been born.

19. This result is obtained when the question is asked when the child is aged two or younger. If the question is asked when the child is aged three to five, the overall incidence of unwanted pregnancy is considerably lower, and if anything, the pregnancy is more likely viewed as unwanted if the child is female.

20. Control variables for the ECLS-B regressions are age (single month), birth state, mother's age (single year), education, foreign birth and indicators for whether the mother is Black or Hispanic. Control variables for the NLSCY regressions are child's age effects (single month), mother's age effects (single year), mother's education (four categories), mother's foreign birth, dummy variables for province, urban size (five categories), and year of birth.

21. The estimates of these postpartum outcomes and the following estimates for parenting practices first appeared in Baker and Milligan (2011).
22. The variables are formed from the survey variables that record responses on a four-point scale ranging from rarely or never (<1 day per week) to most or all of the time (5–7 days per week).
23. Postpartum problems include hemorrhage, infection, depression for more than 14 days, and hypertension.
24. These scales have been used previously in studies of child development (e.g., Baker, Gruber, and Milligan 2008).
25. The parents are asked to rate the "difficulty" of child on a scale from very easy to highly difficult to deal with.

References

Abrevaya, Jason. 2009. "Are There Missing Girls in the United States? Evidence from Birth Data." *American Economic Journal: Applied Economics* 1(2): 1–34.

Adewuya, Abiodun O., Femi O. Fatoye, Bola A. Ola, Omowumi R. Ijaodola, and Stella-Maris O. Ibigbami. 2005. "Sociodemographic and Obstetric Risk Factors for Postpartum Depressive Symptoms in Nigerian Women." *Journal of Psychiatric Practice* 11(5): 353–358.

Almond, Douglas, Janet Currie, and Valentina Duque. 2018. "Childhood Circumstances and Adult Outcomes: Act II." *Journal of Economic Literature* 56(4): 1360–1446.

Almond, Douglas, Joseph J. Doyle Jr., Amanda E. Kowalski, and Heidi Williams. 2010. "Estimating Marginal Returns to Medical Care: Evidence from At-Risk Newborns." *Quarterly Journal of Economics* 125(2): 591–634.

———. 2011. "The Role of Hospital Heterogeneity in Measuring Marginal Returns to Medical Care: A Reply to Barreca, Guidi, Lindo, and Waddell." *Quarterly Journal of Economics* 126(4): 2125–2131.

Almond, Douglas, Lena Edlund, and Kevin Milligan. 2013. "Son Preference and the Persistence of Culture: Evidence from South and East Asian Immigrants to Canada." *Population and Development Review* 39(1): 75–95.

Angelov, Nilolay, Per Johansson, and Erica Lindahl. 2016. "Parenthood and the Gender Gap in Pay." *Journal of Labor Economics* 34(3): 545–579.

Angrist, Joshua D., and William N. Evans. 1998. "Children and Their Parents' Labor Supply: Evidence from Exogenous Variation in Family Size." *American Economic Review* 88(3): 450–77.

Baker, Michael, and Kirsten Cornelson. 2018. "Gender-Based Occupational Segregation and Sex Differences in Sensory, Motor and Spatial Aptitudes." *Demography* 55(5): 1749–1775.

———. 2019. "The Tall and the Short of the Returns to Height." NBER Working Paper No. 26325. Cambridge, MA: National Bureau of Economic Research.

Baker, Michael, Jonathan Gruber, and Kevin Milligan. 2008. "Universal Child Care, Maternal Labor Supply, and Family Well-Being." *Journal of Political Economy* 116(4): 709–745.

Baker, Michael, and Kevin Milligan. 2008. "Maternal Employment, Breast-feeding and Health: Evidence from Maternity Leave Mandates." *Journal of Health Economics* 27(4): 871–887.

———. 2011. "Sex Differences in the Care of Young Children in Canada and the U.S." Working paper. Vancouver and Toronto: University of British Columbia and University of Toronto.

———. 2016. "Boy-Girl Differences in Parental Time Investments: Evidence from Three Countries." *Journal of Human Capital* 10(4): 399–441.

———. 2019. "The Long-Run Impacts of a Universal Child Care Program." *American Economic Journal: Economic Policy* 11(3): 1–26.

Barcellos, Silvia Helena, Leandro S. Carvalho, and Adriana Lleras-Muney. 2014. "Child Gender and Parental Investments in India: Are Boys and Girls Treated Differently?" *American Economic Journal: Applied Economics* 6(1): 157–189.

Barreca, Alan, Melanie Guidi, Jason Lindo, and Glen Waddell. 2011. "Saving Babies? Revisiting the Effect of the Very Low Birth Weight Classification." *Quarterly Journal of Economics* 126(4): 2117–2123.

Barker, David J. 1990. "The Fetal and Infant Origins of Adult Disease." *British Medical Journal* 301(6761): 1111.

Bertrand, Marianne, and Jessica Pan. 2013. "The Trouble with Boys: Social Influences and the Gender Gap in Disruptive Behavior." *American Economic Journal: Applied Economics* 5(1): 32–64.

Bharawaj, Prashant, Katrine V. Loken, and Christopher Neilson. 2013. "Early Life Health Interventions and Academic Achievement." *American Economic Review* 103(5): 1862–1891.

Blau, Francine D., Peter Brummund, and Albert Yung-Hsu Liu. 2013. "Trends in Occupational Segregation by Gender 1970–2009: Adjusting for the Impact of Changes in the Occupational Coding System." *Demography* 50(2): 471–492.

Borghans, Lex, Bart H. Golsteyn, James J. Heckman, and Huub Meijers. 2009. "Gender Differences in Risk Aversion and Ambiguity Aversion." *Journal of the European Economic Association* 7(2–3): 649–658.

Borooah, Vani K. 2004. "Gender Bias among Children in India in Their Diet and Immunization against Disease." *Social Science and Medicine* 58(9): 1719–1731.

Chyn, Eric, Samantha Gold, and Justine Hastings. 2021. "The Returns to Early-Life Interventions for Very Low Birth Weight Children." *Journal of Health Economics* 75.

Cortes, Guido Matias, Nir Jaimovich, and Henry Siu. 2018. "The End of Men and the Rise of Women in the High-Skilled Labor Market." NBER Working Paper No. 24274. Cambridge, MA: National Bureau of Economic Research.

Dahl, Gordon B., and Enrico Moretti. 2008. "The Demand for Sons." *Review of Economic Studies* 75(4): 1085–1120.

Das Gupta, Monica. 1987. "Selective Discrimination against Female Children in Rural Punjab, India." *Population and Development Review* 13(1): 77–100.

Daysal, N. Meltem, Marianne Simonsen, Mircea Trandafir, and Sanni Breining. Forthcoming. "Spillover Effects of Early-Life Medical Intervention." *Review of Economics and Statistics.*

De Tychey, Claude, Serge Briançon, Joëlle Lighezzolo, Elisabeth Spitz, Bernard Kabuth, Vallerie De Luigi, Catherine Messembourg, Françoise Girvan, Aurore Rosati, Audrey Thockler, and Stephanie Vincent. 2007. "Quality of Life, Postnatal Depression and Baby Gender." *Journal of Clinical Nursing* 17(3): 312–332.

Ekuklu, Galip, Burcu Tokuc, Muzaffer Eskiocak, Ufuk Berberoglu, and Ahmet Saltik. 2004. "Prevalence of Postpartum Depression in Edirne, Turkey, and Related Factors." *Journal of Reproductive Medicine* 49(11): 908–914.

Ernst, Mareike, Iris Reiner, Achim Fieß, Ana N.Tibubos, Andreas Schulz, Juliane Burghardt, Eva M. Klein, Elmar Brähler, Philipp S. Wild, Thomas Münzel, Jochem König, Karl J. Lackner, Norbert Pfeiffer, Matthias Michal, Jörg Wiltink, and Manfred E. Beutel. 2020. "Sex-Dependent Associations of Low Birth Weight and Suicidal Ideation in Adulthood: A Community-Based Cohort Study." *Scientific Reports* 10: 12969. https://doi.org/10.1038/s41598-020-69961-5 (accessed March 4, 2021).

Fine, Cordelia. 2010. *Delusions of Gender: How Our Minds, Society, and Neurosexism Create Difference.* New York: W.W. Norton & Company.

Fort, Margherita, Andrea Ichino, and Giulio Zanella. 2020. "Cognitive and Noncognitive Costs of Day Care at Age 0–2 for Children in Advantaged Families." *Journal of Political Economy* 128(1): 158–205.

Ganatra, Bela, and Siddhivinayak Hirve. 1994. "Male Bias in Health Care Utilization for Under-Fives in a Rural Community in Western India." *Bulletin of the World Health Organization* 72(1): 101–104.

Glynn, Laura M., Elysia P. Davis, Christine D. Schetter, Aleksandra Chicz-Demet, Calvin J. Hobel, and Curt A. Sandman. 2007. "Postnatal Maternal Cortisol Levels Predict Temperament in Healthy Breastfed Infants." *Early Human Development* 83(10): 675–681.

Goldin, Claudia. 2014. "A Grand Gender Convergence: Its Last Chapter." *American Economic Review* 104(4): 1091–1119.

Gray, John. 1992. *Men Are from Mars, Women Are from Venus.* New York: Harper Collins.

Heckman, James J., and Ganesh Karapakula. 2019. "The Perry Preschoolers at Late Midlife: A Study in Design-Specific Inference." NBER Working Paper No. 25888. Cambridge, MA: National Bureau of Economic Research.

Heckman, James J., and Stefano Mosso. 2014. "The Economics of Human Development and Social Mobility." *Annual Review of Economics, Annual Reviews* 6(1): 689–733.

Hyde, Janet. S. 2014. "Gender Similarities and Differences." *Annual Review of Psychology* 65: 373–398.

Kleven, Henrik Jacobsen, Camille Landais, and Egholt Søgaard Jakob. 2018. "Children and Gender Inequality: Evidence from Denmark." *American Economic Journal: Applied Economics* 11(4): 181–209.

Kraemer, Sebastian. 2000. "The Fragile Male." *British Medical Journal* 321: 1609–1612.

Liu, Y., S. Kaaya, J. Chai, D. C. McCoy, P. Surkan, M.M. Black, A.L. Sutter-Dallay, H. Verdoux, and M.C. Smith-Fawzi. 2017. "Maternal Depressive Symptoms and Early Childhood Cognitive Development: A Meta-Analysis." *Psychological Medicine* 47(4): 680–689.

Lordan, Grace, and Jörn-Steffen Pischke. 2018. "Does Rosie Like Riveting? Male and Female Occupational Choices." IZA Discussion Paper No. 10129. Bonn: IZA.

Lundberg, Shelly. 2005. "Sons, Daughters and Parental Behavior." *Oxford Economic Papers* 21(3): 340–356.

Lundberg, Shelly, Sabrina W. Pabilonia, and Jennifer Ward-Batts. 2007. "Time Allocation of Parents and Investments in Sons and Daughters." Working paper. Seattle: University of Washington.

Lundberg, Shelly, and Elaina Rose. 2002. "The Effects of Sons and Daughters on Men's Labor Supply and Wages." *Review of Economics and Statistics* 84(2): 251–268.

———. 2003. "Child Gender and the Transition to Marriage." *Demography* 40(2): 333–349.

Madigan, Sheri, Hannah Oatley, Nicole Racine, R.M. Pasco Fearon, Lea Schumacher, Emis Akbari, Jessica E. Cooke, and George M. Tarabulsy. 2018. "A Meta-Analysis of Maternal Prenatal Depression and Anxiety on Child Socioemotional Development." *Journal of the American Academy of Child & Adolescent Psychiatry* 57(9): 645–657.

McDougall, Janette, David J. DeWit, and G. Edward Ebanks. 1999. "Parental Preferences for Sex of Children in Canada." *Sex Roles* 41(7–8): 615–626.

Myers, Sarah, and Sarah E. Johns. 2019. "Male Infants and Birth Complications Are Associated with Increased Incidence of Postnatal Depression." *Social Science & Medicine* 220: 56–64.

Niederle, Muriel, and Lise Vesterlund. 2007. "Do Women Shy Away from Competition? Do Men Compete Too Much?" *Quarterly Journal of Economics* 122(3): 1067–1101.

Pande, Rohini P. 2003. "Selective Gender Differences in Childhood Nutrition and Immunization in Rural India: The Role of Siblings." *Demography* 40(3): 395–418.

Patel, Vikram, Merlyn Rodrigues, and Nandita DeSouza. 2014. "Gender, Poverty, and Postnatal Depression: A Study of Mothers in Goa, India." *American Journal of Psychiatry* 159(1): 43–47.

Price, Joseph. 2008. "Parent-Child Quality Time: Does Birth Order Matter?" *Journal of Human Resources* 43(1): 240–265.

Raley, Sara, and Suzanne Bianchi. 2006. "Sons, Daughters, and Family Processes: Does Gender of Children Matter?" *Annual Review of Sociology* 32(1): 401–421.

Salk, Rachel A., and Janet S. Hyde. 2012. "Contemporary Genetics for Gender Researchers: Not Your Grandma's Genetics Anymore." *Psychology of Women Quarterly* 36(4): 395–410.

Stevenson, D. K., J. E. Tyson, S.B. Korones, C.R. Bauer, B.J. Stoll, L.A. Papile, J. Verter, A.A. Fanaroff, W. Oh, R.A. Ehrenkranz, S. Shankaran, E.F. Donovan, L.L. Wright, and J.A. Lemons. 2000. "Sex Differences in Outcomes of Very Low Birthweight Infants: The Newborn Male Disadvantage." *Archives of Disease in Childhood-Fetal and Neonatal Edition* 83(3): F182–F185.

Xie, Ri-hua, Guoping He, Aizhong Liu, Jacques Bradwejn, Mark Walker, and Shi Wu Wen. 2007. "Fetal Gender and Postpartum Depression in a Cohort of Chinese Women." *Social Science & Medicine* 65(4): 680–684.

Yang, Suengmi, Richard M. Martin, Emily Oken, Mikhail Hameza, Glen Doniger, Shimon Amit, Rita Patel, Jennifer Thompson, Sheryl L. Rifas-Shiman, Konstantin Vilchuck, Natalia Bogdanovish, and Michael S. Kramer. 2018. "Breastfeeding during Infancy and Neurocognitive Function in Adolescence: 16-Year Follow-up of the PROBIT Cluster-Randomized Trial." *PLOS Medicine* 15(4): e1002554. https://doi.org/10.1371/journal.pmed.1002554 (accessed March 5, 2021).

Yeung, Wei-Jun. J., John F. Sandberg, Pamela Davis-Kean, and Sandra L. Hofferth. 2001. "Children's Time with Fathers in Intact Families." *Journal of Marriage and Family* 63(1): 136–154.

5

Household Structure and Socioeconomic Mobility

The Role of Mothers

Sarah Kroeger
University of Notre Dame

RECENT TRENDS IN HOUSEHOLD STRUCTURE

Despite the strong correlation between household structure and economic outcomes, little is known about the interaction between maternal marital status and intergenerational socioeconomic mobility. This is an increasingly important public policy issue, particularly for researchers and practitioners working to reduce poverty. Many scholars have argued that low economic mobility exacerbates societal inequalities over time (Andrews and Leigh 2009; Piketty 2000), and that marriage markets play a central role in this dynamic (Schwartz 2010). As single motherhood continues to become more prevalent for low-income women, an interaction between marital status and economic status on children's outcomes could further widen gaps in income, education, and health outcomes.

The modal household structure in the United States has changed substantially over the past half century. In 1960 nearly three quarters of children grew up with two parents who were both in their first marriage, and only 9 percent of children lived with a single parent. By 2014 those levels had shifted to only 46 percent of children living with two parents in their first marriage, while 7 percent lived with cohabiting parents and 26 percent lived with a single parent (Pew Research Center 2015).[1] Figure 5.1 depicts the changes in marital and extramarital births since 1940, using data from the Centers for Disease Control and Prevention National Center for Health Statistics (NCHS Vital Statistics Reports,

Figure 5.1 Extramarital Births in the United States, 1940–2018

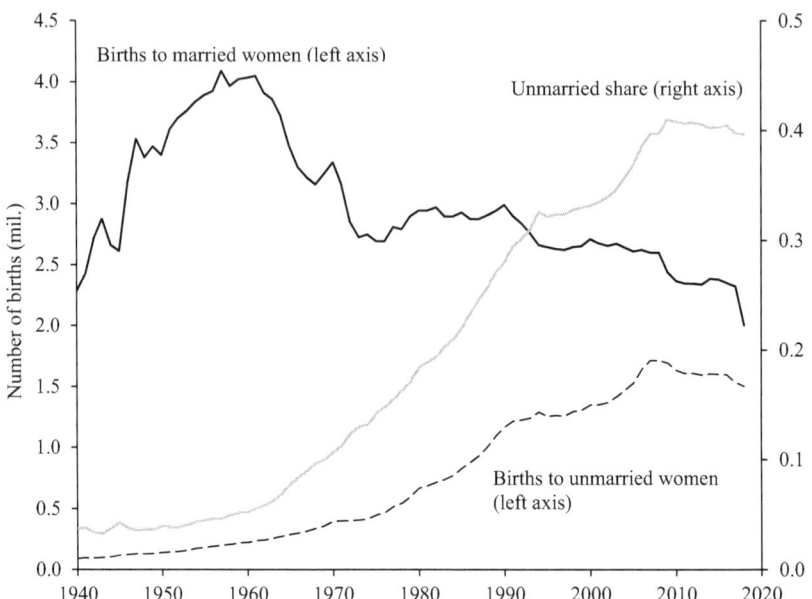

SOURCE: Author's calculations using the Center for Disease Control Vital Statistics, 1940–2018.

1940–2018). Currently, just under 40 percent of births occur outside of marriage, up from only 5.3 percent in 1960. This structural shift is due to the combined effects of increasing divorce rates, declining marriage rates, and a rise in nonmarital childbearing.

The secular trend in extramarital births is noteworthy because of the strong correlation between maternal marital status and the socio-economic outcomes of children. Children of single mothers are more than three times as likely to live in poverty than children of married mothers,[2] and hence also more likely to experience low birth weight and other adverse health outcomes (Aizer 2017), lower income and education levels (Addo, Sassler, and Williams 2016; Amato 2005; Duncan and Brooks-Gunn 1997; Ginther and Pollack 2004; Lopoo and DeLeire 2014; McLanahan and Sandefur 1994); and higher rates of teen pregnancy, delinquency, and out-of-marriage childbearing themselves (Whitbeck, Simons, and Kao 1994).

Single Parenthood and Poverty

There are several plausible explanations for why growing up with a single parent could directly lead to worse outcomes for children: single parents—typically mothers—engage in less time parenting, are younger, and are less likely to have a college degree than their married counterparts (Vernon 2010; Williams et al. 2011). All three of these characteristics are linked to poorer child outcomes, but the mechanism of these pathways may simply be that they each increase the likelihood of poverty. For example, on aggregate, married women tend to show more time spent engaged in direct parenting activities than do single mothers, but Kendig and Bianchi (2008) show that this difference is largely attributable to economic status rather than marital status. Similarly, maternal age at first birth and maternal education are both highly correlated with a mother's poverty status (Kearney and Levine 2015; López Turley 2003). Among children born to the youngest group of mothers, outcomes are particularly unfavorable. After controlling for maternal characteristics and socioeconomic background, Aizer, Devereux, and Salvanes (2018) find that teenage childbearing is associated with adverse long-term outcomes for these mothers' children, including lower earnings in adulthood.[3]

Unsurprisingly, a major component of poverty is a lack of education: among those aged 25–40 in the 2017 American Community Survey, those with an associate degree earned 24 percent more than those with only a high school degree. For the same sample, unemployment rates are 27 percent lower for those with an associate degree compared to those with only a high school diploma. These high returns to college degrees make it very difficult for families to break out of poverty without at least some postsecondary education. This disparity points to a clear path for single-parent households into an intergenerational cycle of poverty. Single parents face specific, nonacademic barriers to completing their college degrees: child care costs; complicated scheduling constraints; and the emotional burden of balancing work, family, and school (Cerven 2013; Cruse et al. 2018). Single parents tend to start college later than students without children (Goldrick-Rab and Sorensen 2010), and age at entrance is negatively correlated with success (Taniguchi and Kaufman 2005). In addition, as of December 2019, eligibility for federal support programs (such as TANF and SNAP) require that single-parent recipients work at least 20 hours per week. College enrollment does not automatically fulfill these work requirements, and in fact usually makes program participation more difficult (Schott and Pavetti 2013).

More fundamentally, single parenthood increases the number of family members supported by a sole adult worker, raising the risk of poverty by construction. As a result, marriage can increase the total household resources available for children, presumably leading to greater investment in their human capital. Single parents are also likely to be significantly time constrained (Son and Bauer 2010). In light of these dynamics, maternal marital status serves as a useful proxy for several forms of disadvantage that predict worse outcomes for children.

If marriage has any causal impact on child poverty or child mobility, we would expect to see a simultaneous movement in these outcomes mirroring the shift in marriage patterns. At the same time, if maternal education or economic security can counteract any potential adverse effect of having children outside of marriage, we should see a difference in the predictive power of maternal status on children's outcomes between married and unmarried mothers. Many scholars, including Zhan and Pandey (2004a,b), Pandey, Zhan, and Kim (2006), and Beeler (2016), have hypothesized that improving maternal education is the most effective and sustainable policy response to raise children out of poverty, and there is some empirical evidence to support the dominant role of maternal education in combating intergenerational poverty (Black, Devereux, and Salvanes 2005; Chevalier et al. 2013). However, more policy-directed research is needed in order to nudge government agencies, lawmakers, and organizations to shape programs with this focus.

In this chapter, I will first summarize the theoretical and empirical relationships between maternal marital status and child outcomes, then establish baseline estimates for mother-child intergenerational mobility, and finally estimate how these mobility coefficients vary by maternal marital status.

CAN MATERNAL MARITAL STATUS CHANGE CHILD OUTCOMES?

The interdependence between marital status and household poverty as well as the highly nonrandom nature of marriage make it difficult to disentangle the causal channels between marital status and adverse outcomes for children. Empirically, being born to married parents is certainly a predictor of higher levels of education and higher lifetime earnings in one's own adulthood. However, parents' marital status appears to improve the child's own outcomes only to a limited extent. Kearney and Levine (2017) show that maternal socioeconomic status is predictive of a stratified "marriage premium" for both children's income and earnings. They present a model showing how marriage for a lower-resourced mother increases the probability that her children will escape poverty or graduate from high school, but has little correlation with more advanced socioeconomic outcomes. In contrast, among children born to mothers with college degrees, maternal marital status is generally not predictive of poverty or high school completion, but is highly correlated with both the child's college graduation rates and a high level of household income for the child at age 25.

The intuition behind the stratified marriage premium comes from assortative matching in the marriage market.[4] Women from lower socioeconomic backgrounds search for a marriage partner among a relatively low-resourced pool of men. If these low-income women remain unmarried, the household resources available to their children are very sparse. However, marrying a partner from this pool of men can increase household resources by only a modest amount. Advanced outcomes such as college graduation and higher levels of income appear to require a minimum level of resources typically seen only when there are two high-status parents present. A college-educated mother, for example, is likely to ensure that her children graduate high school and live above the poverty level whether she marries or not. But if a woman marries a partner from the pool of college-educated men, it increases the chances that her child's later life outcomes are positive, such as achieving advanced degrees and high levels of household income during adulthood.

A growing body of empirical literature points to the long-run growth in nonmarital births as a product of women's preferences in an evolving marriage market. Wilson and Neckerman (1986) and Wilson (1987) were the first prominent studies to highlight declining job opportunities for African American men as the driving force behind the decrease in marriage rates and simultaneous increase in nonmarital births observed post-1960. Other studies (Autor, Dorn, and Hanson 2019; Black, McKinnish, and Sanders 2003; Kearney and Wilson 2018) find further empirical support for this hypothesis by connecting location-specific economic shocks and subsequent changes in nonmarital births. Gray, Stockard, and Stone (2006) use a structural model to demonstrate that the shift in nonmarital births is primarily driven by changes in marriage behavior rather than a change in population fertility. These studies support a rational choice view of nonmarital childbirth and suggest that simply increasing marriage rates would not necessarily decrease child poverty or improve mobility rates for low-income households.

MATERNAL EDUCATION AND NONMARITAL BIRTHS

As a first step in understanding the complex relationship between marriage and child outcomes, it is useful to consider some broad secular trends in nonmarital births and mothers' education levels. The concentration of nonmarital childbearing among lower-educated women has persisted over time in a wide range of surveys. Figure 5.2 shows nonmarital share of births by maternal education, as calculated from the Current Population Survey.[5] These data are sample-based estimates of the population rates and use household responses at a point in time during the child's first year of life. As a result, the year-to-year estimates may differ somewhat from the population aggregates as reported in the Vital Statistics data (used in Figure 5.1), which report information from the time of each birth. However, the trend in the unmarried share of births is consistent with the Vital Statistics rate.

As in Figure 5.1, Figure 5.2 depicts a steady increase in nonmarital births for both college- and high school–educated women from 1970 through the 2010s. This rate is notably higher for women with only a high school degree. Although births by college-educated unmarried women have increased since their extreme rarity in the 1970s, this still remains less than 10 percent of all births in the United States and

Figure 5.2 Nonmarital Share of Births by Maternal Education

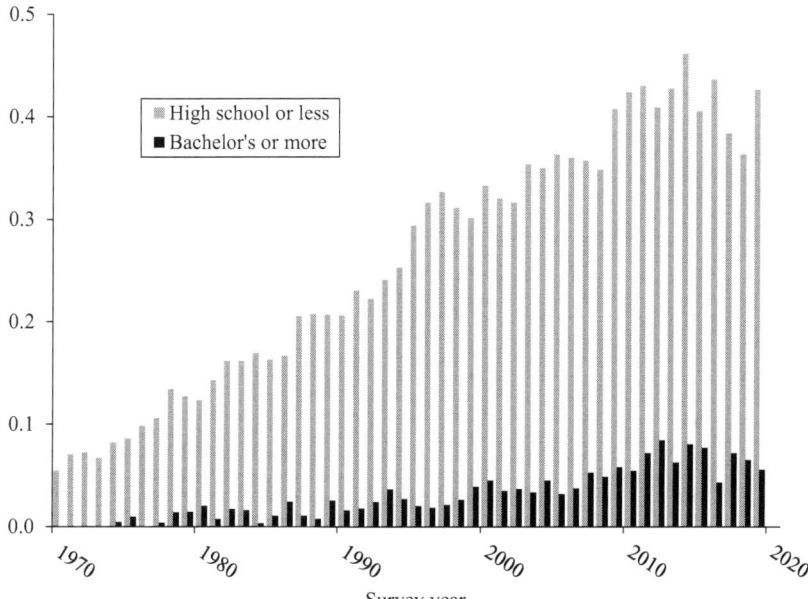

SOURCE: Author's calculations using data from the Current Population Survey, 1970–2019.

has grown more slowly than the category of nonmarital births to less-educated mothers.

Importantly, the average education level of single mothers in the United States has not remained fixed over time. In some ways, single mothers as a demographic group are less disadvantaged today than they were 50 years ago. Over the same time period that nonmarital births were rising, college graduation rates for U.S. women also increased rapidly. Figure 5.3 shows the share of new mothers with a four-year college degree (BA or BS) or higher. In 1970, only 8.5 percent of new mothers held a college degree, while 41 percent of women who gave birth in 2019 held at least a bachelor's degree. Given that a substantial number of nonmarital births each year are to highly educated mothers, a natural question arises as to whether maternal education can compensate for any disadvantages of single motherhood.

Figure 5.3 Share of New Mothers with College Degrees

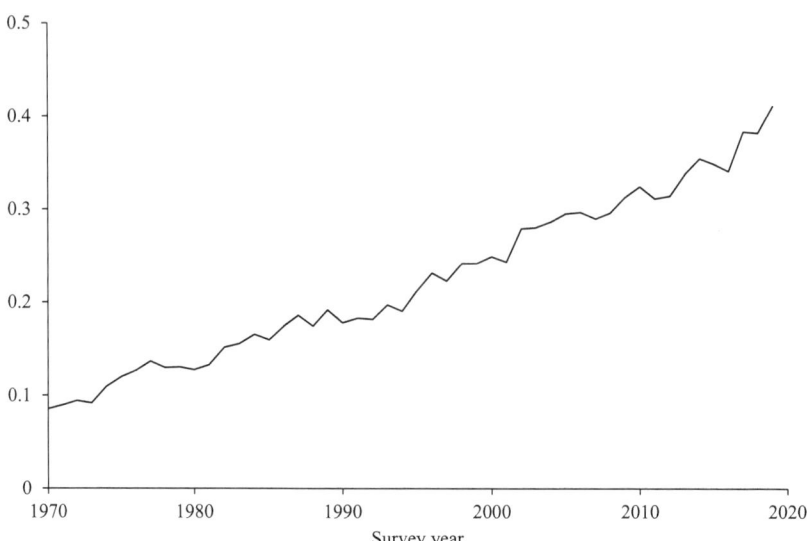

SOURCE: Author's calculations using data from the Current Population Survey, 1970–2019. New mothers are defined as mothers who gave birth in the 12 months prior to the survey and includes mothers who also have older children.

MATERNAL MARITAL STATUS AND INTERGENERATIONAL MOBILITY

How does maternal marital status interact with the intergenerational correlations in household income and education? To investigate this question, I first establish the baseline correlations between parent and child education and income within the Child/Young Adult Survey (CYA) of the National Longitudinal Survey of Youth 1979 (NLSY79) (Bureau of Labor Statistics 2019). The CYA is a unique longitudinal survey that is structured as follows. In 1979, the Bureau of Labor Statistics launched the NLSY79, a nationally representative sample of individuals born between 1957 and 1964.[6] In 1979, when the first wave of the survey was administered, the NLSY79 respondents were between

14 and 22 years old. Starting in 1986, a separate survey of all children born to female respondents of the NLSY79 was initiated.

These correlations, or intergenerational elasticities, have been well measured in a broad range of datasets, and the estimates derived from the NLSY79 sample are in line with earlier studies. To estimate the baseline elasticity coefficient, I regress child birth cohort–adjusted outcomes on maternal birth cohort–adjusted mother outcomes. In this context, the main outcomes of interest are income and education. Within this data, the schooling-schooling elasticity between the mother and child generation is around 0.26 (Figure 5.4), and the intergenerational income elasticity is approximately 0.45 (Figure 5.5). These estimates are similar to what other studies of U.S. data have found, at least within samples of biological children and parents.[7]

Figure 5.4 Regression-Adjusted Intergenerational Correlation, Schooling

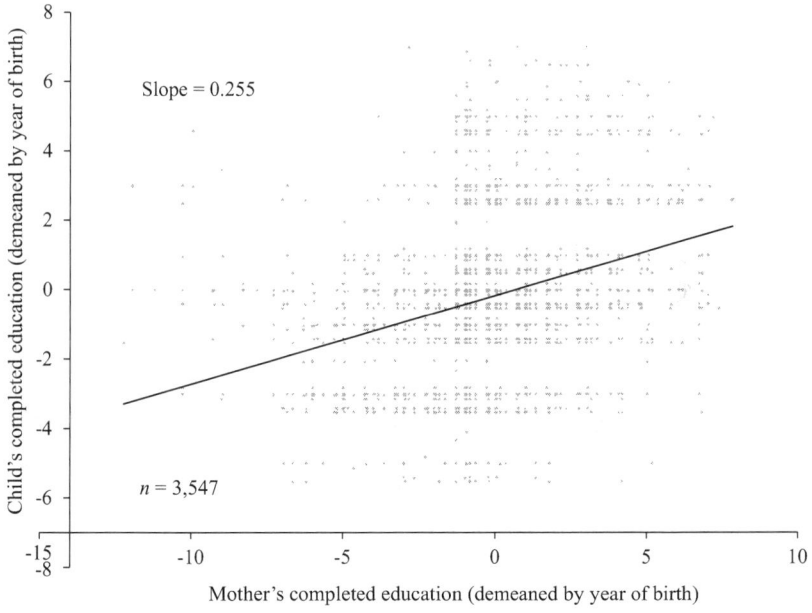

SOURCE: Data are from the Children of the NLSY79 Survey, 1979–2016. Slope represents the coefficient when child's completed education in years is regressed on mother's years of completed education. Years of schooling are demeaned within birth cohort.

Figure 5.5 Regression-Adjusted Intergenerational Correlation, Household Income

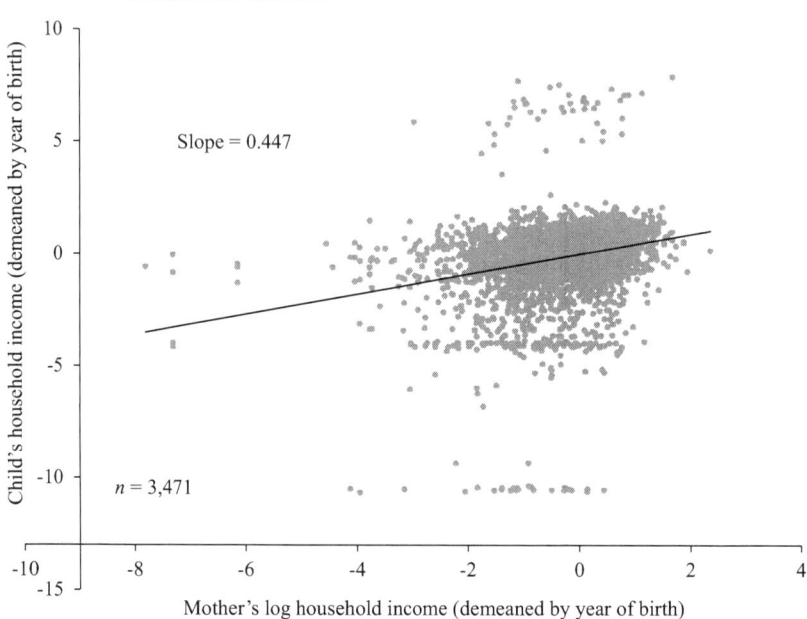

SOURCE: Data are from the Children of the NLSY79 Survey, 1979–2016. Child's log household income regressed on mother's household log income. Both parent and child generations income are adjusted to 2016 dollars. Child's real household income is averaged over all years available between ages 25 and 41, then demeaned by child's birth cohort. Mother's real household income is averaged over all years available between ages 25 and 51 and demeaned by mother's birth cohort.

Figure 5.6 shows the intergenerational correlation coefficient for education for children whose mothers were married at the time of birth versus children whose mothers were unmarried when they were born. The lower spot estimate (0.243) for households with married mothers indicates a higher level of educational mobility in these households. For unmarried mothers, the educational correlation is slightly higher at 0.299, suggesting less mobility for the children of single-mother households. However, the pattern of mobility is reversed for household income measures, as shown in Figure 5.7. In this case, households with unmarried mothers show a lower intergenerational income elasticity (more mobility), while married-mother households display a higher

Figure 5.6 Intergenerational Education Correlation, by Maternal Marital Status

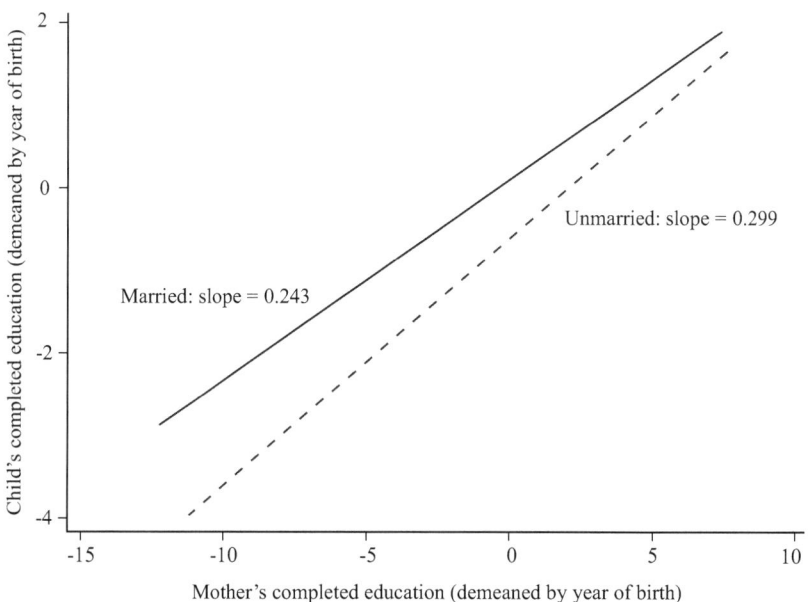

SOURCE: Underlying data are from the NLSY79 and the CYA-Children of the NLSY79.

elasticity (less mobility). Notably, income mobility is quite low for both single-mother and married-mother households: 0.361 and 0.411, respectively, and these coefficients are not statistically different from each other.

While these results may seem contradictory at first, they point to the subtle differences in the influence of maternal income versus maternal education. A reasonable interpretation of these estimates is that maternal education becomes a more important determinant of child outcomes when mothers are unmarried. This is intuitive, since we would expect maternal intergenerational effects to be especially pronounced for mothers who are the only caregiver for their child. But with respect to household income, the relationship is more nuanced. Low-income single mothers will automatically qualify for more financial support—as well as nonfinancial programs, such as child care, rental assistance, or food support—than their married counterparts. This is consistent with slightly greater income mobility for single mothers as compared to married mothers.

**Figure 5.7 Intergenerational Household Income Correlation, by
Maternal Marital Status**

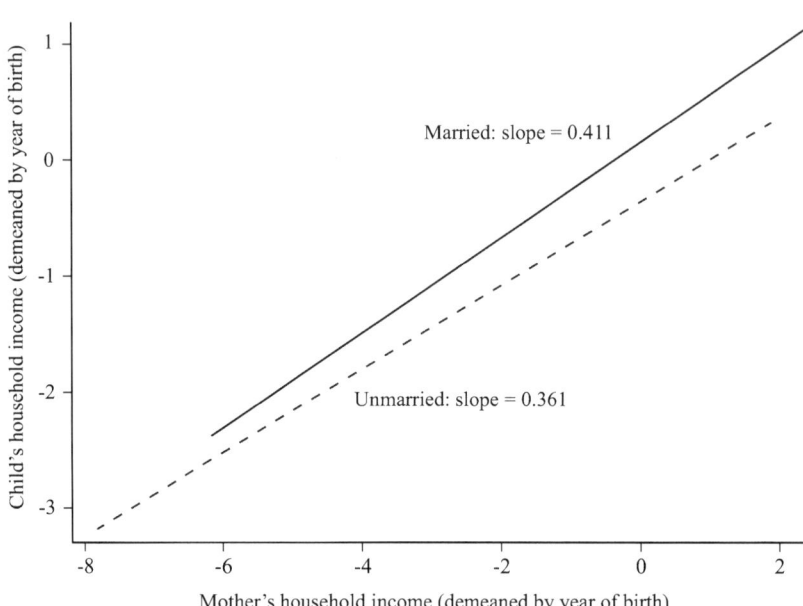

SOURCE: Underlying data are from the NLSY79 and the CYA-Children of the NLSY79.

Overall, maternal marital status in these data remains an over-whelmingly strong predictor for a child's household income in adulthood. Figure 5.8 shows the household income distributions of respondents in the CYA, separated by their mother's marital status during their childhood. Panel A of Figure 5.8 shows the distribution of household income during adulthood for the children of mothers who were married for less than 30 percent of the time while their child was between ages 0 and 18. In Panel B, the histogram depicts the (adulthood) household income distribution for those whose mothers were married for 70 percent or more of their childhood years. As before, in order to smooth out any year-to-year fluctuations, adult household income is a mean of income observed between ages 25 and 41.

The distribution for children of unmarried mothers is heavily skewed toward the lower tail, with over 34 percent of this subsample falling into the bottom 20 percent of the full income distribution. In

Figure 5.8 Household Income Distributions by Maternal Marital Status

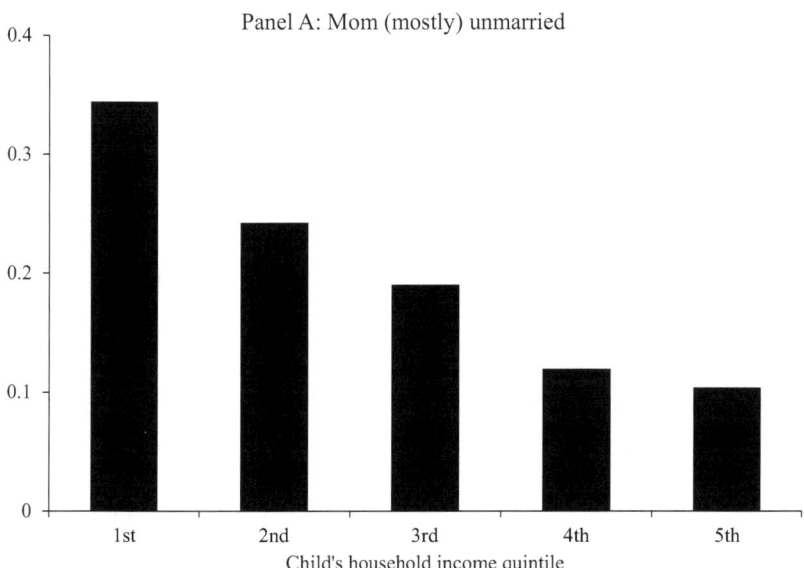

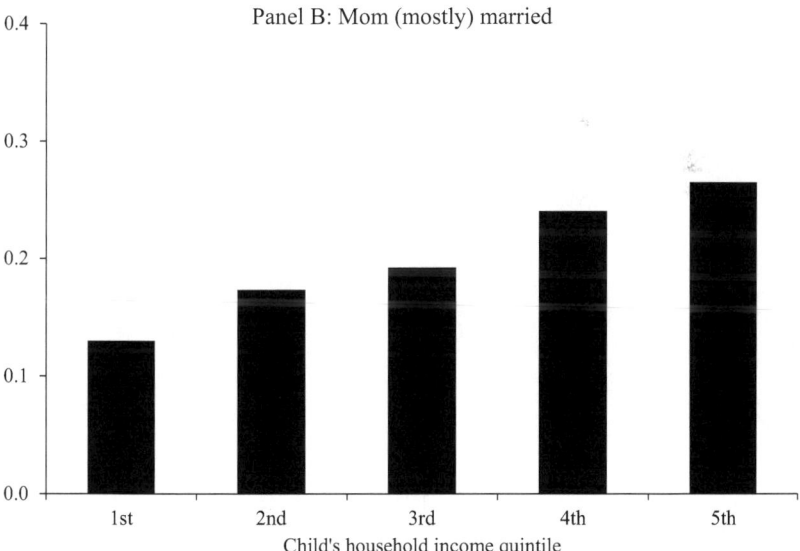

SOURCE: Data are from the Children of the NLSY79 Survey, 1979–2016

contrast, only 10 percent of the children with unmarried mothers reach the 80th percentile of income or better. The distribution of the children with married mothers shows the opposite gradient: 13 percent fall into the poorest quintile, and 26 percent are in the top income category. This means that a child of a married mother is 2.6 times more likely to be in the top category than the child of a single mother. Similarly, the chances of being in the poorest category are nearly three times greater for children with unmarried mothers. These odds are corroborated by the aggregate poverty statistics drawn from national surveys such as the Current Population Survey or the American Community Survey (see the first section in this chapter).[8]

Finally, regression analysis allows us to quantify the conditional effect of maternal marital status on child socioeconomic outcomes, and more precisely differentiate the direct effect of a mother's marriage from the interactive effect of maternal marriage on the transmission of human capital.[9] Table 5.1 explores this decomposition in the context of education. In column 1, child's education is regressed on mother's education as well as a full set of birth cohort dummies for both the mother and child. Child's sex is also included as a covariate. The coefficient on mother's schooling is 0.298, which represents the intergenerational elasticity of education.[10]

Table 5.1 Marital Status and Intergenerational Elasticity of Education

DV: Child's years of school	(1)	(2)	(3)
Mom years of school	0.298***	0.303***	0.272***
	(0.017)	(0.019)	(0.024)
Mother married at child's birth		0.670***	0.628***
		(0.090)	(0.092)
Mom college × mom married at birth			0.388**
			(0.180)
Observations	3,547	2,801	2,801
Mean of Y	12.97	13.04	13.04

NOTE: * $p < 0.1$; ** $p < 0.05$; *** $p < 0.01$. Child's sex, mother year of birth dummies, and child year of birth dummies included in all regressions. All regressions utilize NLSY custom sample weights. Robust standard errors are in parentheses.

SOURCE: Underlying data are from the NLSY79 and NLSY Child/YA, downloaded in 2019. Regression parameters are author's estimates using Stata 14.

Column 2 adds an indicator of whether a mother was married at the time of the child's birth.[11] Being born to a married mother is associated with a mean increase to a child's years of education of 0.67 years, around 5 percent of the sample mean of 13 years of schooling. There is an amplifying effect of marriage on the impact of her education for her children. Column 3 includes the interaction of maternal education and maternal marriage. For the sake of clearer interpretation, mother's education is measured as a binary variable to indicate the completion of at least one year of college. This coefficient indicates that maternal marriage increases the effect of a mother's college education by 0.39 years of school. The results imply that the predicted difference in completed education between the child of a single mother with a high school education and the child of a married mother with two years of college is equal to 1.56 years of school, or 12 percent of the sample mean.[12]

Table 5.2 examines the same interaction between maternal marital status and a mother's economic status with respect to children's household earnings in adulthood. The dependent variable in this case is the mean of all observed years of real household earnings while the child was aged 25 to 41. In the NLSY79, positive household earnings are reported for about two-thirds of the young adult respondents, and the majority (75 percent) of those who report positive earnings report multiple years of household earnings. The baseline specification in Table 5.2, column 1, is a regression of mean household earnings for the child reported between the ages of 25 and 41, regressed on mean household earnings for the mother reported between the (mother's) ages 25 and 51. Age and birth cohort controls for both mother and child are included, as well as indicators for each generation to identify reports of zero earnings. The coefficient in column 1 indicates a baseline intergeneration income elasticity of approximately 0.5. This estimate is statistically significant at the 1 percent level and is in line with other household-household correlation estimates (Chadwick and Solon 2002; Black and Devereaux 2011).

Following the structure of Table 5.1, columns 2 and 3 add maternal marital status and then the interaction of maternal marital status and maternal income, respectively. The direct effect of being born to a married mother increases yearly income by about 0.4 points, or 4 percent of the sample mean. In column 3, the added interaction effect is defined as the product of the indicator for a married mother and an indicator that

Table 5.2 Marital Status and Intergenerational Income Elasticity

DV: Child's household log income	(1)	(2)	(3)
Mom household log income	0.513***	0.436***	0.421***
	(0.033)	(0.039)	(0.040)
Mother married at child's birth		0.415***	0.390***
		(0.070)	(0.071)
Mom high income × mom married			0.138
at birth			(0.091)
Observations	3,471	2,745	2,745
Mean of Y	10.06	10.05	10.05

NOTE: * $p < 0.1$; ** $p < 0.05$; *** $p < 0.01$. Mother year of birth dummies and child year of birth dummies included in all regressions. All regressions utilize NLSY custom sample weights. Robust standard errors are in parentheses.

SOURCE: Underlying data are from the NLSY79 and NLSY Child/YA, downloaded in 2019. Regression parameters are author's estimates using Stata 14.

is equal to 1 if the mother's household income was in the top quintile of the parent sample income distribution. As in Table 5.1, the interaction term is based on two binary variables in order to support a straightforward interpretation of the estimated coefficient. The positive sign on the interaction term suggests a premium income effect of marriage for mothers in the top income quintile; however, the coefficient is not statistically significant, and this result does not rule out the possibility that there is no difference in intergenerational elasticity for married and unmarried mothers.

As a final measure of the interaction between marital status and intergenerational correlations, Table 5.3 examines income mobility at the extreme points of the distribution, the upper and lower quintiles. The top panel of Table 5.3 reports the coefficients for the role of maternal marital status in the regression of child's high-income status on mother's high-income status. As above, high-income status is defined as household income that is at or above the 80th percentile of income within the study sample. The high-income indicator has a lower variance than the mean household log income measures, resulting in smaller magnitudes for the intergenerational elasticity coefficients. The baseline specification in column 1 indicates that children of high-income mothers are 20 percentage points more likely to experience high-income status themselves. Although this coefficient on mother's high-income

Table 5.3 Marital Status and Intergenerational Income Elasticity

Panel A

DV: Child's HH income in top quintile	(1)	(2)	(3)
Mom HH income in top quintile	0.194***	0.174***	0.127***
	(0.017)	(0.018)	(0.034)
Mother married at child's birth		0.077***	0.065***
		(0.016)	(0.018)
Mom high income × mom married at birth			0.065
			(0.040)
Observations	3,547	2,801	2,801
Mean of Y	0.159	0.161	0.161

Panel B

DV: Child's HH income in bottom quintile	(1)	(2)	(3)
Mom HH income in bottom quintile	0.132***	0.098***	0.121***
	(0.016)	(0.019)	(0.026)
Mother married at child's birth		−0.154***	−0.140***
		(0.016)	(0.020)
Mom low income × mom married at birth			−0.042
			(0.033)
Observations	3,547	2,801	2,801
Mean of Y	0.258	0.258	0.258

NOTE: * $p < 0.1$**; $p < 0.05$; *** $p < 0.01$. Mother year of birth dummies and child year of birth dummies included in all regressions. All regressions utilize NLSY custom sample weights. Robust standard errors are in parentheses. HH = household.

SOURCE: Underlying data are from the NLSY79 and NLSY Child/YA, downloaded in 2019. Regression parameters are author's estimates using Stata 14.

status shrinks slightly when marriage covariates are added to the regression, it remains statistically significant at the 1 percent level and large compared to the sample mean of 0.16.

Mother's marital status at birth is added as a control in the specifications shown in columns 2 and 3. In both columns, maternal marriage is again positively and significantly correlated with child's economic status, with an estimated coefficient of 0.07–0.08. Column 3 examines the interaction of the mother's marital status with parental high-income status on the high-income status of the child. As with the results of Table

5.2, the spot estimate for this interaction term is positive but not sufficiently precise enough to confirm a higher intergenerational income effect for married mothers.

Panel B parallels the specifications in the top panel for the lower end of the distribution, where low-income status is defined as having (birth-year adjusted) household income within the bottom 20 percent of the sample. The results are quantitatively and qualitatively very similar to those in Panel A: while low-income status tends to be transmitted from the mother's generation to the child, maternal marital status does not significantly alter the strength of this correlation. However, the combined maternal effects of being married while also being low income do net out to approximately zero, since the marriage effect decreases the probability of poverty quite substantially by 14 percentage points.

DISCUSSION AND POLICY IMPLICATIONS

Nonmarital births have risen to nearly 40 percent of all births in the United States. This trend is unlikely to reverse, as a result of both changes in the marriage market and cultural norms. The high number of single-mother families in American society presents important public policy challenges. In particular, children of single mothers exhibit considerably worse outcomes on average than children of married mothers. While the mechanism of these relationships is not fully understood, single motherhood can exacerbate the symptoms of poverty and pose additional challenges for low-income women and their children. Programs that help single mothers complete a postsecondary degree could be among the most persistent and cost-effective strategies to end the cycle of intergenerational poverty. Encouragingly, a growing number of colleges and nonprofit organizations are now working to support college retention and completion among single-parent students.[13]

The analysis in this chapter demonstrates that while single motherhood is a strong predictor of poverty in the subsequent generation, college degrees for single mothers can mitigate this effect. Firstly, maternal schooling has a very large effect on child education, particularly in a single-parent household setting. For the typical mother in the NLSY79/CYA sample, the difference between 12 and 16 years of education is associated with an increase of about 1.2 years of schooling for her child. In comparison, being married is associated with only an additional 0.6 years of schooling for a woman's child. Secondly, maternal schooling has a larger effect for children of single mothers compared to the children of married mothers. In contrast, we do not observe any significant interactive effects between maternal marital status and parental income, suggesting that additional household income does not show a disproportionate effect for the children of single mothers.

The policy responses needed to address poverty are not straightforward or easily implemented. However, the strong correlation between poverty and household structure may offer a feasible approach that is also politically attainable. Because maternal education has the ability to change outcomes for generations, supporting postsecondary degree completion for single mothers should be viewed as a low-cost, high-return investment.

Notes

1. An additional 15 percent of children live with two parents, at least one of whom has been married before.
2. Author's calculations using the 2019 Current Population Survey, Annual Social and Economic Supplement of the Current Population Survey. Poverty rate for children under 18 living with a single mother is 40 percent, compared to 12 percent for children living with a married mother. In the American Community Survey (2017 five-year estimate), 40 percent of single mothers lived below the federal poverty line compared to 10 percent of married mothers.
3. This impact is driven in large part by the negative characteristics of the men who father these children.
4. For simplicity, this model assumes all partnerships occur between opposite genders.
5. The CPS includes education data for infants' mothers starting in 1970, as long as the mother lived in the same household as the child. Education data are available only in the CDC Vital Statistics for births occurring after 1995.
6. The NLSY79 survey is sponsored and directed by the U.S. Bureau of Labor Statistics and managed by the Center for Human Resource Research at the Ohio State University. Interviews are conducted by the National Opinion Research Center (NORC) at the University of Chicago.
7. Black, Devereux, and Salvanes (2005), Davis and Mazumder (2019), and Sacerdote (2004) find similar estimates for schooling in the United States. For comparable income effects, see Solon (1992) and Chetty et al. (2014). Mazumder (2018) offers a more complete summary of U.S. studies.

8. The figure is qualitatively very similar when the mother's marital status at the time of the child's birth is used. The 30 percent threshold was chosen to balance out the sizes of the two subsamples used for the graph. Using cutoffs closer together (less than 40 percent versus greater than 60 percent) dampens the slopes of the graphs, as expected. Note that the histogram for the full sample would show equal probability (0.2) for each income quintile.
9. The term *effect* is used here in a general sense and should not be taken as a causal estimate, given the nonrandom nature of marriage.
10. The slight difference in this coefficient compared to the slope of the line of best fit in Figure 5.4 arises from the difference in level regressions including year of birth dummies (Table 5.1) versus the correlational coefficient of demeaned schooling levels (Figure 5.4).
11. Marital status at the child's birth is highly correlated with marital status at older ages. This is confirmed both in the NLSY79 and in other datasets (see Kearney and Levine 2017).
12. $(2 \times 0.27) + 0.63 + 0.39 = 1.56$
13. A few examples of such programs are the Uplifting Parents Program of Rapid City, South Dakota; the Jeremiah Program, based in Minneapolis, Minnesota; and the federal CCAMPIS program on select college campuses.

References

Addo, Fenaba R., Sharon Sassler, and Kristi Williams. 2016. "Reexamining the Association of Maternal Age and Marital Status at First Birth with Youth Educational Attainment." *Journal of Marriage and Family* 78(5): 1252–1268.

Aizer, Anna. 2017. "The Role of Children's Health in the Intergenerational Transmission of Economic Status." *Child Development Perspectives* 11(3): 167–172.

Aizer, Anna, Paul J. Devereux, and Kjell G. Salvanes. 2018. "Grandparents, Moms, or Dads? Why Children of Teen Mothers Do Worse in Life." NBER Working Paper No. 25165. Cambridge, MA: National Bureau of Economic Research.

Amato, Paul R. 2005. "The Impact of Family Formation Change on the Cognitive, Social, and Emotional Well-Being of the Next Generation." *Future of Children* 15(2): 75–96.

Andrews, Dan, and Andrew Leigh. 2009. "More Inequality, Less Social Mobility." *Applied Economics Letters* 16(15): 1489–1492.

Autor, David, David Dorn, and Gordon Hanson. 2019. "When Work Disappears: Manufacturing Decline and the Falling Marriage Market Value of Young Men." *American Economic Review: Insights* 1(2): 161–178.

Beeler, Sydney. 2016. "Undergraduate Single Mothers' Experiences in Postsecondary Education." *New Directions for Higher Education* 2016(176): 69–80.

Black, Dan A., Terra G. McKinnish, and Seth G. Sanders. 2003. "Does the Availability of High-Wage Jobs for Low-Skilled Men Affect Welfare Expenditures? Evidence from Shocks to the Steel and Coal Industries." *Journal of Public Economics* 87(9–10): 1921–1942.

Black, Sandra E., and Paul J. Devereux. 2011. "Recent Developments in Intergenerational Mobility." In *Handbook of Labor Economics,* vol. 4, part B, David Card and Orley Ashenfelter, eds. Amsterdam: North Holland, pp. 1487–1541.

Black, Sandra E., Paul J. Devereux, and Kjell G. Salvanes. 2005. "Why the Apple Doesn't Fall Far: Understanding Intergenerational Transmission of Human Capital." *American Economic Review* 95(1): 437–449.

Bureau of Labor Statistics. 2019. "Children of the NLSY79, 1979–2016." Columbus: Center for Human Resource Research, the Ohio State University.

Cerven, Christine. 2013. "Public and Private Lives: Institutional Structures and Personal Supports in Low-Income Single Mothers' Educational Pursuits." *Education Policy Analysis Archives* 21(17):1–29.

Chadwick, Laura, and Gary Solon. 2002. "Intergenerational Income Mobility among Daughters." *American Economic Review* 92(1): 335–344.

Chetty, Raj, Nathaniel Hendren, Patrick Kline, and Emmanuel Saez. 2014. "Where Is the Land of Opportunity? The Geography of Intergenerational Mobility in the United States." *Quarterly Journal of Economics* 129(4): 1553–1623.

Chevalier, Arnaud, Colm Harmon, Vincent O'Sullivan, and Ian Walker. 2013. "The Impact of Parental Income and Education on the Schooling of Their Children." *IZA Journal of Labor Economics* 2(8): 1–22.

Cruse, Lindsey Reichlin, Barbara Gault, Joo Yeoun Suh, and Mary Ann DeMario. 2018. "Time Demands of Single Mother College Students and the Role of Child Care in Their Postsecondary Success." Washington, DC: Institute for Women's Policy Studies. https://iwpr.org/publications/single-mothers-college-time-use/ (accessed February 1, 2020).

Davis, Jonathan, and Bhashkar Mazumder. 2019. "The Decline in Intergenerational Mobility after 1980." Working Paper No. WP-2017-5. Chicago: Federal Reserve Bank of Chicago.

Duncan, Greg J., and Jeanne Brooks-Gunn, eds. 1997. *Consequences of Growing Up Poor*. New York: Russell Sage Foundation.

Ginther, Donna K., and Robert A. Pollack. 2004. "Family Structure and Children's Educational Outcomes: Blended Families, Stylized Facts, and Descriptive Regressions." *Demography* 41(4): 671–696.

Goldrick-Rab, Sara, and Sara Kia Sorensen. 2010. "Unmarried Parents in College." *Future of Children* 20(2): 179–203.

Gray, Jo Anna, Jean Stockard, and Joe A. Stone. 2006. "The Rising Share of Nonmarital Births: Fertility Choice or Marriage Behavior?" *Demography* 43(2): 241–253.

Kearney, Melissa S., and Phillip B. Levine. 2015. "Investigating Recent Trends in the U.S. Teen Birth Rates." *Journal of Health Economics* 41: 15–29.

———. 2017. "The Economics of Nonmarital Childbearing and the Marriage Premium for Children." *Annual Review of Economics* 9: 327–352.

Kearney, Melissa S., and Riley Wilson. 2018. "Male Earnings, Marriageable Men, and Nonmarital Fertility: Evidence from the Fracking Boom." *Review of Economics and Statistics* 100(4): 678–690.

Kendig, Sarah M., and Suzanne M. Bianchi. 2008. "Single, Cohabitating, and Married Mothers' Time with Children." *Journal of Marriage and Family* 70(5): 1228–1240.

López Turley, Ruth N. 2003. "Are Children of Young Mothers Disadvantaged Because of Their Mother's Age or Family Background?" *Child Development* 74(2): 465–474.

Lopoo, Leonard M., and Thomas DeLeire. 2014. "Family Structure and the Economic Wellbeing of Children in Youth and Adulthood." *Social Science Research* 43(1): 30–44.

Mazumder, Bhashkar. 2018. "Intergenerational Mobility in the United States: What We Have Learned from the PSID." *Annals of the American Academy of Political and Social Science* 680(1): 213–234.

McLanahan, Sara, and Gary D. Sandefur. 1994. *Growing Up with a Single Parent: What Hurts, What Helps*. Cambridge, MA: Harvard University Press.

Pandey, Shanta, Min Zhan, and Youngmi Kim. 2006. "Bachelor's Degree for Women with Children: A Promising Pathway to Poverty Reduction." *Equal Opportunities International* 25(7): 488–505.

Pew Research Center. 2015. "Parenting in America: Outlook, Worries, Aspirations Are Strongly Linked to Financial Situation." https://www.pewsocial trends.org/2015/12/17/parenting-in-america (accessed October 9, 2020).

Piketty, Thomas. 2000. "Theories of Persistent Inequality and Intergenerational Mobility." *Handbook of Income Distribution* 1(8): 429–476.

Sacerdote, Bruce. 2004. "What Happens When We Randomly Assign Children to Families?" NBER Working Paper No. 10894. Cambridge, MA: National Bureau of Economic Research.

Schott, Liz, and Ladonna Pavetti. 2013. "Changes in TANF Work Requirements Could Make Them More Effective in Promoting Employment." Washington, DC: Center on Budget and Policy Priorities. https://www.cbpp.org/research/family-income-support/changes-in-tanf-work-requirements-could-make-them-more-effective-in (accessed October 9, 2020).

Schwartz, Christine R. 2010. "Earnings Inequality and the Changing Association between Spouses' Earnings." *American Journal of Sociology* 115(5): 1524–1557.

Solon, Gary. 1992. "Intergenerational Income Mobility in the United States." *American Economic Review* 82(3): 393–408.

Son, Seohee, and Jean W. Bauer. 2010. "Employed Rural, Low-Income, Single Mothers' Family and Work over Time." *Journal of Family and Economic Issues* 31(1): 107–120.

Taniguchi, Hiromi, and Gayle Kaufman. 2005. "Degree Completion among Nontraditional College Students." *Social Science Quarterly* 86(4): 912–927.

Vernon, Victoria. 2010. "Marriage: For Love, for Money . . . and for Time?" *Review of Economics of the Household* 8(4): 433–457.

Whitbeck, Les B., Ronald L. Simons, and Meei-Ying Kao. 1994. "The Effects of Divorced Mothers' Dating Behaviors and Sexual Attitudes on the Sexual Attitudes and Behaviors of their Adolescent Children." *Journal of Marriage and the Family* 56(3): 615–621.

Williams, Kristi, Sharon Sassler, Adrianne Frech, Fenaba Addo, and Elizabeth Cooksey. 2011. "Nonmarital Childbearing, Union History, and Women's Health at Midlife." *American Sociological Review* 76(3): 465–486.

Wilson, William Julius. 1987. *The Truly Disadvantaged*. Chicago: University of Chicago Press.

Wilson, William Julius, and Kathryn M. Neckerman. 1986. "Poverty and Family Structure: The Widening Gap between Evidence and Public Policy Issues." In *Fighting Poverty: What Works and What Doesn't*, Sheldon Danziger and Daniel H. Weinberg, eds. Cambridge, MA: Harvard University Press, pp. 232–259.

Zhan, Min, and Shanta Pandey. 2004a. "Economic Well-Being of Single-Mothers: Work First or Postsecondary Education?" *Journal of Sociology and Social Welfare* 31(3): 87–112.

———. 2004b. "Postsecondary Education and Economic Well-Being of Single Mothers and Single Fathers." *Journal of Marriage and Family* 66(3): 661–673.

6

Race and Intergenerational Mobility in the United States

Bhashkar Mazumder
Federal Reserve Bank of Chicago

One of the most salient issues in American society is the persistent gap in socioeconomic outcomes between Blacks and whites. It has now been over 150 years since slavery was abolished and more than 60 years since *Brown vs. Board of Education* ended state-sponsored segregation of schools. Yet, racial gaps across a broad range of measures remain large and enduring. For example, in 2018 the Black–white gap in median household income was 41 percent.[1] That same gap in 1972 was 42 percent. These income inequalities are also reflected in the wide racial disparities in health that have become increasingly evident during the coronavirus pandemic of 2020 (Chowkwanyun and Reed 2020). Similarly, striking differences in treatment by the police and the criminal justice system toward people of color have led to widespread protests in the United States.

One important way to determine how long it will take for Black–white income gaps to close is to study the intergenerational income transmission process and how it differs across racial groups. Despite the importance of this issue, relatively few studies compare racial differences in intergenerational mobility. One explanation for the dearth of research is data limitations—few publicly available data sets contain a large enough sample of Black families that are followed over two generations with detailed measures of income or other socioeconomic indicators. The papers in the economics literature that use these publicly available sources (e.g., Bhattacharya and Mazumder 2011; Davis and Mazumder 2018; Fox 2016; Hertz 2005; Mazumder 2014) suggest that there are very large racial differences in mobility for cohorts born from the 1950s to 1970s. Not only do Blacks in the bottom of the income distribution experience much less upward mobility than whites,

171

but Blacks in the top of the income distribution experience significantly higher rates of downward mobility. Thus, economic progress for Blacks is much less likely to be sustained. Davis and Mazumder (2018) also look at broad regional differences in the United States and show that there is no region in the country where low-income Blacks have greater opportunity than low-income whites.

The findings mentioned here, which have used mostly longitudinal survey data covering broad swaths of the life cycle for two generations, have been recently confirmed by researchers with access to population-wide administrative data covering more recent cohorts of individuals born from 1978 to 1983 (Chetty et al. 2020).[2] Chetty et al. (2020) also are able to utilize their massive samples to highlight much more granular geographic differences in racial mobility and have shared these data with the research community through the Opportunity Atlas.

In this chapter, I introduce new evidence documenting that the racial mobility gaps were just as large for cohorts born shortly after World War II, who entered the labor market during the 1970s, as it has been for cohorts born around 1960, who entered the labor market during the sharp rise in inequality during the 1980s. This suggests that modern changes in the economy, such as skill-biased technological change and unionization—which may have reduced intergenerational mobility overall (Davis and Mazumder 2020)—have not affected racial gaps in mobility. Collins and Wanamaker (forthcoming) look back even further in time using historical census data and conclude that large racial mobility gaps have long characterized American society.

The implications of these racial gaps in intergenerational mobility are profound for the future of American society. Mazumder (2014) conducts an exercise that attempts to extrapolate how the rates of intergenerational mobility among cohorts born largely in the 1960s would affect the distribution of income among Blacks and whites in the long run and suggests that, "in the steady state, 39 percent of Blacks would occupy the bottom quintile of the income distribution and only 8 percent would be in the top quintile. This finding suggests that rather than convergence, Blacks will remain perpetually disadvantaged in American society if mobility patterns continue to evolve as they have for the cohorts studied in this article" (p. 9).

Given these findings, it is clear that a fundamental priority should be to understand the sources of these large racial gaps in intergenerational mobility. In this chapter, I review some of the major relevant studies in the economics literature and attempt to draw lessons on what factors have contributed to the racial gaps in intergenerational mobility, and how policy can potentially address these causes.

I begin by discussing how the literature has studied racial gaps in intergenerational mobility. I then highlight how the literature has evolved over time to use increasingly better data and methodology. I also discuss new research that documents historical patterns in racial disparities in mobility. I then turn to studies on changes over time in Black–white differences in intergenerational mobility. Finally, I discuss how research has investigated the different mechanisms underlying these racial differences, and also the potential role for policy.

EVOLUTION OF RESEARCH ON OVERALL RACIAL MOBILITY GAPS

Much of the early research on intergenerational mobility was done by sociologists who were interested in studying the changes in the social status of families over a generation. This is likely why the term *social mobility* is used when referring to intergenerational mobility in income or other economic outcomes.[3] This body of research uses occupation as the main measure of social status. The landmark paper on intergenerational occupational mobility is Blau and Duncan (1967), who use data from the 1962 Occupational Change in a Generation Survey. They find that for whites, the occupation of parents mattered for determining the occupation of children as adults, suggesting that persistence of social class is an important phenomenon in the United States. In contrast, Blau and Duncan find that Black children had worse occupations regardless of their parents' occupation, suggesting that class was less important than discrimination in explaining the outcomes of Blacks. A rich literature in sociology continues to examine patterns in social mobility using occupation.

As far as I am aware, Linda Datcher (1981) was the first economic researcher to examine differences in the intergenerational transmission of socioeconomic outcomes by race. Notably, Datcher (later Datcher-Loury) was the first African American woman to receive a PhD in economics from MIT. Datcher (1981) uses the Panel Study of Income Dynamics (PSID) and runs regressions of adult outcomes on family background characteristics, separately by race and sex. She finds that Black families are much less successful than white families in passing on parental economic success from one generation to the next, presaging some of the findings in later research.

Subsequent work by Corcoran and Adams (1997) compares racial differences in the likelihood of escaping poverty. The authors also use the PSID to further consider how covariates affect the intergenerational transmission of poverty. They find that poverty is much more likely to be transmitted among Black families and show that economic factors during childhood, such as local unemployment rates, are important mediators.

Neither of these studies, however, directly measures intergenerational income mobility using the methodological approaches and types of measures that are now standard in the economics literature. The modern approach pioneered in studies by Solon (1992) and Zimmerman (1992) uses nationally representative longitudinal surveys that utilize several years of income in each generation and summarize mobility using a few key parameters, such as the intergenerational elasticity or transition probabilities. The latter is a set of measures that shows the likelihood of moving from one point in the income distribution to another over a generation.

The first study using this framework to examine racial differences in intergenerational mobility was by Hertz (2005), using the PSID. Since the nationally representative portion of the PSID has few Black families (Solon 1992), Hertz also includes the oversample of poorer households in the Survey of Economic Opportunity portion of the PSID. Using a regression framework, he shows that there are large racial gaps in children's income as adults, conditional on their parents' permanent income. He finds that the expected income of Black children with identical levels of parent income to whites is 40 percent lower. He also compares racial differences in transition probabilities, which show the likelihood of moving from one point in the income distribution to another over a generation. Hertz finds that 42 percent of Black children who were born to parents in the bottom decile of the income distribution remain in the bottom decile as adults. The comparable figure for whites is just 17 percent. These racial differences were clearly quite striking and were the first use of transition probabilities in the literature on income mobility to document the lack of opportunity for Blacks.

Hertz's work played a major role in pushing the literature forward, but there were some limitations to the analysis. First, with respect to data, given the concerns about the representativeness of the PSID sample for Blacks, it was important to replicate these findings with larger, nationally representative intergenerational samples of Black families. Second, there are some methodological drawbacks to using transition probabilities. This includes the arbitrariness of the quantiles in the income distribution on which to focus and the "floor-ceiling" problem—that individuals in the lowest quantile group cannot move lower, and similarly those starting in the top group can't move higher.

Bhattacharya and Mazumder (2011) and Mazumder (2014) introduce a new methodological approach to study racial differences in intergenerational mobility by considering mobility in ranks. They also use improved data sources such as the National Longitudinal Survey of Youth 1979 (NLSY79) and the Survey of Income and Program Participation matched to administrative data from Social Security earnings records (SIPP-SSA).[4] They also make another important contribution—they introduce many important covariates into the analysis to better understand the mechanisms behind the racial differences in intergenerational mobility.

In addition to estimating transition probabilities, Bhattacharya and Mazumder (2011) present a novel measure of upward rank mobility (URM)—namely, the likelihood that individuals will surpass their parents' place in the distribution by a given amount, conditional on their parents being at or below a given percentile.

(6.1) $URM_{\tau,s} = \Pr(Y_1 - Y_0 > \tau \mid Y_0 \leq s)$

In the basic case where $\tau = 0$, and $s =$ the 50th percentile, this is simply the probability that a child growing up in the bottom half of the distribution exceeds her parents' place in the distribution.[5] One can then compare this URM measure for Blacks to whites. Similarly, one can construct a measure of downward rank mobility (DRM) using an analogous approach:

(6.2) $DRM_{\tau,s} = \Pr(Y_0 - Y_1 > \tau \mid Y_0 \leq s)$

Mazumder (2014) shows that there are striking differences in URM and DRM between whites and Blacks in the United States. In particular, for any cutoff in the bottom half of the parent income distribution (10th, 20th, 30th, 40th, or 50th), the probability that a white child's rank will exceed his parents' rank is significantly higher than the corresponding figure for a Black child. For example, among white families starting in the bottom quintile in the NLSY, 84 percent of children will exceed their parents' rank. In contrast, only 75 percent of Black children will. If we increase τ to be 0.2, to focus only on larger moves upward in rank, then we find that among families starting in the bottom quintile, 60 percent of white children will experience URM compared to just 36 percent of Black children. Mazumder (2014) shows that these upward mobility estimates are very similar when using administrative earnings records and including a broader set of birth cohorts with the SIPP-SSA data.

Mazumder (2014) also presents comparable estimates for downward mobility using various percentile cutoffs of parental income for families in the top half of the income distribution. The racial differences are not quite so stark for the downward mobility measure, which simply asks whether the child percentile income rank is lower than the parent rank. For example, among NLSY families with above median parent income, 69 percent of white children will experience DRM compared with 79 percent of Black children. If we look at larger downward moves in rank, by setting $\tau =$ to 0.2, we see a much larger racial gap. Under this definition, only 41 percent of white children starting in the top half of the income distribution experience downward mobility to 59 percent of Black children.

These results make it very clear that Blacks are disadvantaged in both directions when it comes to intergenerational income mobility. They experience significantly lower upward mobility and significantly higher downward mobility. An important question is, What do these mobility disadvantages imply for closing the Black–white gap in income in the long run? To assess this, Mazumder (2014) calculates a complete quintile to quintile transition matrix of the probabilities of movement across the income distribution across generations for both whites and Blacks. For example, this analysis shows that 51 percent of Blacks who start in the bottom quintile will remain there as adults compared with just 26 percent of whites. The matrices imply that if this mobility process continued over time, the "steady state" distribution of income would converge to one in which there is a permanent Black underclass, where 39 percent of Blacks would perpetually remain in the bottom quintile and only 8 percent in the top quintile. This is, of course, a stunning and sobering finding and suggests that there is a fundamental lack of opportunity for African Americans in the United States.

More recent groundbreaking work by Chetty et al. (2020) presents even greater detailed evidence of racial disparities in intergenerational mobility by using nearly population-wide data from administrative data for recent cohorts. Building on previous work by Chetty et al. (2014), Chetty et al. (2020) also focus on rank-based estimators of intergenerational mobility, but these are different from Bhattacharya and Mazumder (2011). Specifically, they examine the "rank-rank slope," also known as the Spearman correlation, as well as the conditional expected rank of children throughout the parent income rank distribution. They find, for example, that the expected rank of Black children whose parents were at the 25th percentile is about 13 percentiles lower than the expected rank of white children.

An important contribution of Chetty et al.'s (2020) work is to show that there are key differences in racial mobility gaps by gender. They find virtually no differences in expected rank when using the individual incomes of women but large differences when using men's.

However, perhaps the most significant contribution of Chetty et al. (2020) is that they document highly localized geographic patterns in intergenerational mobility by race, and they have worked with the U.S. Census Bureau to share these statistics with the research community as part of the Opportunity Atlas. They show that sometimes there are sizable mobility differences among Blacks who grew up in neighborhoods just a few miles apart from one another within the same city.

Davis and Mazumder (2018) perform a similar analysis using broader regional categories based on the nine census divisions with survey data from the NLSY and find that there is no region in the country where the children of poor Blacks are expected to do better than poor whites. Figure 6.1 plots the regional differences in the expected rank of children whose parents were at the 25th percentile. Interestingly, the racial gaps are highest in the Northeast regions (New England and Middle Atlantic), where the expected ranks of white children are about 20 percent higher than for Black children. In contrast, the gaps are closer to 10 percent in the two regions covering the Southeastern portion of

Figure 6.1 Expected Child Rank at the 25th Percentile, by Race and Region

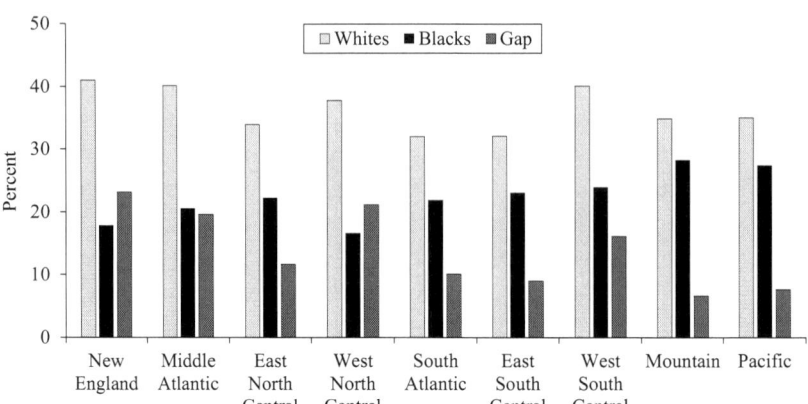

SOURCE: Based on data in Table 3 in Davis and Mazumder (2018).

the United States (South Atlantic and East South Central). Davis and Mazumder point out that although intergenerational mobility for the overall population tends to be low in the Southeast, it is because of the low mobility of whites in these regions. Blacks in this part of the country actually experience modestly higher rates of mobility than Blacks in the Northeast or the Midwest. Overall, however, mobility for Blacks tends to be highest in the West (Mountain and Pacific), where the racial gap in the expected rank is less than 10 percentiles.

TIME PATTERNS IN THE RACIAL GAP IN INTERGENERATIONAL MOBILITY

An important question emerges when trying to understand the extent to which the racial gap in intergenerational mobility has changed over time: Has intergenerational mobility been improving over time in the United States with changing policies, such as Civil Rights–era laws, or is the lack of opportunity an enduring feature of the American economy? Nearly all the research in the previous section has focused on racial differences among Blacks and whites born largely after 1960 and who entered the labor market largely after 1980. One obvious possibility is that perhaps mobility among Blacks was even worse looking back further in time.

To address this, I will present some new empirical results based on previous work with Jonathan Davis. Davis and Mazumder (2020) use data from various National Longitudinal Surveys (NLS) produced by the Bureau of Labor Statistics. The first set of surveys began in 1966 and enables them to track a large sample of men and women born roughly around 1950 from adolescence into adulthood. A subsequent survey, the NLSY79, similarly allows them to track a large set of individuals who were born in the early 1960s. Davis and Mazumder's main finding is that there was a pronounced decline in intergenerational mobility in the United States across these cohorts. The intergenerational income elasticity rose from 0.21 to 0.50, while the rank-rank slope rose from 0.24 to 0.36. However, they did not examine differences by race.

In Figure 6.2, I extend the Davis and Mazumder (2020) analysis by looking at the intergenerational relationship in expected ranks for both Blacks and non-Blacks. The black lines show the relationship for Blacks, while the gray lines show the analogous relationship for non-Blacks. The solid lines are for the earlier cohorts who were born around 1950, and the dashed lines represent the later cohorts born in the early 1960s. While the lines have pivoted a bit between the early cohorts and later cohorts, creating a steeper slope now for both Blacks and non-Blacks, there is little evidence that the racial gap has closed. The more recent cohort of Blacks has continued to experience significantly lower mobility than non-Blacks. For example, the racial gap in the expected rank at the 25th percentile improved only by about 1.3 percentiles, going from a gap of 11.7 percentiles for the earlier cohorts to 10.4 percentiles for the more recent cohorts.

While it is extremely challenging to study intergenerational mobility before the second half of the twentieth century because of the lack of both longitudinal and income data, two recent papers have made clever use of data to make inroads into this question. Collins and Wanamaker (forthcoming) study historical patterns in intergenerational mobility among Blacks and whites going all the way back to the late nineteenth century by creating intergenerational links between the 1880 and 1900 censuses, as well as links between the 1910 and 1930 censuses.

Figure 6.2 Child Rank versus Parent Rank, by Race and Cohort

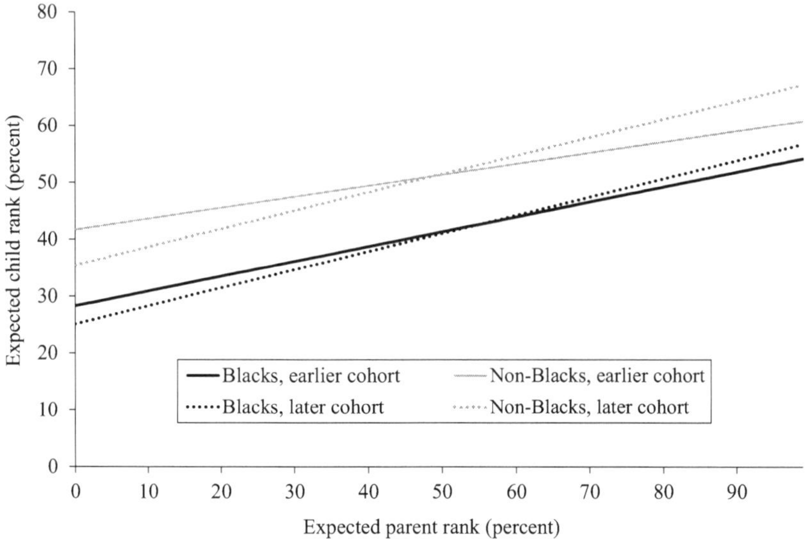

SOURCE: Based on data from Davis and Mazumder (2018).

Since income is unavailable, they impute income based on occupation, region, and gender. One of their main measures of mobility is the URM measure from Bhattacharya and Mazumder (2011) described earlier in the chapter, which measures the probability that a child exceeds his parents' percentile in the income distribution by a given amount. Collins and Wanamaker also estimate the conditional expected rank following Chetty et al. (2014). Additionally, they utilize other more modern datasets such as Occupational Changes in a Generation in 1962 and 1973, and the NLSY in 1979 to produce comparable estimates for more recent periods.

Collins and Wanamaker (forthcoming) find that in every time period, whites in the bottom decile of the income distribution experience substantially greater upward mobility than Blacks. They also find that the extent of this mobility gap did not improve dramatically over time. Looking at the conditional expected rank, they observe a similar pattern of a sharp disadvantage for Blacks that changes little over time. Specifically, they find that, in terms of expected rank in the occupational income distribution conditional on their father's rank, the size of the Black disadvantage has remained large and relatively consistent from the late nineteenth to the end of twentieth century, at around 20 percentile points.

Card et al. (2018) also study historical racial differences in intergenerational mobility at a point in time. Their analysis uses a very different methodology that focuses on educational mobility and uses teenagers who co-reside with their parents in the 1940 census. They show that the vast majority of children at this time lived at home with their parents until the age of 18 and finished their schooling before leaving home. They find vast geographic differences in the probability that a child will attain at least the eighth grade, conditional on their parents' having less than six years of schooling. This measure of upward mobility for Blacks was as high as 90 percent in California and some upper Midwest states and as low as 10 percent in Mississippi and South Carolina. While Card et al. do not examine time trends, their methodology provides a potentially promising new way to look at time trends in upward mobility using other censuses and datasets.

SOURCES OF RACIAL GAPS IN INTERGENERATIONAL MOBILITY

In this section, I explore some of the explanations offered for the large racial disparity in intergenerational mobility and describe the empirical evidence that has been brought to bear thus far.

Human Capital

From the perspective of economics, most theoretical models of intergenerational income mobility consider how human capital investments on the part of parents and the public sector shape the intergenerational associations between parents and children (e.g., Solon 2004). Intergenerational income persistence can be high and mobility low if poorer families face "borrowing constraints" and do not optimally invest in the human capital of their children. On the other hand, public provision of schools and access to early childhood education programs can potentially offset insufficient family investments. Therefore, if Black families face more difficulty than whites in investing in human capital development, or if there is racial inequity in public provision of human capital, then this could at least partially explain mobility gaps. Given the glaring historical legacy of slavery and government-sanctioned segregation and other discriminatory policies, these are highly plausible explanations for the vast gaps in intergenerational mobility.

In order to study this empirically, researchers will often focus on clear markers of human capital such as educational attainment, test scores, noncognitive skills, and health to see how much these disparities can contribute to the disparities in intergenerational mobility. Bhattacharya and Mazumder (2011) and Mazumder (2014) find that much of the gap in upward mobility between Blacks and whites could be accounted for by test scores measured during adolescence. Specifically, these studies use the percentile score on the Armed Forces Qualifying Test (AFQT), which was given to a nationally representative sample of youth in the NLSY. Mazumder shows that the much higher rates of downward mobility among Blacks starting in the top half of the distribution can be explained by differences in test scores. Mazumder finds that educational attainment differences in the parent and child generation can also explain some of the upward and downward mobility gaps.

There are some important caveats to using test scores. First, Lang and Manove (2011) point out that, conditional on AFQT scores, Blacks have higher education levels than whites, suggesting that researchers should also control for education, which these studies have not done. Rodgers and Spriggs (1996) also point to potential racial biases in the AFQT, and therefore the possibility that gaps in AFQT scores may reflect more than just cognitive skills. It is also critical to emphasize the proper interpretation of the finding that test scores can account for racial gaps in mobility. Previous studies have shown that environmental conditions, including hospital access at birth (Chay, Guryan, and Mazumder 2009) and school quality (Aaronson and Mazumder 2011), can affect test scores. Therefore, AFQT should be viewed as reflecting a wide array of influences that are as malleable and potentially affected by social policies.

Another interesting dimension to this issue of the role of test scores is the finding by Chetty et al. (2020) that the racial gaps in intergenerational mobility are large for men but small or nonexistent for women.

In their studies, Bhattacharya and Mazumder (2011) and Mazumder (2014) had pooled men and women together and used family income rather than individual income. Since there are racial test score gaps for both men and women but no racial mobility gap for women, this may tend to raise doubt about whether test scores can really explain the mobility gap. One potentially important issue is whether there is differential selection by race in labor force participation by women. For example, if Black women with high test scores are more likely to work than white women with high test scores, then this differential section could explain some of the smaller racial mobility gap among women. Future research should reexamine this and other aspects of the gender dimension of the racial mobility gap.

Other research bolsters the idea that human capital may be important for intergenerational mobility that does not rely on test scores. Johnson (2016) shows that racial gaps in upward mobility based on the URM measure described earlier were narrowed because of school desegregation policies, school finance reform policies, and the rollout of Head Start. Biasi (2019) also finds evidence that school finance reform policies improved intergenerational mobility, although she doesn't focus on racial gaps. Other historical research also provides results that are consistent with these findings. Card et al. (2018) find that school quality measures are strongly correlated with upward mobility in education and use a border analysis to argue that these associations are causal. In work in progress, I am currently finding results showing that the Rosenwald schools built largely during the 1920s led to an increase in intergenerational educational mobility.

Wealth

Economic theory that emphasizes credit constraints as a possible explanation for low mobility through suboptimal human capital investment also implies that wealth may be another factor to consider. Indeed, the fact that there are vast differences in wealth between white and Black Americans suggests that this is highly plausible. For example, using data from the Survey of Consumer Finances, Dettling et al. (2017) show that the median net worth of Blacks is just 15 percent of that of whites.

Fox (2016) explores the relationship between wealth and the prospects of upward and downward mobility among Black and white families using the PSID. Interestingly, she finds heterogeneous patterns. Among low-income whites, families with low levels of wealth experience lower upward mobility, but no such pattern is evident among low-income Black families. In fact, home ownership is negatively associated with upward mobility for such Black families. In contrast, among high-income Black families, wealth reduces downward mobility. However, higher wealth has no effect on the downward mobility of high-income whites. In contrast to Fox (2016), Mazumder (2011) and Chetty et al. (2020) find evidence that accounting for wealth does reduce the racial gap in upward mobility modestly among lower-income families. For example, Chetty et al. find that accounting for wealth as best they can in their data reduces the racial gap in the conditional expected rank at the 25th percentile from 9.1 percentiles to 8.0 percentiles. They conclude that "differences in wealth between Black and white families are unlikely to explain their starkly different rates of intergenerational mobility" (p. 751).

It has long been suggested that one key reason why Blacks have been unable to build wealth is because of the practice of so-called redlining, where banks have sometimes been unwilling to provide mortgages, or the Federal Housing Administration would not insure mortgages in predominantly Black neighborhoods (e.g., Coates 2014). In recent work, Aaronson, Hartley, and Mazumder (2020) show that the introduction of maps drawn by the Home Owners Loan Corporation during the 1930s did indeed lead to a reduction in home ownership and home values in neighborhoods that were "redlined" by these maps. In subsequent work, Aaronson, Hartley, and Mazumder (2021) use the Opportunity Atlas measures produced by Chetty et al. (2020) to show that these redlining maps have also been linked to reduced rates of intergenerational mobility in neighborhoods many decades later.

Family Structure

Many researchers have hypothesized that perhaps the high rates of single female–headed households among Black families have affected their prospects of joining the middle class and experiencing upward mobility (e.g., Haskins 2013). Mazumder (2014) finds some evidence for this notion using data from the Survey of Income and Program

Participation matched to Social Security Administration detailed earnings records (SIPP-SSA). Although living with two parents throughout childhood has no effect on upward mobility for poor white families, it does appear to improve upward mobility for Black families. Mazumder (2014) finds that approximately 58 percent of children from Black families in the bottom quintile who grow up with two parents are able to escape the bottom quintile as adults. This compares to just 42 percent of children who spend some of their childhood raised by a single parent. On the other hand, family structure does not appear to influence downward mobility among high-income families for either racial group. Chetty et al. (2020) find a modest difference in the racial gap in the conditional expected rank at the 25th percentile when they control for parental marital status. The gap falls from 10 to 9.3 percentiles. They find almost no reduction in the racial gap at the 75th percentile, which also is roughly consistent with Mazumder's (2014) finding of no effect on downward mobility from the top.

Labor Market Institutions

One potentially important factor that has not been studied, as far as I am aware, is the effect on the racial mobility gap of various labor market institutions, such as unionization, the decline in manufacturing, the minimum wage, and monopsony power. One reason for the absence of research is that it may be difficult to isolate meaningful variation and to formulate a credible research design to identify causal effects. For example, changes in unionization have been slow moving and fairly national in scope. Nevertheless, studies of labor market institutions may be an avenue for researchers who can construct clever methods to identify effects.

THE ROLE OF POLICY

Given that the evidence thus far suggests that human capital development plays at least some important role in explaining the racial gap in mobility, we should consider what types of human capital policies are of value. First, there is growing evidence that interventions early in life have potentially large payoffs. This starts with the in utero period, where a growing body of research shows that prenatal exposures such as poor nutrition, disease, stress, violence, alcohol, smoking, lead, extreme heat, pollution, and maternal bereavement all have been linked to worse outcomes later in life (Mazumder 2016). These factors also often impact children who are exposed in the first year or two of life. In practice, this suggests that some policies that are already part of the existing safety net, such as SNAP, WIC, and Medicaid, should be bolstered, and additional programs, such as home-visitation programs by nurses and other child development professionals, should be pursued. All of these would likely help more disadvantaged groups in society and help reduce the racial gap in mobility.

Reducing exposure to air pollution, water pollution, and lead in Black communities is another important area where there may be large gains to be made in fostering intergenerational mobility through improvements in childhood health.

In addition, as discussed in the previous section, a growing body of research strongly suggests that educational policies—early childhood education programs such as Head Start, school finance equalization, and efforts to integrate schools and improvements in teacher quality— can all play an important role in improving upward mobility prospects for Black children.

A policy that may help alleviate credit constraints among Black families and also reduce the influence of racial wealth disparities is Child Development Accounts, or "Baby Bonds" (e.g., Cassidy et al. 2019). Baby bonds are essentially trust accounts funded by the government and provided at birth to every child. These assets can be used to finance investments in children's higher education, home purchases, or to start a business. An experimental program of Child Development Accounts has begun in Oklahoma. More experiments of this type, along with additional research, would be useful to see if these programs have long-term beneficial effects.

Of course, there are many other possible policy interventions, and this section is not meant to provide an exhaustive list. There is a tremendous opportunity for research to better understand how the United States can take action to improve equality of opportunity for Black Americans.

CONCLUSION

A growing literature in economics has emerged that documents striking racial gaps in intergenerational mobility. African Americans experience dramatically lower levels of upward mobility from the bottom of the income distribution, as well as significantly higher levels of downward mobility from the top. If the disparities in these mobility rates continue into the future, they imply that Black Americans would be a permanent underclass in society and that income gaps would not converge.

Research examining trends in mobility rates by race also suggests that there has been relatively little improvement over time. Looking back as far as our current data allow, Blacks have never been as intergenerationally mobile as whites. It is also evident when comparing regions that there is no region where it is better to be poor and Black than to be poor and white in terms of the prospects for upward mobility.

One of the key contributing factors to low mobility among Blacks is the large disparity in human capital development that is rooted in the legacies of slavery, segregation, and other racial policies. Policies that improve school quality, equalize funding, or provide early childhood education have successfully reduced racial disparities in intergenerational mobility. In addition, there is some evidence that vastly unequal levels of wealth have influenced the racial mobility gap to some degree, though there is room for better research in this area. Recent work suggests that areas that were historically redlined have lower prospects for upward mobility today. Finally, there is some evidence that children from low-income Black families with two parents present in the home have higher rates of upward mobility than those with a single parent.

Many types of policies could reduce the racial mobility gaps, beginning with those that can improve human capital development very early in life and continuing with policies that affect disparities in schooling. Reducing exposure to pollution and lead is also an important area for policy. Finally, policies that provide child development accounts, or baby bonds, may help address the racial wealth gap by alleviating credit constraints and, in turn, encourage upward mobility. Future research should continue to explore and evaluate these policies.

Notes

1. Calculations based on data contained in Table A2 of U.S. Census Bureau (2019).
2. Mazumder (2014) also uses administrative earnings data.
3. For example, Paul Krugman often refers to studies of intergenerational income mobility as *social mobility* (e.g., Krugman 2019).
4. Bhattacharya and Mazumder (2011) use only the NLSY, whereas Mazumder (2014) uses both the NLSY and the SIPP-SSA.
5. Bhattacharya and Mazumder (2011) show that when using the full sample (i.e., pooling all subgroups), the URM measure is meaningful only if there is some cutoff, *s*, used to condition the sample.

References

Aaronson, Daniel, Daniel Hartley, and Bhashkar Mazumder. 2020. "The Effects of the 1930s HOLC 'Redlining' Maps." *American Economic Journal: Economic Policy* 13(4): 355–392.

———. 2021. "The Long-Run Effects of the 1930s HOLC 'Redlining' Maps on Place-Based Measures of Economic Opportunity and Socioeconomic Success." *Regional Science and Urban Economics* 86.

Aaronson, Daniel, and Bhashkar Mazumder. 2011. "The Impact of Rosenwald Schools on Black Achievement." *Journal of Political Economy* 119(5): 821–888.

Bhattacharya, Debopam, and Bhashkar Mazumder. 2011. "A Nonparametric Analysis of Black–White Differences in Intergenerational Income Mobility in the United States." *Quantitative Economics* 2(3): 335–379.

Biasi, Barbara. 2019. "School Finance Equalization Increases Intergenerational Mobility: Evidence from a Simulated-Instruments Approach." NBER Working Paper No. 25600. Cambridge, MA: National Bureau of Economic Research.

Blau, Peter M., and Otus Dudley Duncan. 1967. *The American Occupational Structure*. New York: John Wiley and Sons.

Card, David, Ciprian Domnisoru, and Lowell Taylor. 2018. "The Intergenerational Transmission of Human Capital: Evidence from the Golden Age of Upward Mobility." NBER Working Paper No. 25000. Cambridge, MA: National Bureau of Economic Research.

Cassidy, Christa, Rachel Heydemann, Anne Price, Nathaniel Unah, and William Darity Jr. 2019. "Baby Bonds: A Universal Path to Ensure the Next Generation Has the Capital to Thrive." Durham, NC: Samuel Dubois Cook Center on Social Equity, Duke University.

Chay, Kenneth, Jonathan Guryan, and Bhashkar Mazumder. 2009. "Birth Cohort and the Black–White Achievement Gap: The Role of Health Soon after Birth." Working paper. Chicago: Federal Reserve Bank of Chicago.

Chetty, Raj, Nathaniel Hendren, Maggie R. Jones, and Sonya R. Porter. 2020. "Race and Economic Opportunity in the United States: An Intergenerational Perspective." *Quarterly Journal of Economics* 135(2): 711–783.

Chetty, Raj, Nathaniel Hendren, Patrick Kline, and Emmanuel Saez. 2014. "Where Is the Land of Opportunity? The Geography of Intergenerational Mobility in the United States." *Quarterly Journal of Economics* 129(4): 1553–1623.

Chowkwanyun, Merlin, and Adolph L. Reed. 2020. "Racial Health Disparities and Covid-19—Caution and Context." *New England Journal of Medicine* 383: 201–203.

Coates, Ta-Nehisi. 2014. "The Case for Reparations." *Atlantic*, June. https://www.theatlantic.com/magazine/archive/2014/06/the-case-for-reparations/361631/ (accessed February 8, 2021).

Collins, William J., and Marianne H. Wannamaker. Forthcoming. "African American Intergenerational Economic Mobility Since 1880." *American Economic Journal: Applied Economics*.

Corcoran, Mary, and Terry Adams. 1997. "Race, Sex, and the Inter-generational Transmission of Poverty." In *Consequences of Growing Up Poor*, Greg J. Duncan and Jeanne Brooks-Gunn, eds. New York: Russell Sage Foundation, pp. 461–517.

Datcher, Linda. 1981. "Race/Sex Differences in the Effects of Background on Achievement." In *Five Thousand American Families: Patterns of Economic Progress,* vol. 9, Martha S. Hill, Daniel H. Hill, and James N. Morgan, eds. Ann Arbor: Institute for Social Research, University of Michigan, pp. 359–390.

Davis, Jonathan, and Bashkar Mazumder. 2018. "Racial and Ethnic Differences in the Geography of Intergenerational Mobility." Available at SSRN: https://ssrn.com/abstract=3138979 or http://dx.doi.org/10.2139/ssrn.3138979 (accessed November 30, 2021).

———. 2020. "The Decline in Intergenerational Mobility after 1980." Stone Center on Socio-Economic Inequality Working Paper. New York: City University of New York.

Dettling, Lisa, Joanne Hsu, Lindsay Jacobs, Kevin Moore, and Jeffrey Thompson. 2017. "Recent Trends in Wealth-Holding by Race and Ethnicity: Evidence from the Survey of Consumer Finances." *FEDS Notes*, September 27. Washington, DC: Board of Governors of the Federal Reserve System.

Fox, Liana. 2016. "Parental Wealth and the Black–White Mobility Gap in the U.S." *Review of Income and Wealth* 62(4): 706–723.

Haskins, Ron. 2013. "Three Simple Rules Poor Teens Should Follow to Join the Middle Class." Brookings Institution, March 13. https://www.brookings .edu/opinions/three-simple-rules-poor-teens-should-follow-to-join-the -middle-class/ (accessed February 9, 2021).

Hertz, Tom. 2005. "Rags, Riches, and Race: The Intergenerational Economic Mobility of Black and White Families in the United States." In *Unequal Chances: Family Background and Economic Success*, Samuel Bowles, Herbert Gintis, and Melissa Osborne Groves, eds. Princeton: Princeton University Press, pp. 165–191.

———. 2008. "A Group-Specific Measure of Intergenerational Persistence." *Economic Letters* 100(3): 415–417.

Isaacs, Julia B., Isabel V. Sawhill, and Ron Haskins. 2008. "Getting Ahead or Losing Ground: Economic Mobility in America." Washington, DC: Brookings Institution and Pew Charitable Trusts.

Johnson, Rucker C. 2016. "Can Schools Level the Intergenerational Playing Field? Lessons from Equal Educational Opportunity Policies." In *Economic Mobility: Research & Ideas on Strengthening Families, Communities & the Economy*, Federal Reserve Bank of St. Louis and the Board of Governors of the Federal Reserve System, eds. St. Louis, MO; and Washington, DC: Federal Reserve Bank of St. Louis and the Board of Governors of the Federal Reserve System, pp. 290–324.

Krugman, Paul. 2019. "Socialism and the Self-Made Woman." *New York Times*, February 28. https://www.nytimes.com/2019/02/28/opinion/ivanka -trump-social-mobility.html (accessed April 15, 2021).

Lang, Kevin, and Michael Manove. 2011. "Education and Labor Market Discrimination." *American Economic Review* 101(4): 1467–1496.

Lee, Chul-In, and Gary Solon. 2009. "Trends in Intergenerational Income Mobility." *Review of Economics and Statistics* 91(4): 766–772.

Mazumder, Bhashkar. 2011. "Black–White Differences in Intergenerational Economic Mobility in the United States." Federal Reserve Bank of Chicago Working Paper No. 2011-10. Chicago: Federal Reserve Bank of Chicago.

———. 2014. "Black–White Differences in Intergenerational Economic Mobility in the United States." *Economic Perspectives* 38(1): 1–18.

———. 2016. "What Should Be Done to Increase Intergenerational Mobility in the US? In *The U.S. Labor Market Questions and Challenges for Public Policy*, Michael R. Strain ed. Washington, DC: American Enterprise Institute, pp. 14–28.

Neal, Derek A., and William R. Johnson 1996: "The Role of Premarket Factors in Black–White Wage Differences." *Journal of Political Economy* 104(5): 860–895.

Rodgers, William M. III, and William E. Spriggs. 1996. "What Does the AFQT

Really Measure: Race, Wages, Schooling and the AFQT Score." *Review of Black Political Economy* 24(4): 13–46.

Solon, Gary. 1992. "Intergenerational Income Mobility in the United States." *American Economic Review* 82(3): 393–408.

———. 2004. "A Model of Intergenerational Mobility Variation over Time and Place." In *Generational Income Mobility in North America and Europe*, Miles Corak, ed. Cambridge: Cambridge University Press, pp. 38–47.

U.S. Census Bureau. 2019. "Historical Income Tables: Families." Washington, DC: Department of Commerce. https://www.census.gov/data/tables/time-series/demo/income-poverty/historical-income-families.html   (accessed October 6, 2020).

Zimmerman David. 1992. "Regression Toward Mediocrity in Economic Stature." *American Economic Review* 82(3): 409–829.

7

Accounting for Race Differences in How Family Structure Shapes the Transition into Adulthood

Paula Fomby
University of Michigan

In the United States, young adults raised in stably married two-parent families complete college, enter full-time employment, and delay family formation more often than peers raised in other family forms (Fomby and Bosick 2013; Hofferth and Goldscheider 2010). These events and statuses mark the transition into adulthood and are associated with positive long-term economic, physical, and emotional well-being. Yet two in five contemporary U.S. children grow up in other living arrangements, a disparity that largely cleaves along racial, ethnic, and social class lines (Payne 2019). Given the perceived long-term gains to growing up with stably married parents and children's divergent experiences of family composition, a substantial social science literature has emerged over the last 50 years to explore what sets parents' marriage apart from other forms of family organization as a context for child rearing and why or whether family structure matters for the transition into adulthood.

While robust, this literature is characterized by two shortcomings. The first is the expectation that the married two-parent family remains the appropriate reference point in a context of increasingly heterogeneous family forms (Powell et al. 2016). The second is that the average observed gains to residing in a stable two-parent family—and the perceived cost to growing up in an alternative family form—are not the same for everyone. Rather, these relationships are contingent on historical period, national context, and children's sociodemographic characteristics, including race and gender (Aquilino 1991; Fomby, Mollborn, and Sennott 2010; Heuveline and Timberlake 2004). Together, these shortcomings highlight the need for a conceptual and methodological approach that recognizes the emerging plurality of family forms and the moderating effects of social location to sharpen or blunt the effect of family structure on child and young adult development.

To illustrate this perspective, I focus on the relationship between family structure in childhood and the transition into adulthood among two groups that make this transition after a lifetime of largely divergent experiences: non-Hispanic white and Black young adults in the United States. In this chapter I describe historical trends in family structure and the transition into adulthood and research how these circumstances are associated overall and for white and Black youth. I then describe and critique the framework that has informed scholarship on racial differences in family structure and the transition into adulthood over the past half century. Finally, I offer examples from four areas of social science research that have pushed back on the predominant model and that offer guidance for new directions in scholarship:

1) family income;

2) the role of social and economic institutions in shaping the contingent gains to family structure by race;

3) culturally inclusive measurement of family process; and

4) improved theory, measurement, and analysis on racial differences in the role of extended kinship and social networks in shaping children's and young adults' well-being.

TRENDS IN FAMILY STRUCTURE BY RACE

Much of contemporary scholarship positions family organization in the mid-twentieth century as a normative standard and seeks to explain why American families pivoted to alternative family forms in the ensuing decades. Yet household and family organization in the post–World War II era (roughly 1946–1964) was largely a historical aberration. Compared to previous periods, this era was marked by earlier and nearly universal marriage, high fertility both in terms of the proportion of women ever having children and the number of children born per woman, and declining child and adult mortality. As a result, by 1960, most people lived in married-couple households and 88 percent of children lived with both parents (U.S. Census Bureau 2012, 2019b). Divorce, spousal death, and remarriage featured in the family structure landscape, but these events were dwarfed by high rates of first marriage, and most children spent the majority of childhood in two-parent families. A short-lived nexus of circumstances, including explosive national economic growth (Nelson 1991), low male unemployment (Bureau of Labor Statistics 2020b), the expansion of consumer credit markets (Logemann 2008), and broad access to subsidized home loans and postsecondary education through the GI Bill (Bound and Turner 2002; Fetter 2013) enabled young families to thrive in a growing middle class through the mid-1960s. Much of the effort to describe the pace and pattern of family change since then has been built on elucidating the structural and cultural tensions and strictures that underlay that context and contributed to its eventual erosion.

Substantial upheaval in family composition over the past 60 years has changed family organization, largely through a rapid rise in the divorce rate in the 1970s and 1980s and the emergence of childbearing in cohabitation as an alternative to marriage in the late 1980s and 1990s. Today, 40 percent of children aged 0–17 years in the United States live outside a married two-parent family (Payne 2019). Further, children experience frequent change in family structure. On average, they experience at least one change through parents' union dissolution or new union formation by age 12, and only 44 percent of children live with both married parents from birth to early adolescence (S. Brown, Stykes, and Manning 2016). This shift has drawn attention to a plurality of alternative family forms distinguished by parents' legal union status, parents' gender, the relatedness of children in a shared household, and nonresidential parents' new family formation after a divorce or separation (Manning, S. Brown, and Stykes 2014; Powell et al. 2016). A large body of research has considered, for example, how children fare when they are raised by cohabiting parents (S. Brown 2004) or stepparents (Ganong and Coleman 2004); with stepsiblings or half siblings in their own or in a nonresident parent's household (Fomby, Goode, and Mollborn 2016; Halpern-Meekin and Tach 2008); with an unpartnered father or unpartnered mother (Bzostek and Berger 2017; Krueger et al. 2015); or when they experience their parents' repeated union formation and dissolution (Cavanagh and Fomby 2019). Almost always, children in these family statuses are compared to children living with both married parents and their biological siblings, even as this group has become an increasingly selective and shrinking statistical norm.

Yet even when the married two-parent family was at its statistical peak, it was not an experience shared equally by white and Black children. In 1960, over 90 percent of white children aged 17 years or younger resided with both parents, compared to two-thirds of Black children. And while fewer than 2 percent of children in that era had a never-married parent, Black children were about five times more likely than white children to live with a separated or divorced mother even by age 1 (Ruggles et al. 2020).

Black and white children in the United States have continued to experience distinctive family structure patterns as the national profile of family composition has evolved. These differences remain most pronounced in comparing the distribution of single-mother and married-parent families. The share of Black children residing with two parents decreased by half between 1960 and the mid-1990s, reaching 33 percent before regaining to about 44 percent in 2019. An equal share of Black children resided with an unpartnered mother in that year. The share of white children residing with two parents declined steadily but less sharply and plateaued at about 73 percent in the mid-2000s, with about one in five white children living with an unpartnered mother in 2019 (see Figure 7.1). These patterns are consistent with a growing divide in marriage rates between Black and white women over the past 50 years (Raley, Sweeney, and Wondra 2015). Children with Black parents also experience more frequent change in family structure compared to white children, in part because parents are more often unpartnered or cohabiting at birth compared to white families, and those family structures are less stable over time compared to marriage (S. Brown, Stykes, and Manning 2016). Notably, contemporary Black and white families are similar in the share of children aged 0–17 years residing with cohabiting parents, stepparents, or an unpartnered father (Payne 2019).

The decline in stable two-parent marriage and the emergence of alternative family forms over the past 50 years have occurred against a backdrop of far-reaching structural and cultural change, including the introduction and legalization of reliable contraception, the liberalization of divorce laws, women's rising educational attainment, deindus-

Figure 7.1 Residence with Two Parents or Mother Only, Black and White Children, 0–17 Years, 1960–2019

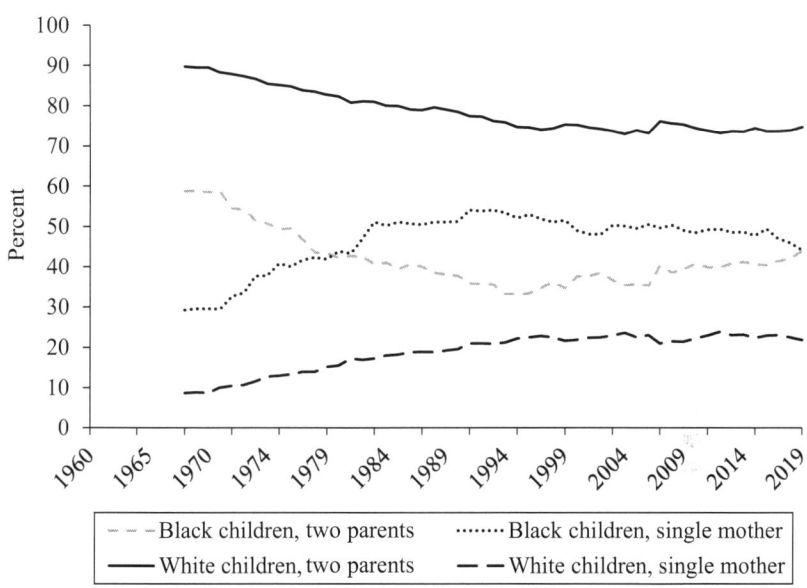

SOURCE: U.S. Census Bureau, Current Population Survey, March and Annual Social and Economic Supplements, Table CH-1.

trialization, real wage stagnation, increasing labor market returns to education, growth in upper-tail income and wealth inequality, welfare reform, and rising rates of incarceration. In this context, adults who enter stable marriage and have children with only a single partner are increasingly likely to be white and college-educated, while the diversity of alternative family forms is occupied by nonwhite adults who have finished high school or some college (S. Brown, Stykes, and Manning 2016; Cherlin 2014; Guzzo 2014; McLanahan 2004; McLanahan and Percheski 2008; Payne 2019; Raley, Sweeney, and Wondra 2015). Yet systems such as the labor market, child care, education, health insurance and health care, criminal justice, estate law, federal and local taxation, and entitlement programs continue to reflect, enable, and advantage married two-parent families with shared children (Cherlin 2009; Cott 2000). Thus, the same social, economic, and cultural conditions that give rise to a stratified system of family structure in turn reinforce that stratification in ways that are detrimental and impactful for children who grow up outside of stably married two-parent families. In the United States, this impact falls disproportionately on Black children.

TRENDS IN THE TRANSITION TO ADULTHOOD BY RACE

The evolution of U.S. family structure is of consequence to the extent that family organization in childhood directly or indirectly facilitates or hinders children's long-term well-being. An often-used metric to evaluate such well-being considers the timing, sequence, and content of significant events that are broadly recognizable as markers of the transition into adulthood. In the United States, these markers include setting up an independent household apart from parents, finishing formal schooling, entering the labor force, entering a cohabiting union or marriage, and experiencing a first birth (Arnett 2000). The salience of these markers to young adults' subjective sense of well-being and the notion that there is a universally "right" pathway through this transition have increasingly come into question (Bynner 2005; DeLuca, Clampet-Lundquist, and Edin 2016; Silva 2013), but they continue to remain meaningful as precursors to and correlates of later life physical and mental health, security, and social connectedness.

At the population level, the timing and sequence of transition into adulthood events differ substantially for Black and white young adults. With regard to completed education, earlier disparities in high school graduation have nearly closed, with 90 percent of white and 88 percent of Black adults 25 years and older having earned a high school diploma. But as access to college has expanded over the past 50 years, the share of Black adults who have completed college has consistently remained 10 percentage points lower than that of white adults. Today, 26 percent of Black adults aged 25 and older and 36 percent of same-age white adults hold a bachelor's degree or higher (U.S. Census Bureau 2020). Early labor force participation is also divergent: Black teens and young adults (aged 16–24) are about twice as likely to be neither employed nor in school compared to their white peers (Ross and Svajlenka 2016). Reflecting these early differences in human capital accumulation, median annualized weekly earnings for workers 25 years and older are more than 20 percent lower for Black compared to white workers (Bureau of Labor Statistics 2020a).

Black and white young adults also experience substantially different patterns of independent living and family formation. Black young adults are less likely to move out of and more likely to return to their parents' homes during young adulthood compared to whites, a pattern associated with Black adults' less frequent early stable employment and union formation, more limited family economic resources to finance setting up a separate household, and greater closeness to and need for support from parents (Lei and South 2016). Compared to white young adults, Black young adults have children earlier and marry less often and later in the life course. Although teen childbearing has declined dramatically and ages at first birth and marriage have risen for all women in the past three decades, mean age at first birth remains about two years earlier for Black women compared to white women (25.1 years versus 27.2 years in 2018; Martin et al. 2019), and median age at marriage remains about 2.5 years higher (30.4 years for Black women versus 27.9 years for white women in 2017; Payne 2019). Reflecting these patterns, about 70 percent of Black women's births occur outside marriage, and two-thirds of those nonmarital births also occur outside a cohabiting union. Among white women, the comparable statistics are 28 percent and 33 percent respectively (Martin et al. 2019). Black women are also about two-thirds as likely as white women to describe their births as on time and intended (Guzzo 2017).

FAMILY STRUCTURE AND THE TRANSITION INTO ADULTHOOD

The preceding review illustrates dramatic qualitative differences in the experience of family structure during childhood and in the transition into adulthood among white and Black youth. At the population level, is racial variation in young adulthood experiences at least partially a function of divergent family structure experiences in childhood? For this to be true, scholarship would need to present evidence that childhood family structure either directly or indirectly influences young adult outcomes, and that any observed effects operate similarly for both Black and white youth.

Indeed, descriptive portraits of family change coupled with rigorous, theoretically informed hypothesis testing have demonstrated that families are varied and complex in their organization and in the ways they imprint children's and adolescents' well-being and the transition into adulthood. In particular, a substantial volume of descriptive research has demonstrated that the experience of growing up outside a stably married two-parent family—and particularly the experience of residing with a single mother—is associated with a variety of challenges. These include a higher likelihood of high school dropout and lower likelihood of college enrollment and completion (Martin 2012; McLanahan and Sandefur 1994; Sassler et al. 2013; Wojtkiewicz and Holtzman 2011; Ziol-Guest, Duncan, and Kalil 2015); earlier and more frequent nonmarital childbearing (Musick 2002; Wu and Martinson 1993); an elevated risk of early union formation and union instability (Amato et al. 2008; Amato and Patterson 2017; Hofferth and Goldscheider 2010; Ryan et al. 2009); more frequent downward income mobility (Bloome 2017); and lower life satisfaction (Amato and Keith 1991; Amato, Loomis, and Booth 1995).

A variety of theories have been put forward to explain these descriptive associations. Perhaps foremost in public discourse, research has documented that diminished or unstable family economic resources and a higher risk of poverty contribute to young adults' educational disadvantage and early transition to adulthood in single-parent families (Fomby and Kravitz-Wirtz 2019; McLanahan and Percheski 2008; McLanahan and Sandefur 1994; Wojtkiewicz and Holtzman 2011). Other theoretical perspectives emphasize mediating factors that arise from family structure status. One branch considers the quality and quantity of time that families invest in children (Astone and McLanahan 1991; Hofferth and Anderson 2003; Hofferth et al. 2007; Kalil and Mayer 2016; Kalmijn 2015; McLanahan, Tach, and Schneider 2013), while another emphasizes the effect of adults' conflicted relationships and complex and contingent family roles on their interactions with children (Cherlin et al. 1991; Cherlin 2004; Musick and Meier 2010; Tach, Mincy, and Edin 2010; Townsend 2002). Beyond the household, children experience stigma attached to nonmarital family structures when families engage with other social institutions such as schools

(Fomby and Mollborn 2017) and experience more frequent residential and school mobility compared to peers who remain in the same family structure throughout childhood (Fomby and Sennott 2013). Each of these mechanisms appears to independently and partially explain the association between specific family structure arrangements and children's adjustment in the eventual transition into adulthood.

However, an important caveat to this body of work is the persistent finding that time outside a two-parent stable marriage is less strongly associated with the timing, sequence, and context of transition into adulthood events for Black compared to white youth. With regard to educational attainment, time with a single parent, the experience of parents' union dissolution, and exposure to repeated family structure change are each more weakly associated or not significantly associated with academic performance in high school (Heard 2007); high school completion (Cross 2020; Perkins 2019; McLanahan and Sandefur 1994); and college enrollment and completion (Amato and Keith 1991) among Black adolescents compared to white. These same family structure circumstances and events are also less predictive of adolescent delinquency and young adult illegal behavior among Black compared to white youth (Bosick and Fomby 2018; Cavanagh and Fomby 2019; Fomby and Cherlin 2007; Fomby, Mollborn, and Sennott 2010); early sexual initiation (Wu and Thomson 2001; Fomby, Mollborn, and Sennott 2010); early and unplanned nonmarital childbearing (Fomby, Mollborn, and Sennott 2010; Musick 2002; Wu 1996; Wu and Martinson 1993); and entry into early cohabitation or marriage (Bosick and Fomby 2018). This pattern is consistent with related research that finds weaker effects of family structure on development and well-being during adolescence (McLanahan and Percheski 2008; Sun and Li 2007).

Collectively, racial differences in the magnitude of family structure effects on child and young adult development raise critical questions about how we understand this relationship. To the extent that families and family structure matter for children's and young adults' well-being, I posit that they do not actually matter more for one socially defined group than another. Rather, I argue that the social construction of the family as it is theorized, measured, and articulated in social science research and public expression reflects the biases of the actors who predominate in that discourse. In the United States, this has meant that scholarship on the family has taken as a given that the two-parent nuclear household that prevails among white families is the optimal and most salient family context for well-being. This approach has overlooked the strengths of other family forms and also has overlooked the ways that white and Black families engage with other social institutions that contribute to or constrain human development. Below I consider one example of how mid-twentieth-century public discourse about the nexus of race, family structure, and the transition into adulthood has shaped subsequent research on this topic. I also highlight opportunities to develop a new approach that is a more inclusive and accurate portrayal of family structure in all its diversity among American families.

FRAMING SCHOLARSHIP ON RACIAL DIFFERENCES IN FAMILY STRUCTURE

Differences in Black and white children's experiences of family structure attracted national attention in 1965 with the publication of Daniel Patrick Moynihan's report to the Office of Policy Planning and Research in the U.S. Department of Labor, *The Negro Family: The Case for National Action.* Moynihan, a sociologist and assistant secretary of labor, described the U.S. Black community as a "tangle of pathology" characterized by high rates of poverty, unemployment, and crime. He identified the disproportionately high share of female-headed households in predominantly Black neighborhoods as the cause of community disorganization, contending that "the Negro community has been forced into a matriarchal family structure which, because it is too out of line with the rest of the American society, seriously retards the progress of the group as a whole" (Moynihan 1965, p. 29).

Moynihan's report was spurred by President Lyndon Johnson's War on Poverty, an ambitious set of federal programs designed to remove or ameliorate the effects of structural barriers to upward economic mobility in poor families. The report recognized that historical and structural conditions—including slavery, Jim Crow laws, residential and occupational segregation, discrimination, and racism—preceded both the prevalence of female-headed households and social and economic disadvantage in Black communities. And the objective of the report was to motivate investments that would secure stability and resources in Black families (p. 48). The report and the call to action were deeply progressive for the time. In particular, compared to the Depression-era New Deal program that was designed to reduce unemployment and benefit the average American household, War on Poverty programs targeted those who were excluded from the country's broad postwar economic prosperity (Bailey and Duquette 2014).

Yet the Moynihan report also made four tenuous connections that continue to be reflected in the framework social scientists use to motivate research questions and analytical approaches in order to understand the relationships between race and ethnicity, family structure, and the transition into adulthood in the United States. First, the report put family structure—particulary single-parent, female headship—on the causal pathway to long-term negative outcomes for children. Second, it identified female headship as an inherently "weak" (p. 30) family structure arising from men's historical social and economic disengagement. Third, it identified female headship as an endemic feature of low-income Black communities that placed those communities outside the structural and cultural framework that sustained white and middle-class families' daily lives. Fourth, it made the implicit assumption that the two-parent nuclear family is always the most salient and optimal family system for children. Together, these connections have informed a social science and public policy agenda to solve the perceived problem of nonmarital family structure as a contributor to intergenerational disadvantage, and particularly to racial disparities in achievement. I refer to this perspective as the *deficit model* for studying the impact of family structure on child well-being, a phrase borrowed from education research and evaluation (Harry and Klingner 2007).

The deficit model is premised on the expectation that disparities in child well-being and the transition into adulthood between two groups can be explained by one group's departure from normative standards that are considered by the majority group to be prerequisite to success. Further, this departure from normative standards is held to originate from and inhere within individuals or families through a process detached from the broader social and economic context in which they are embedded. In the case of Moynihan's assessment of the role of father absence in shaping child outcomes in poor Black families, he opined that "three centuries of injustice have brought about deep-seated structural distortions in the life of the Negro American. At this point, the present tangle of pathology is capable of perpetuating itself without assistance from the white world" (p. 47). Without intervention, he argued, a system of father absence from poor Black families and the perceived attendant negative consequences for children would persist even if the structural conditions that had contributed to the system's emergence were no longer in place.

LIMITATIONS OF THE DEFICIT MODEL IN FAMILY SCHOLARSHIP

Father Absence and Family Income

The tenuous connections initially articulated in the Moynihan report have been reified as a set of specious assumptions in the deficit model that have subsequently undergirded empirical research on the relationship between race, childhood family structure, and the transition into adulthood during the past five decades. Perhaps most critical among these is the contention that higher rates of father absence from children's households is a direct and irreducible cause of compromised transition into adulthood among Black compared to white youth.

In a set of publications in the 1980s, Sara McLanahan (1983, 1985, 1988) offered a direct and substantive critique of this contention. This research leveraged nationally representative longitudinal, intergenerational data with an oversample of families headed by unmarried Black women to illustrate that economic strain and family stress, more so than father absence, explained the observed association between growing up with a single parent and an elevated risk of poverty in early adulthood. (Also see McLanahan, Tach, and Schneider [2013] for a comprehensive review of the estimated causal effect of father absence on a variety of child and young adult outcomes.) In a later review piece, McLanahan and Percheski (2008) emphasized that the intertwined relationship between single-parent status and poverty in the United States had disproportionately affected Black and Latino children, citing evidence that recent historical change in family structure accounts for a larger share of the change in child poverty among non-Hispanic Black families than among Hispanic or non-Hispanic white families (Iceland 2003) and that the poverty rates of Black and Puerto Rican children would be about one-third lower if their distribution across family structures were the same as in the total population of children (Lichter, Qian, and Crowley 2005).

Collectively, this work contributed to reorienting research and racialized public discourse about the relationship between family structure and poverty. It deviated from a pathologized view of "broken families" as an irreversible consequence of historic circumstances to one that emphasized the capacity for public policy to bolster children's and parents' well-being through income rather than through prescribed family structures. Further, it emphasized that public policy action or inaction to prevent exposure to poverty and to remediate its effects would continue to disproportionately influence the well-being of Black children. Multidisciplinary scholarship led by Greg Duncan further refined this argument by documenting the enduring effect of poverty during early childhood on later cognitive achievement (Duncan and Magnuson 2005) and employment, earnings, and nonmarital childbearing in early adulthood (Duncan, Ziol-Guest, and Kalil 2010; Duncan et al. 1998) and demonstrating the compensatory effects of direct unconditional cash transfers to families in poverty and interventions in early childhood education (Duncan, Ludwig, and Magnuson 2007; Duncan, Magnuson, and Votruba-Drzal 2014).

This research spurred subsequent scholarship that has mapped out how poverty, financial hardship, financial strain, and other stressors influence family process in single-parent and other alternative family forms to compromise children's and young adults' well-being. This work has strived to close racial disparities in family well-being by identifying strategies that reduce poverty-related stress exposure and remediating its effects where it occurs. Like the deficit model popularized by Moynihan, contemporary work recognizes the continuing role of social, economic, and legal institutions in shaping divergent opportunities and constraints in the structure and organization of white and Black families. Yet those contextual factors are rarely made explicit in empirical models. And by using the two-parent family as the normative comparison group, this work collectively continues to valorize that family form. To the extent that Black children are significantly more likely to spend at least part of childhood outside parents' stable marriage compared to white children, this approach continues to present nonwhite children's family structure as a social problem to be solved through intervention and correction. Further, tests of hypothesized mediating mechanisms continue to regard the measurement of family process and family resources as scientifically neutral, despite incomplete population representation in the creation of those measures, thus potentially misspecifying the relationship between family structure and family process in nonwhite families. As a result, while the theories and motivation for scholarship on the family structure, race, and young adult outcomes have become more nuanced since the Moynihan report was published more than 50 years ago, the strategy to empirically describe these relationships in quantitative research continues to resemble the logic of the deficit model and to implicitly pathologize Black family organization. I discuss these limitations below.

Contingent Gains to Family Structure by Race

Much of the empirical research grounded in the deficit model assumes that the relationship between family structure and child outcomes can be validated, understood, and interpreted apart from the broader social and economic context in which families are embedded. Under this approach, research to understand disparities in Black and white young adult outcomes as a function of family structure—and particularly as a function of single motherhood—artificially bounds the research question at the perimeter of family membership.

For example, one goal of the 1996 Personal Responsibility and Work Opportunity Reconciliation Act, more commonly referred to as welfare reform, was to promote entry into stable marriage as a strategy to increase family income, limit welfare dependency, and improve well-being and status attainment in low-income families with children (U.S. House of Representatives 1996). Marriage promotion policy was largely ineffective in encouraging couples to become and to remain married, and among low-income single mothers, those who married were unlikely to select partners with high earnings (Graefe and Lichter 2008; but see Bzostek, McLanahan, and Carlson 2012).

But even beyond the general lack of success of marriage promotion initiatives, the policy design overlooked race differences when considering the impact that two household income earners compared to one may have on family income in the short term and on intergenerational upward mobility in the long term. In particular, while poverty rates are lower and median family income is higher in married-parent compared to single-parent families across racial and ethnic groups, the income gains to marriage are smaller for Black compared to non-Hispanic white families (U.S. Census Bureau 2019a). The Black–white wealth gap among college-educated married adults of childbearing age with or without a college education is even more acute (Darity et al. 2018) and equally persistent (Aliprantis and Carroll 2019). Further, even in Black families with moderate incomes, children are substantially more likely than their white counterparts to earn less and to accumulate less wealth than their parents when they reach adulthood, a pattern of downward intergenerational mobility that holds irrespective of parents' marital status and that is particularly strong for Black boys (Chetty et al. 2020; Pfeffer and Killewald 2019).

Thus, the economic gains to marriage for Black and white families are unequal. A substantial literature suggests that these weaker gains are not the result of group differences in the attributes of Black compared to white families, but to enduring group differences in school quality, educational achievement, employment opportunity and discrimination, labor force attachment, and contact with the criminal justice system that contribute to Black men's lower earnings and availability for marriage relative to white men's (O'Neill 1990; Pager 2003; Pager, Bonikowski, and Western 2009; Sellers and Shelton 2003; Wilson 1987). Research models that overlook such racial variation in attachment to and engagement with social and economic institutions beyond the family household introduce a profound problem of omitted variable bias that potentially misspecifies the effect of family structure on children's well-being and contributes to policies that are misaligned with population need. In the case of children in low-income Black families that are disproportionately disadvantaged in broader social contexts, such an approach may overestimate the observed negative effect of growing up with a single parent and fail to explain the unequal impact of living with two married parents on outcomes in early adulthood compared to white children. That is, among Black children, the economic costs to living with a single parent or experiencing repeated change in family structure may be less and the gains to living stably with two parents may be weaker compared to white families. This pattern partially explains why time outside a two-parent family is less predictive of transition to adulthood events like high school completion, sexual initiation, and nonmarital childbearing among Black compared to white youth (Cross 2020; Fomby, Mollborn, and Sennott 2010).

Validity in Family Process Measurement

Current applications of the deficit model also assume that the validity of scales and indices to tap psychosocial constructs extends to populations that were not included in the creation of those measures. In particular, the deficit model identifies behaviors, attitudes, and activities that have been found to predict children's healthy development in white, middle-class families and evaluates the extent to which the absence of those characteristics in other family types contributes to explaining disparities in child and young adult outcomes. Yet these metrics may not be equally valid or salient in all populations or, even if equally valid, may not co-vary with the variables whose relationships they are expected to mediate in the same way across racial and ethnic categories (Henrich, Heine, and Norenzayan 2010). In such cases, the deficit model both fails to explain the mechanisms that drive racial and ethnic disparities in child outcomes and fails to explore why potential mediators function differently across groups, thus missing the opportunity to interrogate the generalizability and validity of assumptions derived from family theory to explain variation in young adult outcomes.

One example is the expansive literature on parenting style, defined by the balance of strictness and emotional warmth that parents demonstrate to children in everyday interactions. This construct was developed from laboratory- and home-based observation of child-parent interactions in convenience or clinical samples during the mid-twentieth century (Baumrind 1966; Maccoby and Martin 1983), and subsequent work has demonstrated that it lacks comparable salience outside the United States and even among nonwhite families within the United States. In particular, in the U.S. context, authoritative parenting, characterized by the presence of both strictness and emotional warmth in parents' interactions with children, is more weakly associated with child behavior problems and academic achievement in Black compared to non-Hispanic white families, and authoritarian parenting, characterized by strictness and less frequent emotional warmth, is not associated with these outcomes for Black children in meta-analyses (Deater-Deckard et al. 2011; Pinquart and Kauser 2018). Nevertheless, the construct of parenting style is widely used to explain population variation in behavior problems (Pinquart 2017) and academic achievement (Pinquart 2016), including as a hypothesized mediator of the relationship between family structure and child and adolescent outcomes (Bastaits and Mortelmans 2016; Fine, Voydanoff, and Donnelly 1993). Similar criticisms of racial bias have been made against the standard measurement of self-reported mental health, stress appraisal, and genetic expression to explain why these constructs appear to operate differently on family functioning and well-being in Black compared to white families (L. Brown et al. 2019; Henrich, Heine, and Norenzayan 2010; Rosenfield and Mouzon 2013).

Extended Kin and Social Embeddedness

As noted above, the Moynihan report asserted that the stable, two-parent nuclear family household is the optimal family configuration for children. Not coincidentally, this was the modal white family structure at the time the report was produced. Much research employing the deficit model carries this assumption forward by measuring family structure in terms of the presence, biological relatedness, and marital status of parents in a child's household. This work often ignores the presence of coresident kin as well as the proximity and involvement of non-coresident kin and friends in active social networks. Yet recent quantitative work and a large body of qualitative research have highlighted the salience of these relationships in Black family life across the socioeconomic spectrum. This work also illustrates that such relationships are neutral or positive for the well-being of Black youth but more often are associated with deleterious outcomes for white youth, largely because of differential selection into extended kin coresidence and activation of social networks by race. Below I summarize extant research on racial differences in extended kin coresidence, nonresident father involvement, and engagement with cross-household social networks to make the case that much more research from this perspective is required to reflect the diversity of family composition and family process in the United States.

Extended kin coresidence

With regard to coresidence with extended kin, a growing body of research has used information from household rosters reported in national survey data to consider the full composition of children's households rather than focusing only on the presence or absence of a child's biological parents to define family structure. Here, the innovation is in the definition and measurement of family membership. To date, theoretically motivated expectations about why the presence or absence of extended kin may be similar to or different from the presence or absence of parents in a child's household is not yet well established. Like other conventional empirical research, this work tends to use nuclear family structure and the social organization of white families as the reference group to describe and explain Black family organization. Despite these limitations, growing attention to the relationship between extended kin coresidence and child and young adult well-being presents new opportunities to enrich family theory and research with existing secondary data.

Recent scholarship in this area has demonstrated that about 1 in 9 minor children in Black families lives in a three-generation household with at least one grandparent, compared to 1 in 20 children in white families nationally (Pilkauskas and Cross 2018). Racial disparities in extended kin coresidence emerge when children are young. At age two, for example, approximately 35 percent of Black children and 13 percent of white children lived with a grandparent, aunt or uncle, or other relative in the early 2000s (Mollborn, Fomby, and Dennis 2012). These spells of extended kin coresidence persist across the span of childhood, particularly in Black families. Among today's young adults, 57 percent of those in Black families had ever lived with a grandparent, aunt or uncle, or other relative by age 18, compared with 20 percent of young adults raised in white families (Cross 2018). Contemporary Black young adults were also more likely to experience change in extended kin household composition during childhood (0.7 entrances into or exits from a Black child's household by extended kin before age 18 compared to 0.28 such transitions for white children) (Perkins 2019).

More than a compositionally distinct feature of Black compared to white children's households, extended kinship and change in such kinship is associated with positive child development and young adult outcomes. During early childhood, coresidence with grandparents in

Black families is associated with higher cognitive scores and better parent-reported behavior compared to nuclear family organization, but the opposite is true for children in white families (Mollborn, Fomby, and Dennis 2011). By the end of adolescence, higher rates of extended kin coresidence partially explain why Black children raised by single mothers are more likely to complete high school compared to white children growing up with a single mother (Cross 2020). Extended kin coresidence is also one aspect of Black adolescents' access to social embeddedness that appears to reduce the risk of early sexual initiation and unintended childbearing following parents' own repeated union dissolution and repartnering (Fomby, Mollborn, and Sennott 2010). To date, there is little research to rigorously examine why extended kin coresidence may be more advantageous in Black compared to white families, but there is some evidence that white families are more likely than Black families to enter extended family organization in response to stressors such as financial strain or a health crisis (Mollborn, Fomby, and Dennis 2011) and that extended kin coresidence is more uniformly distributed across the socioeconomic spectrum in Black compared to white families (Cross 2018).

Nonresident father involvement

Beyond the residential household, Black families' social embeddedness with kin and nonkin networks living elsewhere facilitates transfers of practical, financial, and emotional support in the interest of children's development. This work emphasizes that in research on family organization, the family household poses a meaningful but somewhat arbitrary boundary around the family members who are relevant to children's daily lives (Seltzer 2019; Seltzer et al. 2005). A salient example is how research accounts for the presence of nonresident fathers in children's lives. The Moynihan report conceptualized Black fathers' absence from children's primary households as an indicator of their total erasure. Family scholars have since refuted that characterization and have documented heterogeneous patterns of nonresident father involvement with children, with the majority of nonresident fathers consistently or increasingly in contact with their children over time (Cheadle, Amato, and King 2010; Edin and Nelson 2013). Other work has documented that Black men's contact with their nonresident children is on par with or exceeds white fathers' contact, and that Black fathers are more engaged as coparents with the mothers of their biological children (Ellerbe, Jones, and Carlson 2018; King, Harris, and Heard 2004; Mincy, Edin, and Tach 2009), belying an enduring cultural trope of nonresident Black fathers' indifference to their children's care. Qualitative research focused on Black men's nonresident fatherhood has highlighted men's adherence to widely shared values of fatherhood as provider, teacher, and role model to children in the face of obstacles, including conflict with former partners and kin, unreliable earnings, and the perception of operating within an impersonal punitive child support system (Edin and Nelson 2013; Hamer 2001; Julion et al. 2007; Threlfall, Seay, and Kohl 2013).

Social network embeddedness

More broadly, the social networks in Black families headed by single mothers have been characterized as an example of superorganization, or a system of strong ties with kin and nonkin across households that is posited to offer a better strategy to manage the hardships of minority life compared to the siloed nuclear family organization that predominates in white families (Sarkisian and Gerstel 2011). The super-organization thesis recognizes nonresident Black fathers' higher levels of involvement with children compared to white peers as described above, but also emphasizes patterns of informal reciprocity that prevail between women and their kin and peers that operate in place of predictable and affordable formal and institutionalized mechanisms to facilitate childrearing. This may include pooling or exchanging child care, transportation, or housing, or providing small-scale loans (Hofferth 1984; Hogan, Hao, and Parish 1990; Sarkisian and Gerstel 2004). There is some evidence in quantitative research that Black adolescents' social embeddedness in neighborhoods, churches, and schools partially explains why they are less likely than their white peers to engage in delinquent behavior, have sex early, or have an early nonmarital birth when they experience frequent family change (Fomby, Mollborn, and Sennott 2010). But to date, there is a dearth of literature to consider how Black families use their social embeddedness with extended family and nonkin to support young adults' development, or to assess how such connections may hinder the transition into adulthood.

Carol Stack's *All Our Kin* (1974) offered the first ethnographic portrait of resource sharing among kin and friends in the social networks of Black, single-mother families in a U.S. midwestern city. This portrait highlighted the inadequacy of conventional survey-based methods, which focus on family systems in households, to adequately characterize Black mothers' access and obligation to effective family and social connections in other spheres. A large body of ethnographic and qualitative work has continued to highlight the interdependent relationships among kin and kin-like groups across households as a coping strategy among poor, mostly unpartnered mothers (Domínguez and Watkins 2003; Edin and Kefalas 2005; Edin and Lein 1997; Hays 2003; Newman 1999). While much of this work does not focus explicitly on race differences in family organization, the experiences of low-income single Black women often feature significantly. Thus, while this work is informative, nuanced, and policy relevant, it often observes research participants at a particular intersection of race, class, and marital status, foregoing the opportunity to explore the role of extended kinship in other Black family forms and social locations.

Over the past two decades, other ethnographic and qualitative scholarship has redressed this limitation by focusing on middle-class and married Black families, including the extended kin networks and neighborhoods in which they are embedded (Dow 2019; Lacy 2007; McDonald and Cross-Barnet 2018; Pattillo 1999, 2005; St. Vil, McDonald, and Cross-Barnet 2018). Like lower-income or unpartnered Black parents, relatively advantaged Black families draw upon and provide coresidence, child care, advice, and emotional support within families, particularly when children are young (St. Vil, McDonald, and Cross-Barnet 2018; also see Cross 2018). More prosperous Black families' residential proximity to poorer Black neighborhoods in the context of residential racial segregation also fosters community organization and embeddedness across the socioeconomic gradient (Pattillo 1999; Domínguez and Watkins 2003).

Ethnographic and qualitative research also emphasizes that engagement in a superorganized family system carries costs as well as benefits. Informal systems of exchange and support carry strong expectations of enforceable trust and balanced reciprocity (M. Nelson 2000), and participation can require substantial emotional labor, time, and opportunity costs (Domínguez and Watkins 2003). Further, social networks may not be protective or supportive on balance. For example, young Black mothers who evacuated New Orleans after Hurricane Katrina reported feeling unexpectedly liberated from the perceived obligations and expectations of the social networks they left behind and relished the independence they achieved in a new setting that offered greater structural opportunity (Bosick 2015).

It is also important to note that Black families' reliance on extended kin and nonkin networks arose in a context of institutional and structural exclusion, and the capacity to leverage that social embeddedness to parents', children's, and young adults' advantage continues to be constrained by exposure to bias, discrimination, and limited structural opportunity. This is reflected in part in Black families' more homogenous social networks with regard to residential location, educational attainment, occupation, and employment status compared to white families' (Wilson 1987). Where networks are more diverse, more advantaged network members provide a bridge to access resources and connections that otherwise would not be directly attainable (Cross 2018; Domínguez and Watkins 2003). But those more advantaged network members also engage in boundary setting for a variety of reasons, including distrust of other network members (Smith 2005) and identity management as Black professionals (Lacy 2007) and middle-class parents (Dow 2019). This boundary setting requires substantial emotional labor and can also foreclose opportunities to activate network access among less advantaged network members. Together, this work suggests that attention to the resources and stressors that inhere in Black extended family and quasi-family networks can offer additional insight into how families scaffold or inhibit the transition into adulthood, but this area of scholarship remains mostly unexplored in qualitative or quantitative research.

CONCLUSION

At the population level, Black and white youth in the United States reach the transition into adulthood after a lifetime of divergent family structure experiences. In particular, Black youth are more likely than their white peers to have been born outside marriage or a cohabiting union, and those who are born to partnered parents are more likely to experience their parents' union dissolution and to spend a larger share of childhood living with a single parent. Black and white youth also experience qualitatively different transitions into adulthood with regard to the timing, sequence, and context of events such as leaving home and school, starting work, having children, and entering long-term romantic relationships.

Over the past 50 years, a substantial social science literature has emerged to ask whether and how differences in childhood family structure experience are associated with disparities in transition into adulthood outcomes by race. Much of this research is presented in the framework of what I refer to as a deficit model. This deficit model is premised on the expectation that disparities between Black and white young adults can be explained by Black youths' departure from normative standards that are considered by the majority group to be prerequisite to success. Further, this departure from normative standards is presented as originating from and inhering within individuals or families without regard for the broader social and economic context in which they are embedded. I propose that with regard to questions about the role of family structure in explaining Black/white disparities in young adult outcomes, this framework has survived at least since its appearance in an influential mid-twentieth-century federal report written to inform public policy around the well-being of Black children living with single mothers (Moynihan 1965).

I argue that reliance on the deficit model has contributed to a myopic and truncated view of Black family organization that biases how social science research describes the racial differences in the association between family structure and the transition into adulthood. This is reflected in research that suggests Black children's family structure experience is less consequential for their eventual well-being than for their white peers. To the extent that the structure and routines of families truly matter for the life chances of the people who live in them, one might expect that they would matter equally for Black and white youth. Where this is not the case, the pattern of findings raises questions about the adequacy of extant theory and empirical models and metrics to characterize these relationships.

The preceding review highlights key conclusions from four lines of research that have pushed back against the assertions in Moynihan's thesis and the resulting deficit model. First, family income, rather than father absence, largely explains the poorer outcomes of children and young adults raised by single mothers. As a result, Black children are disproportionately affected by the absence of U.S. child and family policy to increase family income or remediate the effects of financial hardship on children in single-parent families. Arguably, this public choice, rather than a cultural "weakness," contributes to explaining racial disparities in young adult outcomes that are attributable to family structure differences. Second, the gains or costs to residing in a specific family structure during childhood are contingent on race; that is, the gains to living with two stably married parents appear to be greater for white children than for Black children because white adults see greater returns to earned income and wealth accumulation compared to Black adults, even among the college educated. This reflects a deeply entrenched history of racial inequality in access to and engagement with the social and economic institutions that build and reward human, social, and cultural capital in favor of white Americans. Thus, we cannot understand racial differences in how family structure shapes children's well-being without considering how social and economic institutions condition these associations. Third, the metrics used to describe family process in two-parent families and alternative family forms are culturally biased, and thus incompletely or inaccurately describe family routines, parenting styles, and parent mental health in Black compared to white families. Finally, research on family structure that prioritizes the nuclear family household as optimal for children often ignores the presence and role of coresident kin and broader kin and friend networks in shaping child and young adult outcomes, despite the strikingly high prevalence and salience of these connections in Black families.

Scholarship on families, young adulthood, race and ethnicity, and social stratification would be well served to advance theory, measurement, and empirical modeling to better characterize Black family structure, family process, and the role of external institutions in shaping both parents' family formation and young adults' well-being. This should include qualitative and quantitative research that compares Black families of various family structures within and across social class categories rather than relying on comparison to the increasingly selective category of white, stably married two-parent families. It should also include the creation of broadly culturally informed measures of family process. Finally, it should include comprehensive data collection and digestible public use data that describe the complex relationships in children's coresident and non-coresident families beyond relationships to parents and their partners. These efforts will likely yield more accurate depictions of Black family organization and offer significant advances to explicate how family structure and family process contribute to a successful transition into adulthood.

Note

Research reported here was also supported by the Eunice Kennedy Shriver National Institute of Child Health and Human Development under award number R01HD088506.

References

Aliprantis, Dionissi, and Daniel R. Carroll. 2019. "What Is Behind the Persistence of the Racial Wealth Gap?" *Economic Commentary* 2019–03, February 28. Cleveland: Federal Reserve Bank of Cleveland. https://doi .org/10.26509/frbc-ec-201903 (accessed October 6, 2020).

Amato, Paul R., and Bruce Keith. 1991. "Parental Divorce and Adult Well-Being: A Meta-Analysis." *Journal of Marriage and Family* 53(1): 43–58.

Amato, Paul R., Nancy S. Landale, Tara C. Havasevich-Brooks, Alan Booth, David J. Eggebeen, Robert Schoen, and Susan M. McHale. 2008. "Precursors of Young Women's Family Formation Pathways." *Journal of Marriage and Family* 70(5): 1271–1286.

Amato, Paul R., Laura Spencer Loomis, and Alan Booth. 1995. "Parental Divorce, Marital Conflict, and Offspring Well-Being during Early Adulthood." *Social Forces* 73(3): 895–915. https://academic.oup.com/sf/article -abstract/73/3/895/2233877 (accessed October 6, 2020).

Amato, Paul R., and Sarah E. Patterson. 2017. "The Intergenerational Transmission of Union Instability in Early Adulthood." *Journal of Marriage and Family* 79(3): 723–738.

Aquilino, William S. 1991. "Family Structure and Home-Leaving: A Further Specification of the Relationship." *Journal of Marriage and Family* 53(4): 999–1010.

Arnett, Jeffrey Jensen. 2000. "Emerging Adulthood—A Theory of Development from the Late Teens through the Twenties." *American Psychologist* 55(5): 469–480.

Astone, Nan Marie, and Sara S. McLanahan. 1991. "Family Structure, Parental Practices and High School Completion." *American Sociological Review* 56(3): 309–320.

Bailey, Martha J., and Nicolas J. Duquette. 2014. "How Johnson Fought the War on Poverty: The Economics and Politics of Funding at the Office of Economic Opportunity." *Journal of Economic History* 74(2): 351–388.

Bastaits, Kim, and Dimitri Mortelmans. 2016. "Parenting as Mediator between Post-divorce Family Structure and Children's Well-Being." *Journal of Child and Family Studies* 25(7): 2178–2188.

Baumrind, Diana. 1966. "Effects of Authoritative Parental Control on Child Behavior." *Child Development* 37(4): 887–907.

Bloome, Deirdre. 2017. "Childhood Family Structure and Intergenerational Income Mobility in the United States." *Demography* 54(2): 541–569.

Bosick, Stacey J. 2015. "'Pushed Out on My Own': The Impact of Hurricane Katrina in the Lives of Low-Income Emerging Adults." *Sociological Perspectives* 58(2): 243–263.

Bosick, Stacey J., and Paula Fomby. 2018. "Family Instability in Childhood and Criminal Offending during the Transition into Adulthood." *American Behavioral Scientist* 62(11): 1483–1504.

Bound, John, and Sarah Turner. 2002. "Going to War and Going to College: Did World War II and the G.I. Bill Increase Educational Attainment for Returning Veterans?" *Journal of Labor Economics* 20(4): 784–815.

Brown, Lauren, Leah Abrams, Uchechi Mitchell, and Jennifer Ailshire. 2019. "Black-White Differences in Chronic Stress: Does Appraisal Matter for Anxiety and Depressive Symptoms?" *Innovation in Aging* 3 (Suppl 1): S191–S192.

Brown, Susan L. 2004. "Family Structure and Child Well-Being: The Significance of Parental Cohabitation." *Journal of Marriage and Family* 66(2): 351–367.

Brown, Susan L., J. Bart Stykes, and Wendy D. Manning. 2016. "Trends in Children's Family Instability, 1995–2010." *Journal of Marriage and Family* 78(5): 1173–1183.

Bureau of Labor Statistics. 2020a. "Median Usual Weekly Earnings of Full-Time Wage and Salary Workers by Age, Race, Hispanic or Latino Ethnicity, and Sex, Not Seasonally Adjusted (Table 3)." In *Labor Force Statistics from the Current Population Survey*.

———. 2020b. "Monthly Unemployment Rate, 1948–Present (United States)." Washington, DC: Department of Labor. https://data.bls.gov/timeseries/LNS14000000 (accessed April 14, 2021).

Bynner, John. 2005. "Rethinking the Youth Phase of the Life-Course: The Case for Emerging Adulthood?" *Journal of Youth Studies* 8 (4): 367–384. https://doi.org/10.1080/13676260500431628 (accessed April 14, 2021).

Bzostek, Sharon H., and Lawrence M. Berger. 2017. "Family Structure Experiences and Child Socioemotional Development during the First Nine Years of Life: Examining Heterogeneity by Family Structure at Birth." *Demography* 54(2): 513–40. https://doi.org/10.1007/s13524-017-0563-5 (accessed April 14, 2021).

Bzostek, Sharon H., Sara S. McLanahan, and Marcia J. Carlson. 2012. "Mothers' Repartnering after a Nonmarital Birth." *Social Forces* 90(3): 817–841. https://doi.org/10.1093/sf/sos005 (accessed April 14, 2021).

Cavanagh, Shannon, and Paula Fomby. 2019. "Family Instability in the Lives of American Children." *Annual Review of Sociology* 45: 493–513.

Cheadle, Jacob E., Paul R. Amato, and Valarie King. 2010. "Patterns of Nonresident Father Contact." *Demography* 47(1): 205–225.

Cherlin, Andrew J. 2004. "The Deinstitutionalization of American Marriage." *Journal of Marriage and Family* 66 (4): 848–861.

———. 2009. *The Marriage-Go-Round: The State of Marriage and the Family in America Today.* 1st ed. New York: Alfred A. Knopf.

———. 2014. *Love's Labor Lost: The Rise and Fall of the Working Class Family in America.* New York: Russell Sage.

Cherlin, Andrew J., Frank F. Furstenberg, P. Lindsay Chase-Lansdale, Kathleen E. Kiernan, Philip K. Robins, Donna Ruane Morrison, and Julian O. Teitler. 1991. "Longitudinal Studies of Effects of Divorce on Children in Great Britain and the United States." *Science* 252(5011): 1386.

Chetty, Raj, Nathaniel Hendren, Maggie R. Jones, and Sonya R. Porter. 2020. "Race and Economic Opportunity in the United States: An Intergenerational Perspective." *Quarterly Journal of Economics* 135(2): 711–783.

Cott, Nancy F. 2000. *Public Vows: A History of Marriage and the Nation.* Cambridge, MA: Harvard University Press.

Cross, Christina J. 2018. "Extended Family Households among Children in the United States: Differences by Race/Ethnicity and Socio-Economic Status." *Population Studies* 72(2): 235–251.

———. 2020. "Racial/Ethnic Differences in the Association between Family Structure and Children's Education." *Journal of Marriage and Family* 82(2): 691–712.

Darity, William Jr., Darrick Hamilton, Mark Paul, Alan Aja, Anne Price, Antonio Moore, and Caterina Chiopris. 2018. "What We Get Wrong about Closing the Racial Wealth Gap." Durham, NC: Samuel DuBois Cook Center on Social Equity.

Deater-Deckard, Kirby, Jennifer E. Lansford, Patrick S. Malone, Liane Peña Alampay, Emma Sorbring, Dario Bacchini, Anna Silvia Bombi, et al. 2011. "The Association between Parental Warmth and Control in Thirteen Cultural Groups." *Journal of Family Psychology* 25(5): 790–794.

DeLuca, Stefanie, Susan Clampet-Lundquist, and Kathryn Edin. 2016. *Coming of Age in the Other America.* New York: Russell Sage Foundation.

Domínguez, Silvia, and Celeste Watkins. 2003. "Creating Networks for Survival and Mobility: Social Capital among African-American and Latin-American Low-Income Mothers." *Social Problems* 50(1): 111–135.

Dow, Dawn Marie. 2019. *Mothering While Black: Boundaries and Burdens of Middle-Class Parenthood.* Berkeley and Los Angeles: University of California Press.

Duncan, Greg J., Jens Ludwig, and Katherine A. Magnuson. 2007. "Reducing Poverty through Preschool Interventions." *Future of Children* 17(2): 143–160.

Duncan, Greg J., and Katherine A. Magnuson. 2005. "Can Family Socioeconomic Resources Account for Racial and Ethnic Test Score Gaps?" *Future of Children* 15(1): 35–54.

Duncan, Greg J., Katherine A. Magnuson, and Elizabeth Votruba-Drzal. 2014. "Boosting Family Income to Promote Child Development." *Future of Children* 24(1): 99–120.

Duncan, Greg J., W. Jean Yeung, Jeanne Brooks-Gunn, and Judith R. Smith. 1998. "How Much Does Childhood Poverty Affect the Life Chances of Children?" *American Sociological Review* 63(3): 406–423.

Duncan, Greg J., Kathleen M. Ziol-Guest, and Ariel Kalil. 2010. "Early-Childhood Poverty and Adult Attainment, Behavior, and Health." *Child Development* 81(1): 306–325.

Edin, Kathryn, and Maria Kefalas. 2005. *Promises I Can Keep: Why Poor Women Put Motherhood before Marriage.* Berkeley: University of California Press.

Edin, Kathryn, and Laura Lein. 1997. *Making Ends Meet: How Single Mothers Survive Welfare and Low-Wage Work.* New York: Russell Sage Foundation.

Edin, Kathryn, and Timothy Jon Nelson. 2013. *Doing the Best I Can: Fatherhood in the Inner City.* Berkeley: University of California Press.

Ellerbe, Calvina Z., Jerrett B. Jones, and Marcia J. Carlson. 2018. "Race/Ethnic Differences in Nonresident Fathers' Involvement after a Nonmarital Birth." *Social Science Quarterly* 99(3): 1158–1182.

Fetter, Daniel K. 2013. "How Do Mortgage Subsidies Affect Home Ownership? Evidence from the Mid-Century GI Bills." *American Economic Journal: Economic Policy* 5(2): 111–147.

Fine, Mark A., Patricia Voydanoff, and Brenda W. Donnelly. 1993. "Relations between Parental Control and Warmth and Child Well-Being in Stepfamilies." *Journal of Family Psychology* 7(2): 222–232.

Fomby, Paula, and Stacey J. Bosick. 2013. "Family Instability and the Transition to Adulthood." *Journal of Marriage and Family* 75(5): 1266–1287.

Fomby, Paula, and Andrew J. Cherlin. 2007. "Family Instability and Child Well-Being." *American Sociological Review* 72(2): 181–204.

Fomby, Paula, Joshua A. Goode, and Stefanie Mollborn. 2016. "Family Complexity, Siblings, and Children's Aggressive Behavior at School Entry." *Demography* 26(1): 1–26.

Fomby, Paula, and Nicole Kravitz-Wirtz. 2019. "Family Systems and Parents' Financial Support for Education in Early Adulthood." *Demography* 56(5): 1875–1897.

Fomby, Paula, and Stefanie Mollborn. 2017. "Ecological Instability and Children's Classroom Behavior in Kindergarten." *Demography* 54(5): 1627–1651.

Fomby, Paula, Stefanie Mollborn, and Christie A. Sennott. 2010. "Race/Ethnic Differences in Effects of Family Instability on Adolescents' Risk Behavior." *Journal of Marriage and Family* 72(2): 234–253.

Fomby, Paula, and Christie A. Sennott. 2013. "Family Structure Instability and Mobility: The Consequences for Adolescents' Problem Behavior." *Social Science Research* 42(1): 186–201.

Ganong, Lawrence, and Marilyn Coleman. 2004. *Stepfamily Relationships: Development, Dynamics, and Interventions*. New York: Kluwer Academic/Plenum Publishers.

Graefe, Deborah Roempke, and Daniel T. Lichter. 2008. "Marriage Patterns among Unwed Mothers: Before and after PRWORA." *Journal of Policy Analysis and Management* 27(3): 479–497.

Guzzo, Karen Benjamin. 2014. "New Partners, More Kids: Multiple-Partner Fertility in the United States." *ANNALS of the American Academy of Political and Social Science* 654(1): 66–86.

———. 2017. "Unintended Births: Variation across Social and Demographic Characteristics." Family Profile No. 9. Bowling Green, OH: National Center for Family and Marriage Research, Bowling Green State University.

Halpern-Meekin, Sarah, and Laura Tach. 2008. "Heterogeneity in Two-Parent Families and Adolescent Well-Being." *Journal of Marriage and Family* 70(2): 435–51.

Hamer, Jennifer. 2001. *What It Means to Be Daddy: Fatherhood for Black Men Living Away from Their Children*. New York: Columbia University Press.

Harry, Beth, and Janette Klingner. 2007. "Discarding the Deficit Model." *Education Leadership* 64(5): 16–21.

Hays, Sharon. 2003. *Flat Broke with Children: Women in the Age of Welfare Reform*. New York: Oxford University Press.

Heard, Holly E. 2007. "The Family Structure Trajectory and Adolescent School Performance—Differential Effects by Race and Ethnicity." *Journal of Family Issues* 28(3): 319–354.

Henrich, Joseph, Steven J. Heine, and Ara Norenzayan. 2010. "The Weirdest People in the World?" *Behavioral and Brain Sciences* 33(2–3): 61–83.

Heuveline, Patrick, and Jeffrey M. Timberlake. 2004. "The Role of Cohabitation in Family Formation: The United States in Comparative Perspective."
Journal of Marriage and the Family 66(5): 1214–1230.

Hofferth, Sandra L. 1984. "Kin Networks, Race, and Family Structure." *Journal of Marriage and Family* 46(4): 791–806.

Hofferth, Sandra L., and Kermyt G. Anderson. 2003. "Are All Dads Equal?
Biology versus Marriage as a Basis for Paternal Investment." *Journal of
Marriage and Family* 65(1): 213–232.

Hofferth, Sandra L., Natasha Cabrera, Marcia Carlson, Rebekah Levine Coley,
Randal Day, and Holly S. Schindler. 2007. "Resident Father Involvement
and Social Fathering." In *Handbook of Measurement Issues in Family
Research*, Sandra L. Hofferth and Lynne M. Casper, eds. Mahwah, NJ:
Lawrence Erlbaum Associates, pp. 335–374.

Hofferth, Sandra L., and Frances K. Goldscheider. 2010. "Family Structure
and the Transition to Early Parenthood." *Demography* 47(2): 415–437.

Hogan, Dennis P., Ling-Xin Hao, and William L. Parish. 1990. "Race, Kin
Networks, and Assistance to Mother-Headed Families." *Social Forces*
68(3): 797–812.

Iceland, John. 2003. "Why Poverty Remains High: The Role of Income
Growth, Economic Inequality, and Changes in Family Structure, 1949–
1999." *Demography* 40(3): 499–519.

Julion, Wrenetha, Deborah Gross, Gina Barclay-McLaughlin, and Louis Fogg.
2007. "'It's Not Just about MOMMAS': African-American Non-resident
Fathers' Views of Paternal Involvement." *Research in Nursing & Health*
30(6): 595–610.

Kalil, Ariel, and Susan E. Mayer. 2016. "Understanding the Importance of
Parental Time with Children: Comment on Milkie, Nomaguchi, and Denny
(2015)." *Journal of Marriage and Family* 78(1): 262–265.

Kalmijn, Mattijs. 2015. "Family Disruption and Intergenerational Reproduction: Comparing the Influences of Married Parents, Divorced Parents, and
Stepparents." *Demography* 52(3): 811–833.

King, Valarie, Kathleen Mullan Harris, and Holly E. Heard. 2004. "Racial and
Ethnic Diversity in Nonresident Father Involvement." *Journal of Marriage
and Family* 66(1): 1–21.

Krueger, Patrick M., Douglas P. Jutte, Luisa Franzini, Irma Elo, and Mark D.
Hayward. 2015. "Family Structure and Multiple Domains of Child Well-
Being in the United States: A Cross-Sectional Study." *Population Health
Metrics* 13(1): 6. https://doi.org/10.1186/s12963-015-0038-0 (accessed
April 14, 2021).

Lacy, Karyn R. 2007. *Blue-Chip Black: Race, Class, and Status in the New
Black Middle Class*. Berkeley: University of California Press.

Lei, Lei, and Scott L. South. 2016. "Racial and Ethnic Differences in Leaving and Returning to the Parental Home: The Role of Life Course Transitions, Socioeconomic Resources, and Family Connectivity." *Demographic Research* 34(4): 109–142.

Lichter, Daniel T., Zhenchao Qian, and Martha L. Crowley. 2005. "Child Poverty among Racial Minorities and Immigrants: Explaining Trends and Differentials." *Social Science Quarterly* 86(S1): 1037–1059.

Logemann, Jan. 2008. "Different Paths to Mass Consumption: Consumer Credit in the United States and West Germany during the 1950s and '60s." *Journal of Social History* 41(3): 525–559.

Maccoby, Eleanor E., and J.A. Martin. 1983. "Socialization in the Context of the Family: Parent-Child Interaction." In *Handbook of Child Psychology: Vol. 4: Socialization, Personality and Social Development*, 4th ed., Paul H. Mussen and E. Mavis Hetherington, eds. New York: Wiley, pp. 1–101.

Manning, Wendy D., Susan L. Brown, and J. Bart Stykes. 2014. "Family Complexity among Children in the United States." *ANNALS of the American Academy of Political and Social Science* 654(1): 48–65.

Martin, Joyce A., Brady E. Hamilton, Michelle J. Osterman, and Anne K. Driscoll. 2019. "Births: Final Data for 2018." *National Vital Statistics Reports* 68(13): 47.

Martin, Molly A. 2012. "Family Structure and the Intergenerational Transmission of Educational Advantage." *Social Science Research* 41(1): 33–47.

McDonald, Katrina Bell, and Caitlin Cross-Barnet. 2018. *Marriage in Black: The Pursuit of Married Life among American-Born and Immigrant Blacks.* New York: Routledge, Taylor & Francis Group.

McLanahan, Sara. 1983. "Family Structure and Stress: A Longitudinal Comparison of Male and Female-headed Families." *Journal of Marriage and the Family* 45(2): 347–357.

———. 1985. "Family Structure and the Reproduction of Poverty." *American Journal of Sociology* 90(4): 873–901.

———. 1988. "Family Structure and Dependency: Early Transitions to Female Household Headship." *Demography* 25(1): 1–16.

———. 2004. "Diverging Destinies: How Children Are Faring under the Second Demographic Transition." *Demography* 41(4): 607–627.

McLanahan, Sara, and Christine Percheski. 2008. "Family Structure and the Reproduction of Inequalities." *Annual Review of Sociology* 34(1): 257–76.

McLanahan, Sara, and Gary Sandefur. 1994. *Growing Up with a Single Parent: What Hurts, What Helps.* Cambridge, MA: Harvard University Press.

McLanahan, Sara, Laura Tach, and Daniel Schneider. 2013. "The Causal Effects of Father Absence." *Annual Review of Sociology* 39(1): 399–427.

Mincy, Kathryn Edin, Laura Tach, Ronald. 2009. "Claiming Fatherhood:

Race and the Dynamics of Paternal Involvement among Unmarried Men." *ANNALS of the American Academy of Political and Social Science* 621(1): 149–177.

Mollborn, Stefanie, Paula Fomby, and Jeffrey A. Dennis. 2011. "Who Matters for Children's Early Development? Race/Ethnicity and Extended Household Structures in the United States." *Child Indicators Research* 4(3): 389–411.

———. 2012. "Extended Household Transitions, Race/Ethnicity, and Early Childhood Cognitive Outcomes." *Social Science Research* 41(5): 1152–1165.

Moynihan, Daniel Patrick. 1965. *The Negro Family. The Case for National Action.* Washington, DC: Government Printing Office.

Musick, Kelly. 2002. "Planned and Unplanned Childbearing among Unmarried Women." *Journal of Marriage and Family* 64(4): 915–929.

Musick, Kelly, and Ann Meier. 2010. "Are Both Parents Always Better than One? Parental Conflict and Young Adult Well-Being." *Social Science Research* 39(5): 814–830.

Nelson, Margaret K. 2000. "Single Mothers and Social Support: The Commitment to, and Retreat from, Reciprocity." *Qualitative Sociology* 23(3): 291–317.

Nelson, Richard R. 1991. "Diffusion of Development: Post–World War II Convergence among Advanced Industrial Nations." *American Economic Review* 81(2): 271–275.

Newman, Katherine S. 1999. *No Shame in My Game: The Working Poor in the Inner City.* New York: Knopf and the Russell Sage Foundation.

O'Neill, June. 1990. "The Role of Human Capital in Earnings Differences between Black and White Men." *Journal of Economic Perspectives* 4(4): 25–45.

Pager, Devah. 2003. "The Mark of a Criminal Record." *American Journal of Sociology* 108(5): 937–975.

Pager, Devah, Bart Bonikowski, and Bruce Western. 2009. "Discrimination in a Low-Wage Labor Market: A Field Experiment." *American Sociological Review* 74(5): 777–799.

Pattillo, Mary E. 1999. *Black Picket Fences: Privilege and Peril among the Black Middle Class.* Chicago: University of Chicago Press.

———. 2005. "Black Middle-Class Neighborhoods." *Annual Review of Sociology* 31(1): 305–329.

Payne, Krista. 2019. "Children's Family Structure, 2019." Bowling Green, OH: National Center for Family and Marriage Research, Bowling Green State University.

Perkins, Kristin L. 2019. "Changes in Household Composition and Children's Educational Attainment." *Demography* 56(2): 525–548.

Pfeffer, Fabian T., and Alexandra Killewald. 2019. "Intergenerational Wealth Mobility and Racial Inequality." *Socius* 5: 1–2.

Pilkauskas, Natasha V., and Christina Cross. 2018. "Beyond the Nuclear Family: Trends in Children Living in Shared Households." *Demography* 55(6): 2283–2297.

Pinquart, Martin. 2016. "Associations of Parenting Styles and Dimensions with Academic Achievement in Children and Adolescents: A Meta-Analysis." *Educational Psychology Review* 28(3): 475–493.

———. 2017. "Associations of Parenting Dimensions and Styles with Externalizing Problems of Children and Adolescents: An Updated Meta-Analysis." *Developmental Psychology* 53(5): 873–932.

Pinquart, Martin, and Rubina Kauser. 2018. "Do the Associations of Parenting Styles with Behavior Problems and Academic Achievement Vary by Culture? Results from a Meta-Analysis." *Cultural Diversity and Ethnic Minority Psychology* 24(1): 75–100.

Powell, Brian, Laura Hamilton, Bianca Manago, and Simon Cheng. 2016. "Implications of Changing Family Forms for Children." *Annual Review of Sociology* 42(1): 301–322.

Raley, R. Kelly, Megan M. Sweeney, and Danielle Wondra. 2015. "The Growing Racial and Ethnic Divide in U.S. Marriage Patterns." *Future of Children* 25(2): 89–109.

Rosenfield, Sarah, and Dawne Mouzon. 2013. "Gender and Mental Health." In *Handbook of the Sociology of Mental Health*. 2nd ed. New York: Springer Science + Business Media, pp. 277–296.

Ross, Martha, and Nicole Prchal Svajlenka. 2016. "Employment and Disconnection among Teens and Young Adults: The Role of Place, Race, and Education." Washington, DC: Brookings Institution.

Ruggles, Steven, Sarah Flood, Ronald Goeken, Josiah Grover, Erin Meyer, Jose Pacas, and Matthew Sobek. 2020. "IPUMS USA: Version 10.0." IPUMS. https://doi.org/10.18128/D010.V10.0 (accessed April 14, 2021).

Ryan, Suzanne, Kerry Franzetta, Erin Schelar, and Jennifer Manlove. 2009. "Family Structure History: Links to Relationship Formation Behaviors in Young Adulthood." *Journal of Marriage and Family* 71(4): 935–953. https://doi.org/10.1111/j.1741-3737.2009.00645.x (accessed March 17, 2021).

Sarkisian, Natalia, and Naomi Gerstel. 2004. "Kin Support among Blacks and Whites: Race and Family Organization." *American Sociological Review* 69(6): 812–837.

———. 2011. *Nuclear Family Values, Extended Family Lives: The Power of Race, Class, and Gender*. New York: Routledge.

Sassler, Sharon, Kristi Williams, Fenaba Renae Addo, Adrianne M. Frech, and

Elizabeth C. Cooksey. 2013. "Family Structure and High School Graduation: How Children Born to Unmarried Mothers Fare." *Genus* 69(2): 1–33.

Sellers, Robert M., and J. Nicole Shelton. 2003. "The Role of Racial Identity in Perceived Racial Discrimination." *Journal of Personality and Social Psychology* 84(5): 1079–1092.

Seltzer, Judith A. 2019. "Family Change and Changing Family Demography." *Demography* 56(2): 405–426.

Seltzer, Judith A., Christine A. Bachrach, Suzanne M. Bianchi, Carolyn H. Bledsoe, Lynne M. Casper, P. L. Chase-Lansdale, Thomas A. DiPrete, et al. 2005. "Explaining Family Change and Variation: Challenges for Family Demographers." *Journal of Marriage and Family* 67(4): 908–925.

Silva, Jennifer M. 2013. *Coming Up Short: Working-Class Adulthood in an Age of Uncertainty*. Oxford Scholarship Online. https://www.oxfordscholarship.com/view/10.1093/acprof:oso/9780199931460.001.0001/acprof-9780199931460 (accessed October 6, 2020).

Smith, Sandra Susan. 2005. "'Don't Put My Name on It': Social Capital Activation and Job-Finding Assistance among the Black Urban Poor." *American Journal of Sociology* 111(1): 1–57.

St. Vil, Noelle M., Katrina Bell McDonald, and Caitlin Cross-Barnet. 2018. "A Qualitative Study of Black Married Couples' Relationships with Their Extended Family Networks." *Families in Society* 99(1): 56–66.

Stack, Carol B. 1974. *All Our Kin: Strategies for Survival in a Black Community*. New York: Harper & Row.

Sun, Yongmin M., and Yuanzhang H. Li. 2007. "Racial and Ethnic Differences in Experiencing Parents' Marital Disruption during Late Adolescence." *Journal of Marriage and Family* 69(3): 742–762.

Tach, Laura, Ronald Mincy, and Kathryn Edin. 2010. "Parenting as a 'Package Deal': Relationships, Fertility, and Nonresident Father Involvement among Unmarried Parents." *Demography* 47(1): 181–204.

Threlfall, Jennifer M., Kristen D. Seay, and Patricia L. Kohl. 2013. "The Parenting Role of African American Fathers in the Context of Urban Poverty." *Journal of Children & Poverty* 19(1): 45–61.

Townsend, Nicholas W. 2002. *The Package Deal: Marriage, Work, and Fatherhood in Men's Lives*. Philadelphia: Temple University Press.

U.S. Census Bureau. 2012. "Households, Families, Subfamilies, and Married Couples [Table 59]." In *Statistical Abstract of the United States*. Washington, DC: Department of Commerce. https://www.census.gov/library/publications/2011/compendia/statab/131ed/population.html (accessed October 6, 2020).

———. 2019a. "Historical Income Tables: Families [Table F-7]." Washington, DC: Department of Commerce. https://www.census.gov/data/tables/time-series/demo/income-poverty/historical-income-families.html (accessed October 6, 2020).

———. 2019b. "Living Arrangements of Children under 18 Years Old: 1960 to Present (Table CH-1)." Historical Living Arrangements of Children. Washington, DC: Department of Commerce. https://www.census.gov/data/ tables/time-series/demo/families/children.html (accessed October 6, 2020).

———. 2020. "Educational Attainment by Race and Hispanic Origin: 1970 to 2019 [Selected Years]." In *ProQuest Statistical Abstract of the U.S. 2020 Online Edition.* https://statabs-proquest-com.proxy.lib.umich.edu/sa/ docview.html?table-no=256&acc-no=C7095-1.4&year=2020&z=7101400 81EDA5F41EC98A0DFBA1F641B69012A25 (accessed October 6, 2020).

U.S. House of Representatives. 1996. "Personal Responsibility and Work Opportunity Reconciliation Act of 1996 (104 H. Rpt. 3734)." Webpage. 1995/1996. https://www.congress.gov/bill/104th-congress/house-bill/3734/ text (accessed October 6, 2020).

Wilson, William J. 1987. *The Truly Disadvantaged. The Inner City, the Underclass, and Public Policy.* Chicago: University of Chicago Press.

Wojtkiewicz, Roger A., and Mellisa Holtzman. 2011. "Family Structure and College Graduation: Is the Stepparent Effect More Negative than the Single Parent Effect?" *Sociological Spectrum* 31(4): 498–521.

Wu, Lawrence L. 1996. "Effects of Family Instability, Income, and Income Instability on the Risk of a Premarital Birth." *American Sociological Review* 61(3): 386–406.

Wu, Lawrence L., and Brian C. Martinson. 1993. "Family Structure and the Risk of a Premarital Birth." *American Sociological Review* 58(2): 210–232.

Wu, Lawrence L., and Elizabeth Thomson. 2001. "Race Differences in Family Experience and Early Sexual Initiation: Dynamic Models of Family Structure and Family Change." *Journal of Marriage and Family* 63(3): 682–696.

Ziol-Guest, Kathleen M., Greg J. Duncan, and Ariel Kalil. 2015. "One-Parent Students Leave School Earlier: Educational Attainment Gap Widens." *Education Next* 15(2): 37–41.

Authors

Michael Baker is a professor in the department of economics and Canada Research Chair in Economics, Child Development, and Public Policy at the University of Toronto. He is also the academic director of the Toronto Region Statistics Canada Research Data and a research associate of the National Bureau of Economic Research.

Rachel Connelly is the Bion R. Cram Professor of Economics at Bowdoin College. She previously served as the director of the Gender and Women's Studies Program, and is currently the chair of the economics department. She is a research fellow at the IZA, the Institute for the Study of Labor, in Bonn, Germany, and at the Chinese Center for Human Capital and Labor Market Research, Beijing, China.

Paula Fomby is the associate director of the Population Studies Center at the University of Michigan. She is also a research associate professor at the Population Studies Center and the Survey Research Center, Institute for Social Research. She studies how family instability affects child well-being, including how parents' choices and behaviors influence those of their children.

Ariel Kalil is the Daniel Levin Professor of Public Policy at the University of Chicago Harris School of Public Policy. At Harris, she directs the Center for Human Potential and Public Policy and codirects the Behavioral Insights and Parenting Lab. She also holds an appointment as an adjunct professor in the Norwegian School of Economics in Bergen, Norway.

Jean Kimmel is a professor in the Department of Economics at Western Michigan University. She teaches a course on women and the economy, which relies on microeconomics to study marriage, fertility, and employment decisions. Her main research interests are labor economics, female employment, child care, time use, moonlighting, motherhood wage gap, wage determination, and computer access.

Sarah Kroeger is a research assistant professor at the Wilson Sheehan Lab for Economic Opportunities in the department of economics at the University of Notre Dame. Her research interests lie in inequality, intergenerational mobility, and economics of the family. Her recent research examines such topics as women's education, career choice, and gender differences in college completion.

Susan Mayer is professor emeritus at the University of Chicago Harris School of Public Policy and the College. She served as dean of Harris from 2002 to 2009. She has published numerous articles and book chapters on the measurement of poverty, the effect of growing up in poor neighborhoods, and the effect of parental income on children's well-being.

Bhashkar Mazumder is a senior economist and economic advisor in the economic research department and executive director of the Chicago Federal Statistical Research Data Center at the Federal Reserve Bank of Chicago. As a member of the microeconomic team, Mazumder conducts research in labor economics, education, and health. His research has focused on three areas: intergenerational economic mobility, the long-term effects of poor health early in life, and black-white gaps in human capital development.

Index

Note: The italic letters *f, n,* or *t* following a page number indicate a figure, note, or table, respectively, on that page. Double letters mean more than one such consecutive item on a single page.

About the Institute

The W.E. Upjohn Institute for Employment Research is a nonprofit research organization devoted to finding and promoting solutions to employment-related problems at the national, state, and local levels. It is an activity of the W.E. Upjohn Unemployment Trustee Corporation, which was established in 1932 to administer a fund set aside by Dr. W.E. Upjohn, founder of The Upjohn Company, to seek ways to counteract the loss of employment income during economic downturns.

The Institute is funded largely by income from the W.E. Upjohn Unemployment Trust, supplemented by outside grants, contracts, and sales of publications. Activities of the Institute comprise the following elements: 1) a research program conducted by a resident staff of professional social scientists; 2) the Early Career Research Award program, which provides funding for emerging scholars to complete policy-relevant research on labor-market issues; 3) a publications program and online research repository, which provide vehicles for disseminating the research of staff and outside scholars; 4) a regional team that conducts analyses for local economic and workforce development; and 5) the Employment Management Services Division, which administers publicly funded employment and training services as Michigan Works! Southwest in the Institute's local four-county area.

The broad objectives of the Institute's activities are to 1) promote scholarship and evidence-based practices on issues of employment and unemployment policy, and 2) make knowledge and scholarship relevant and useful to policymakers in their pursuit of solutions related to employment and unemployment.

Current areas of concentration for these programs include the causes, consequences, and measures to alleviate unemployment; social insurance and income maintenance programs; compensation and benefits; workforce skills; nonstandard work arrangements; and place-based policy initiatives for strengthening regional economic development and local labor markets.